FOURTH EDITION

Media Debates

GREAT ISSUES FOR THE DIGITAL AGE

EVERETTE E. DENNIS
Fordham University

JOHN C. MERRILL
University of Missouri

THOMSON
™
WADSWORTH

Australia • Canada • Mexico • Singapore • Spain • United Kingdom • United States

Publisher: Holly J. Allen
Assistant Editor: Darlene Amidon-Brent
Editorial Assistant: Sarah Allen
Technology Project Manager: Jeanette Wiseman
Marketing Manager: Mark Orr
Marketing Assistant: Andrew Keav
Marketing Communications Manager: Shemika Britt
Project Manager, Editorial Production: Paul Wells

Art Director: Maria Epes
Print Buyer: Lisa Claudeanos
Permissions Editor: Joohee Lee
Production Service: Scratchgravel Publishing Services
Copy Editor: Margaret C. Tropp
Cover Designer: Bartay
Compositor: Cadmus
Printer: Webcom

Printed in Canada
1 2 3 4 5 6 7 09 08 07 06 05

For more information about our products,
contact us at:
Thomson Learning Academic Resource Center
1-800-423-0563

For permission to use material from this text
or product, submit a request online at
http://www.thomsonrights.com.

Any additional questions about permissions can be
submitted by email to
thomsonrights@thomson.com.

Library of Congress Control Number: 2005923113

ISBN 0-495-00181-3

Thomson Higher Education
10 Davis Drive
Belmont, CA 94002-3098
USA

Asia (including India)
Thomson Learning
5 Shenton Way
#01-01 UIC Building
Singapore 068808

Australia/New Zealand
Thomson Learning Australia
102 Dodds Street
Southbank, Victoria 3006
Australia

Canada
Thomson Nelson
1120 Birchmount Road
Toronto, Ontario M1K 5G4
Canada

UK/Europe/Middle East/Africa
Thomson Learning
High Holborn House
50–51 Bedford Row
London WC1R 4LR
United Kingdom

Latin America
Thomson Learning
Seneca, 53
Colonia Polanco
11560 Mexico
D.F. Mexico

Spain (including Portugal)
Thomson Paraninfo
Calle Magallanes, 25
28015 Madrid, Spain

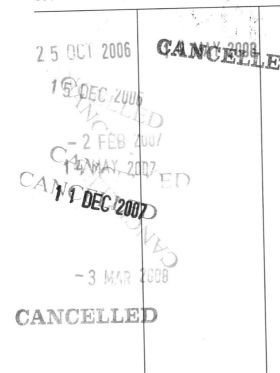
for
dozens

upple-
urces.
d pre-
ies.

Contents

Preface

In what has come to be called the post-9/11 world, in which international terrorism on the world stage influences virtually all human activity in some fashion, the media function as a central nervous system for society and culture. They do so in a fast-changing and increasingly interactive digital age. The media, and especially the news and information media, are both a social institution interacting with other such institutions—business, government, and so on—and a conduit for content that informs individuals, institutions, and society itself.

Thus, in this age of the Internet and new media, the fundamental debates involving communication and society both change and remain the same. Although conceptions of the press and the news media are themselves under scrutiny, many of the issues involving how they perform their functions and the reliability of the content they offer are as lively and vibrant as ever.

Whether the method of delivery is ink on paper, electronic communication, or the digital impulses of the World Wide Web, people continue to care and care deeply about the role media play in society and culture—the way they shape attitudes and opinions and influence politics and consumer behavior. We ask whether the media are getting better or worse, and why. Well beyond the social, commercial, and political roles, people care specifically about the content they get from the media—whether information and news in a newspaper or magazine or on television, opinion on radio, or entertainment at the movies or on cable. Universal concerns about freedom and fairness, for example, are tempered by current conditions but are still at the heart of discussion and debate about the media.

In a global economy, Americans ponder how our media system differs from others in the world. Is it better or worse? The relationships between media and government—who is influencing whom and why, matters of trust, accountability, and our right of access to diverse information and opinions—are always of concern. We worry about media bias and impartiality, matters of race and ethnicity, the nature of news and its foundations, the journalistic profession itself, and those industries so integrally related to media—advertising and public relations.

This book is by no means a history, but it does benefit from historical insights of the many scholars and media commentators we cite as well as our own observations. When the book was first written, media–government disputes were often central to the arguments we traced. Over time, the importance of the economic system, always vital, has become more so as the impact of ownership and greater media concentration loom large. Increasingly, any understanding of the media and questions raised about them center on economic, technological, and regulatory matters, including the interplay of money, the news machines, and the law. They are all interconnected. For example, the changing landscape of digital media has greatly expanded our communication options and dilemmas. These are sometimes seen as technological developments and innovations, but they do not stand alone. The so-called new platforms of the Internet, the World Wide Web, and various broadband and satellite capacities require knowledge of people's media habits, desires, and fears.

Most of us who engage in media debates—whether that involves criticism of a biased news source, sloppy reporting, or a blurring of information and entertainment—are fixed largely on the present and future. The approach in this book raises large questions in the context of current controversies and future scenarios. We hope that people who use this book will bring present-day dilemmas to the larger matter of long-term prospects suggested in these pages. What we talk about today when reflecting on a current headline is part of a larger mosaic of media trends of which we are all a part.

The authors of this book are dedicated learners drawing on decades of scholarly evidence and practical experience. Between us we've written nearly 70 books and hundreds of articles for learned journals and professional magazines. We have worked in the communications field and have regular contact with individuals ranging from entry-level employees to the heads of giant corporations. We have consulted on media and done research in nearly 100 countries and are often quoted in media reports. We have taught in 10 universities and have worked for foundations, think tanks, and other enterprises where knowledge of and experience with the media are valued. Both of us, however, enjoy the continuous debates we have with our students—in person and online. With each edition of this book, thousands of students have engaged us via e-mail, telephone, and letters. This experience and specific information have been factored into the book.

What's new in this the fourth edition of *Media Debates*? A great deal that reflects both the passing show—current events in real time that have changed the media landscape and the issues therein—and the long view of media, which changes incrementally and sometimes subtly but significantly. Since the last edition of this book, media have been involved in a number of swirling controversies, including:

- **The Jayson Blair affair** at the *New York Times*, which involved falsification of information and plagiarism that eventually brought down the paper's top editors and sent shock waves across the news media and media industries generally

- **A war on terrorism,** with global implications for media coverage along with government controls on information that usually augur against freedom of expression
- **Wars in Iraq and Afghanistan** that once again brought back the conflict between secrecy and publicity in an open society, with implications for the news media
- **Continued consolidation and concentration of ownership** in media industries, affecting their operations, content, personnel, and social role
- **Changing styles and standards of journalism** and other media content, affecting such concerns as civic journalism, the ideology of the media, and whether the media are biased or not
- **Political upheaval** as represented in the U.S. presidential election of 2004 and in electoral races elsewhere at home and overseas, once again raising questions about what the role of the news media should be
- **The rise of ideological media,** with the Fox Network and conservative and liberal talk show hosts and networks part of a dramatic, changing media landscape that challenges the old notion that the U.S. media tend toward an objective ideal
- **Globalization of almost everything,** including the media, igniting both quiet changes and street riots, influencing the pace of change and a new economic imperative
- **A redefinition of diversity,** moving it beyond race and ethnicity to gender and even age, affecting how the media do their work and the audiences to whom they appeal
- **The age-old media and democracy conundrum**—how an institution that promotes freedom for others can be so autocratic in its own operations—and hence the question, how free should the media be?

These and other dramatic changes in the media landscape, from the *change of network anchors* to the *rise of reality television* and the *coming of the bloggers*, are all part of the new material offered in this edition.

As we ponder these concerns, it is clear that one can walk through the halls of any school of journalism or communication and hear lectures about the motivations of media owners—unfortunately, by people who have never ventured inside a corporate boardroom and who have never had a conversation with the people they so easily understand and so often denounce. By the same token, it is not hard to find media professionals, such as editors and broadcasters, who immediately dismiss research conducted by university professors, asserting that "they don't know what they are talking about." The authors of this book collectively have met and known the leaders of media industries, the famous and the lesser known in communication, as well as leading scholars, researchers, and other commentators. We have traveled widely both in the United States and on nearly every other continent of the globe and have studied similarities and differences between U.S. media systems and those elsewhere.

The result of this experience is humility about what we really know and understand. The field of communication and media studies is not as easy as some might imagine; rather, it is multifaceted and multidimensional. Different people with different life experiences, perspectives, political outlooks, and indeed vested interests will come to different conclusions. There are, in fact, different ways of knowing the same subject. Nowhere is this more the case than in media, where entry-level reporters will differ sharply with the owners of their enterprise and where news managers see things differently than do people in advertising and public relations. Similarly, in the university, historians of the press will have one view, social science researchers another, and cultural studies and critical theory advocates still another. We believe that no one approach has a franchise on truth and that intelligent assessment, accepting some views and discarding others, is the best course and the one most relevant at this or any other time. Thus, we include some theorists and commentators whose work may not be known to those who pursue a particular ideological course. The material cited is as fresh as books, articles, and essays published the month we sent our work to the publisher and as venerable as ancient philosophers and modern (not just postmodern) critics. We believe that research is about respect, and we fully respect the scholarly efforts of several different research traditions as well as the intelligence gathered from media professionals, commentators, and ordinary citizens. The differences mentioned here are often in play, swirling around the debates between people with different interests and motivations. Thus, it is left to the student to absorb varied perspectives, sift through a range of evidence, and come to his or her own conclusions.

In the field of media studies, there are few fixed points on the compass, few imperatives that are always, under every circumstance, true or false. Communication issues and communication policy, whether expressed at the individual, group, organizational, or societal level, are matters of human decision making. A fact or trend that one person or organizational leader thinks terribly important may seem irrelevant to another. Where one person sees radical change, another sees an exceptional lurch not likely to be repeated. However one resolves a media debate, nonetheless, many of the abiding issues and principles do endure. For that reason, a clear assessment of the issue at hand in the context of institutional memory, history, scholarly assessment, and personal experience will lead to different conclusions and outcomes.

This book was the outgrowth of a conversation between two media scholars and analysts who admired each other's work but often disagreed with the other's conclusions or the way that evidence about a given topic was weighted. When one of us suggested a coauthored book, that seemed highly unlikely until we proposed a debate. There is a danger in this kind of approach, in which one author takes a position and then uses lawyerly case building and the assembling of evidence to support a strong conclusion. The other author follows and tries to demolish the first's argument, evidence, and conclusion. Then there are opportunities for rebuttal. In the end, students are offered divergent models of discourse and are given both study and research questions that ought to be helpful as they reach their own conclusions. This can be risky because as authors we are not simply ladling up our own positions and prejudices but rather are playing the role of advocates for our positions (which may not be our personal views at all) in order to put forth a compelling case for the proposition at hand. In some instances, we have drawn straws for the position; in others, we have picked that side of the case we know best, whether or not it is a personal conviction. We invite students to consider our other published work if they are truly interested in our own views, as opposed to those we champion for the sake of lively discourse here.

The format of the book is straightforward: A neutral description that reflects prevailing sentiment on what the issue under discussion means is followed by both a challenge and a response. In the challenge and response, we have attempted to assemble the best evidence from both scholarly and professional sources to support our positions. Although we've mined a good deal of material that covers several recent decades and also goes back to historical references, we have, at the same time, developed a detailed bibliography of pertinent source material for later consideration. Those suggestions for further reading appear at the end of each chapter.

This book was developed for courses in mass communication, journalism, media studies, and related fields, especially those just beyond the introductory level. Over the years, earlier editions of this book have been used by sophomores, juniors, seniors, graduate students, and media professionals. The book has been used most often as a text in Mass Communication and Society classes and in other classes called, variously, Media and Entertainment Industries, Contemporary Problems (or Issues) in Journalism and Mass Communication, Media Ethics, Communication Ethics and Law, Introduction to Media Studies, and the like.

More than anything, the authors believe that a thoughtful blend of systematic knowledge gleaned from research—ours and that of others—as well as the direct experience of media owners, executives, and professional employees greatly strengthens our own perspectives and the material in this book. Mutual respect among media people, media scholars, other citizens, and institutional leaders makes for a more useful and truly interactive book. That's what we've tried to do here with the help of several generations of students, various faculty colleagues, and media professionals. We are grateful to many colleagues in the academy and industry who have critiqued our work and especially to those who have weighed in on several editions of this book, including Salma Ghanem, University of Texas–Pan American; Bruce Gronbeck, University of Iowa; Kevin Kawamoto, University of Washington; Kent Middleton, University of Georgia;

Carol Reuss, University of North Carolina; Gary Pettey, Cleveland State University; Dominick LaSorsa, University of Texas at Austin; Vince P. Norris, Penn State University; and Dwight Teeter, University of Wisconsin, Milwaukee.

This book also owes a considerable debt to several generations of students whose lively inquiries and blunt assessments shaped what we have written, as well as to many faculty and other professional colleagues who joined vigorously in the debates developed, recreated, and extended here.

About the Authors

Everette E. Dennis and John C. Merrill are widely known authorities on media issues, institutions, and industries. Both have international reputations as authors, scholars, and leaders in communication and media education. Dr. Dennis is the Felix E. Larkin Professor of Communication and Media Industries at Fordham's Graduate School of Business in New York City, and Dr. Merrill is professor emeritus from the School of Journalism at the University of Missouri. Dr. Dennis was founding director of the respected Media Studies Center at Columbia University and founding president of the American Academy in Berlin. He has been a dean at the University of Oregon and taught at the Universities of Minnesota, Kansas State, and Northwestern. Dr. Merrill spent most of his academic career at Missouri, but also served as director and professor of the Manship School of Journalism at Louisiana State University and held a chair at the University of Maryland. He has also taught overseas in several countries. Dennis and Merrill are among the most prolific scholars and researchers in the media studies field, having produced works on media ethics, international communication, media industries, media law, and other topics. Both are recent winners of major awards in their fields of expertise from academic and professional organizations. Both are active scholars and students of the media, with Dr. Merrill serving as a visiting professor at the American University, Cairo, in 2004 and Dr. Dennis completing a major study of the digital strategies of the top 25 media companies the same year, when he also won the coveted Eleanor Blum Award for service to research from the Association for Education in Journalism and Mass Communication.

INTRODUCTION

The media in all forms—from books to broadband—are platforms for content that sparks debate. Sometimes the debate is about the nature of what is communicated, sometimes it is about the way the information has been gathered, and sometimes it is about how the information is understood and used. Arguments wherein one person favors an issue while another opposes it are central to communication and media. By their very existence media often stir controversy, especially as they describe the world around them. Media organizations and their staffs from the largest to the smallest produce content for audiences, and those audiences are rarely passive receivers of information, opinion, and entertainment. Instead they discuss what they see and hear, massage its meaning, and tell their friends and acquaintances about it. Then the trouble begins, as different perspectives, perceptions, and points of view come into play. Such views can be gentle or violent, but they mark human differences that communicators need to know and understand. Well beyond the content of the media and the performance of media people, the larger impact of media as institutions in society is also the stuff of controversy.

People who make up the media audiences quite naturally like to talk about the various media messages directed toward them. Sometimes they do so with considerable knowledge and apparent insight; they have a right to express their views, to put forth their impressions and concerns. This book presents some of the many arguments that arise in regard to the process of mass communication—whether in the media generally, in media institutions such as newspapers and television, in individual communicators such as reporters, producers, photographers, public relations personnel, and advertising executives, or in the messages themselves, both written and visual.

Although many media issues may seem trendy and ephemeral because they themselves are part of the news, they are really part of a larger mosaic of enduring debates that stretch back decades, even centuries in some cases. A county prosecutor tries to stop a reporter from covering a trial. A grieving parent wants

1

the press to leave the scene of a tragedy. A government wants to censor the Internet. A television producer betrays the trust of a source. One side in a regional conflict holds a reporter hostage. An advertiser pulls its commercials from a popular television program. A critic decries a media corporation. Others complain that the media are ageist, dismissive of older people, as that demographic group grows larger and larger. Gays and lesbians say they are portrayed unfairly in television coverage. Residents in a developing country complain that their economy is hampered by their image in the West. These and hundreds of other media issues arise daily and are often debated. At first they seem quite perishable and many are, but all of them are linked to similar controversies that have arisen in the past and that will recur in the future. A text about media does not serve the reader well if, in striving for clarity, it suggests agreement. Issues are not that settled in this field. We are instead aiming to stir up further debate and reader reaction, believing that controversy creates interest and understanding.

Public communication issues are important because they can affect people's lives both directly and indirectly. The content of communication—for example, the image of African Americans, Asian Americans, or Latinos in the media or the coverage of health issues, the economy, or the environment—almost always arouses criticism. The way reporters and other media people perform their jobs, whether or not they are ethical, does too. There is also concern about the way a given medium—such as a radio station, magazine, or newspaper—behaves in its community. The same is true for entertainment and opinion media as well as advertising, marketing, and public relations. There are media debates in recording studios, on soundstages, and in the enclaves of digital media as well as in the newsrooms, production facilities, and boardrooms of many different media industries. Because folklore (as well as reality) says that those who "pay the piper call the tune," the ownership and control of communication is always on the agenda of those who care about the media systems. Beyond these considerations, the social consequences of communication also attract attention and comment. The system of freedom of expression and its relationship with government and other institutions of society are always worthy of hard thought and public scrutiny.

This book examines some of the persistent arguments that puzzle editors, broadcasters, critics, educators, ordinary people, and any who are concerned about the purposes and practices of the mass media in America. We have selected 20 of the most common and recurring themes in debates about media, communications, and journalism. The old distinctions between media—print and broadcast, for example—have nearly been erased by the imperatives of the digital age. Media have truly converged in an age of interactive multimedia and mega media, all of which we explain later. We hope that this book will stimulate the thinking of students and media professionals alike as they confront these issues that have continued to plague, perplex, and excite people over the years. The subjects presented here are organized to encourage the reader to explore the nature, purpose, and operations of mass communication in America. Some of the issues are large with social implications, whereas others border on shoptalk. Taken together, they help us understand the relationship of the communications media to society, as well as the relationship of social forces to the media and communication process.

In selecting the issues presented here, we examined scores of books, articles, bibliographies, and other scholarly inventories to assure ourselves that we were choosing both the most prevalent and the most important arguments for analysis. The 20 issues singled out are developed with more than 100 subsidiary issues. There is no universal, agreed-upon inventory of concepts and issues from which to select, so we have settled on those that have most often been the subject of active debates in the media industries, academe, and professional organizations. We have tried to isolate concepts and issues that persist over time. It is our belief that most short-term issues can be located within the larger arguments of this or earlier times. Although the basic functions and related rights of communication do not change much, they are clearly conditioned by economics, technology, and the legal framework, all of which we factor into our commentaries and arguments.

Whenever possible, we point up the links between the various professional and scholarly controversies, explaining how and why they are interrelated. We begin with freedom of the press, the most fundamental of all issues in any media system. That connects nicely to media and democracy and then on to media and government. We follow in quick succession with economic considerations for the media and the matter of public trust, an essential link between communicators and their audiences. Several connected concepts also considered are the right to know, media bias, and political leanings—ideas often discussed in media coverage of politics. Then we take a look at the digital revolution and the Internet. Although these early chapters are philosophical underpinnings for any media system, their importance is determined by ascertaining the ability of the media to decide the news, position objectively, and shape journalistic ethics. Continuing concern about changing journalistic styles and standards is also examined in the form of civic journalism. So is the ever important matter of communicating race, ethnicity, and gender. Matters of persuasion, public opinion involving advertising, and public relations are also addressed. Then we focus on journalism as a profession, again a vocational application of earlier and more theoretical discussions. While compressing chapters from earlier editions, we've added material on media and national emergencies—including terrorism and war. Finally, we take the issue to the world stage by looking at globalization for the media and communication.

In most instances a lively contemporary controversy can be examined in the context of a conventional tenet or *article of faith* about the media in America. It is not uncommon for antagonisms to flare over whether the prevailing thought about the issue is adequate or needs to be reconsidered or replaced.

We have tried to recreate that spirit in this book. We present the issues in an adversarial style. Without recreating a conventional debate format, we argue two positions by assembling evidence.

This book is a departure from standard journalism texts in several ways. Each of the 20 issues is succinctly defined and explained. The prevailing sentiment on each of them is identified. Then one author challenges the contemporary view and the other offers a response. *Although each of us argues a particular position, we are not necessarily presenting our personal viewpoints. We are acting as advocates for the position, trying to marshal the best evidence possible.* It is important to identify the central questions at the core of the debate and to demonstrate how and why people legitimately reduce a number of complex subjects to stark pro and con arguments. We do this primarily as a catalyst for discussion. We use this procedure because it is the way two people naturally discuss any debatable subject, trivial or significant. But we also indicate that many complexities ought to be considered before anyone comes to a reasoned conclusion, especially in the area of media. Even though resolved through compromise, such decisions require choices that relate evidence, values, and practical solutions to problems.

Just as lawyers advocate the very best case for their clients, we each argue as strongly as we can, based on evidence, for the side of the argument we agreed to represent. And just as the lawyer knows that the client is not always an angel, we know that all issues have many sides and that few arguments are resolved in such stark fashion. Most people, however, when confronted with a media issue, eventually do take sides. Each person decides whether a given story was of high quality or not; whether a reporter was ethical or unethical; whether public relations are generally good; and so on. Media issues belong to people, not to institutions, governments, scholars, or critics. They are matters that affect all of us as members of the many audiences at which media messages are directed. Because we are all targeted by advertisers, editorial pages, television entertainment programs, radio news, and much more, it is vital that we become better consumers of the media by being more critical about the various processes that create public communication, as well as the consequences of this communication. Each of us needs to engage in the debate, to argue about communication that affects us, to try to influence it, and to talk back.

We can start by building awareness of the great media debates. In the end, we all ought to marshal evidence and confront the arguments in our own way for our own purposes. In doing so, we can all reach our own conclusions, recognizing that on these issues there are no right or wrong positions.

FREEDOM OF THE PRESS

At one university, a campus newspaper editor is fired by the administration-dominated publication board for attacking the dean in an editorial. At another, a student blog is shut down for promoting an unpopular and allegedly racist cause. Passions run high in both cases, with profound disagreements on both sides. Words like *censorship* and *freedom* fly back and forth, yet everyone involved in these controversies will say that he or she is a staunch advocate of freedom of speech and press, an idea that surfaces daily in many communities and nations the world over.

Freedom of the press is usually defined as the right to communicate ideas, opinions, and information without government restraint. A deeply held value in the United States and most of the world these days, press freedom is also guaranteed by law in the free-press clause of the First Amendment to the U.S. Constitution, which states:

> Congress shall make no law respecting an establishment of religion, or prohibiting the free exercise thereof; or abridging the **freedom of speech, or of the press;** or the right of the people peaceably to assemble, and to petition the government for redress of grievances.

A central purpose of freedom of the press is to encourage the existence of an educated and informed electorate that can make decisions about public affairs. From early times forward, freedom of the press simply meant the absence of government licensing of printing and publishing. Later it came to mean *no prior restraint* of publication. This is the idea that prepublication censorship is out of bounds. But freedom of the press is really a much broader construction than it immediately appears to be. It is truly *freedom of expression,* broader than the First Amendment guarantees, and this amazes and perplexes people in other countries that have no such explicit law. The First Amendment has protected unpopular speech and communication such as cross burnings and other hate messages, unfair political statements, some pornography, libel that is not malicious, and even the publication of stolen government documents. The test is always whether there is a public benefit or a clear *public interest* in the free flow of information, regardless of whether it is necessarily accurate, fair, or sensible. In no other country is there such a dramatic mandate of freedom, though citizens in other countries often greatly admire this aspect of the American system, whereas their leaders often assuredly do not. The United States assures freedom of expression with legal procedures that make it very difficult for the government—or, for that matter, business—to restrain the press and other media. We even have a process of judicial review that ensures that restrictions on freedom of expression are not vague or overbroad so that government cannot act arbitrarily or capriciously. This is an old doctrine with modern applications, as was demonstrated when the Congress acted to prevent indecent material on the Internet only to see that legislation struck down by the Supreme Court, which saw a more generalized danger to freedom of speech and press in these restrictions.

Freedom of the press is said to assure satisfaction of society's need for a maximum flow of information and opinion and the individual's right of self-fulfillment. Freedom of the press is also a promoter and protector of other rights: In the United States, a free press is regarded as central to the functioning of democratic government and a free citizenry. Of course, freedom of the press also means protection from arbitrary and despotic control.

There is much continuing debate about the essential nature of this concept of freedom, what it actually means, to whom it extends, and whether it is an *individual* or an *institutional* right—that is, does freedom of the press belong to every citizen or only to those organizations that constitute *the press*, such as newspapers, television stations, and even Internet Websites? In large part, the contemporary interpretation of freedom of the press depends on legally sanctioned definitions of such terms as *Congress, no law,* and *press. Press* once meant only the print media, but in an age of broadcast and computer technology, the concept of *the press* has been greatly expanded to include various electronic media, motion pictures, recorded music, and of course, the Internet and other digital forms.

CHALLENGE

Dennis: Press freedom is not a settled issue.

"Freedom of the press" is one of those noble expressions that slide easily off our tongues, though it is not always fully understood or documented. There is a persistent, romantic notion that freedom of the press flourishes in the United States and that it is an essential linchpin of our democratic system of government. Many of us want to believe that, but such a belief eludes the truth. The American press is simply not free in any accurate sense of the word. The press fights for freedom and, from time to time, achieves fragments of freedom, but press freedom is far from full-scale attainment. Press freedom, or more extended freedom of expression, is hardly a settled issue in the United States. Although many First Amendment advocates step forward declaring that a given law or practice will not pass *the First Amendment test*, that is usually their opinion and subject to a public fight, whether in demonstrations, the halls of Congress, or the courts. Students who loved to download music through Napster and other music sites discovered this quite abruptly a few years ago when the music business virtually shut down the popular Internet music portal for violating intellectual property rights. Free media, indeed. In other instances it is not unusual for a local district attorney to prohibit the showing of a controversial film, whether for sexual or religious reasons. Unpopular causes, whether they involve admittedly despicable racists or obscure religious cults, have a tough time in the United States; they're chastised by local citizens and sent on their way. And although it is true that courts sometimes intervene well after the fact and give the wounded cause (or person) relief, it is often too little and too late. The idea that freedom of expression, especially freedom of the press, is a settled issue that the world marvels at is so much nonsense. It is instead a battleground where the fight for freedom must be fought again and again, a process that requires considerable money, time, and patience.

I make this argument knowing that the press in the United States is better off and under fewer restraints than media in most other countries and cultures. I would still argue that bona fide freedom of the press is a distant dream that will probably never be achieved. Why? Because when all of the romantic rhetoric of press freedom is pushed aside, the most basic formulation of freedom of the press is what the great constitutional scholar Thomas Cooley called "the right to publish whatever one may please and to be protected against any responsibility for so doing." Cooley wrote those words in the 19th century in one of the earliest treatises on our constitutional law, but he added this important qualification:

> except so far as such publications, from their blasphemy, obscenity, or scandalous character, may be a public offense, or by their falsehood and malice they may injuriously affect the standing, reputation, or the pecuniary interests of individuals. (Cooley, 1888, 885–86)

Although Judge Cooley's 1888 statement effectively summarizes the battlefield on which many of the fights for press freedom have been waged, it also is a chilling inventory of exceptions that make freedom quite conditional. And all of Cooley's conditions—except blasphemy—are still alive and well in the trial courts, clearly constraining freedom.

In part, confusion over the idea of press freedom stems from the word *freedom* itself. Freedom can mean the total absence of restraint. The term *liberty* comes closer to Cooley's meaning, because liberty is commonly defined as freedom from all restraints except those justly imposed by law. Liberty of the press assumes a system of rights and duties, whereas freedom of the press does not. In the United States Constitution, the framers were not simply stating philosophical maxims, but were trying to devise a workable system of government. Thus, freedom under our system had a narrower focus than liberty. The originators of our legal basis for freedom of the press were the framers of the Constitution, individuals influenced by the Enlightenment philosophers who wrote about the *rights of man* in broad-based, idealized fashion. The framers inserted the words "freedom of speech or of the press" in what is now the First Amendment, but they were doing more than stating a philosophy. Rather, they tried to find practical means of letting the press have considerable latitude, but not unrestrained freedom. Those simple words unleashed a lively, continuing debate. Two factors that have fueled this controversy are:

1. The general lack of agreement about what is meant by freedom of the press
2. The recognition that freedom of the press does not exist in a vacuum, but instead must coexist with other rights accorded to individuals under the Constitution

Only the most naive dreamer could look on the history of the American media and think that they have ever been completely free from restraint. From the earliest times laws were enacted, mainly at the state level, to protect citizens *from* the press, just as the Bill of Rights protects citizens from the government and its police. As Cooley suggested, those restrictions included libel (in police terms, false arrest), invasion of privacy (in police terms, unreasonable search and seizure), and many others. It was generally accepted by society that the press should not be free to destroy reputations, undermine the confidence of the community, promote violence, murder, and mayhem, or incite other activities deemed to be harmful. The debate over the extensions (or limits) of press freedom has often centered on whether that freedom is *absolute* or *conditional*.

The idea of literal or absolute freedom of the press has found few champions more fierce and steadfast than Hugo Lafayette Black, who served on the U.S. Supreme Court from 1937 to 1971. To Justice Black, the First Amendment was a literal command. The First Amendment says that "Congress shall make no law . . . abridging freedom of speech, or of the press," and to Black, no law meant no law. "I am," he wrote, "for the First Amendment from the first word to the last. I believe it means what it says" (Cahn, 1962, 53). Justice Black (and sometimes his colleague Justice William O. Douglas) was often adamant about the absolute nature of the First Amendment. Justice Black's brand of First Amendment absolutism is not limited to the lofty chambers of the Supreme Court. I recall this idea being expressed vehemently by an editor at the *Milwaukee Journal Sentinel.* I was speaking to the staff and speculating about some of the trade-offs that citizens expect from the press as a result of the First Amendment franchise. Red-faced, the editor exploded, telling me that there was nothing about that in the Constitution. "No law, that's what it says," he told me. "Sounds familiar," I replied. Many laws made by Congress and by state legislatures constrain and complicate freedom of the press. They range from libel and privacy statutes to laws governing intellectual property and advertising to the publication of government secrets. Even the resolute Justice Black would sometimes admit that at certain *times*, under certain *circumstances*, and in certain *places*, there could be limits on freedom of expression. So much for the foundations of First Amendment absolutism. Black's position on this issue, even when unyielding, was never the view of a majority of the Supreme Court.

The philosopher Sidney Hook argued that freedom of the press is not absolute and must yield on occasion to the nation's national security needs or to the rights of individuals that collide with notions of press freedom—for example, the right to a fair trial as guaranteed in the Sixth Amendment or the right of privacy.

People take many complex positions involving facts, values, and policies as they explore the intricacies of the concept of press freedom, and almost all of them agree that press freedom is fragile and volatile, lacking real stability. Critics point out the negative nature of the First Amendment that figuratively slaps the hand of Congress in advance but says little about what the powerful executive and judicial branches of the federal government may do. The framers could not have foreseen the so-called strong presidency and the "imperial judiciary." Some critics argue that the First Amendment really means *all government* instead of Congress per se. Even though the Fourteenth Amendment has been interpreted so that it extends the provisions of the Bill of Rights (including press freedom) to the states, it was not until 1925 that the Supreme Court, in *Gitlow v. New York*, told the states not to impair these rights with laws of their own. But even this court ruling and many subsequent decisions that have defined the conditions and contours of so-called press freedom have failed to wipe out a complex series of state and federal laws and court rulings that place severe limits on freedom of the press.

Most people who have studied freedom of the press agree that one of its fundamental conditions in the United States is the doctrine of *no prior restraint* of publication. This doctrine holds that the press must be free to publish what it wishes without interference from the government, while remaining subject to various types of legal scrutiny after the fact. This is, of course, a kind of muted freedom, but even here the record is by no means unsullied.

In *Near v. Minnesota* (1931), the U.S. Supreme Court struck down a gag law in that state and established the principle of **no prior restraint** of the press firmly in American constitutional law. On a number of occasions since, however, the government has attempted to block publication of controversial material. In 1971, for example, the *New York Times* and *Washington Post* published some material about the Vietnam War from classified government documents two weeks before the Supreme Court conceded their right to do so; in the meantime, the *Times* and *Post* were enjoined from further publication. A similar issue arose a few years later when *The Progressive* magazine was prevented from publishing a story about building a hydrogen bomb. In recent years, the Communications Decency Act tried to curtail pornography on the Internet until it was overturned by the Supreme Court. And, in the wake of the 9/11 terrorist acts at the World Trade Center and in Washington, D.C., Congress passed the U.S. Patriot Act, which in an effort to fight terrorism also limited civil liberties as well as curtailing freedom of information. In this instance national security trumped freedom of expression—and ultimately media freedom too.

Although there may have been good reason for the government's actions in these instances, they hardly contributed to a sense of freedom from prior restraint. There are scores of examples in which courts have placed restraining orders and other gag rules on reporters attempting to cover the judicial system. These restraints may be fully justifiable, but in any event, their presence is not press freedom. Of course, such actions are perfectly permissible under our legal system in spite of the First Amendment.

I believe that constraints on press freedom in the public sector by the judiciary, the executive, and the legislative branches of government are only part of the barrier to freedom of the press in the United States. There are also many restrictions in the private sector. These include aspects of contract and property law that severely restrict the press in carrying out its fullest exercise of freedom. In addition, the law of intellectual property (copyright) sometimes inhibits republication of particular material, as in the Napster and MP3 cases. Such constraints as nondisclosure agreements in employment contracts can also impair press freedom.

The noble purposes of press freedom, as envisioned by the Enlightenment philosophers and others since, would clearly elevate society, but in most instances these are still distant goals, not actual accomplishments, not the reality of the situation today or perhaps ever. Some commentators say "the structure is the message" in any consideration of media organizations and their behavior. The structure of the newspaper or broadcast organization dictates rules under which reporters and editors operate. There are conventions against certain kinds of behavior. Some stories get covered; others don't. The written or unwritten rules or newsroom policies, so fully documented in studies of media gatekeepers, are also constraints on freedom. Professionalism itself restrains free will and limits individual choice. Many of us would agree that such private restraints (also called responsibility and ethics) actually limit press freedom, but for the right reasons. Many forces and factors have an impact on shaping the performance of the media. They condition and control. They slow and mute freedom.

Some theorists believe that freedom of the press has a preferred place in our scheme of individual liberty and freedom, because of its symbolic primacy* in the

---

*The number one placement of the First Amendment was really an accident, not the result of calibrated planning by the framers.

Bill of Rights and its importance to the functioning of democratic government, but the fact remains that freedom of the press, if it exists at all, is engaged in continuous bargaining with other rights and interests, both individual and social. This has been called a process of reconciliation, wherein rights exercised by one person or one group can be reconciled with equal opportunity for others to enjoy them. Thus, we have a complex, interrelated system in which rights, principles, practices, and institutions interact. A local newspaper may severely limit my right of privacy today in the name of press freedom, but I may be able to restrain that freedom tomorrow by arguing that pretrial publicity is impairing my right to a fair trial.

The American media live with rules and regulations, conventions and constraints. They enjoy a measure of liberty and have a mechanism that, under most circumstances, allows for the adjudication of disputes that constrain freedom. Freedom of the press presupposes the free flow of information and the free dissemination of a wide spectrum of opinions. In most instances we have a rather muted version of this enlightened view of a free press. A more penetrating look at the many social and psychological factors that can have a chilling effect on freedom—such as the subtle influences of one's peers, bosses or community—yields a haunting indictment of any claim of press freedom. Finally, as we examine the law, there is a subtle message that ought to be understood: Through the years spokespersons for the media have fought vigorously for greater and greater press freedom. If this is necessary, the media are hardly free.

Some of my journalist friends tell me that "nowhere does the Constitution say anything about responsibility; the press has no responsibility to do anything." Perhaps, but the same people are fond of enumerating the rights of the press and the rights of reporters. All rights, as anyone who has studied law knows, usually have corresponding duties. And any system of free expression, which presupposes that there are rights, also assumes that there are duties. Whether these duties are also responsibilities is partly a semantic quibble. However, what appears to be a victory for the press one day, such as the *New York Times* decision rendering it difficult for public officials to sue for libel, later can emerge as a constraint. In a late 1970s Supreme Court case, *Herbert v. Lando*, the *New York Times* standard for defining malice (reckless disregard or knowing falsehood) was used to force a broadcast producer of *60 Minutes* to account for his private thoughts in planning a story. What had been a new right came back to haunt—and also to restrain—the media. Sometimes the intent of the legislature or court in defining and extending freedom can become the loophole by which it later comes back to check the media.

One thoughtful champion of press freedom, Alexander Bickel of Yale Law School, observed that the more we have to define freedom, the less freedom we have. This is not inconsistent with Justice Black's view that we should not have tampered with the command of the framers in the First Amendment. But the fact remains that we have taken considerable license in interpreting its meaning and reach. What remains is hardly a pristine vessel. The charter of press freedom is now somewhat the worse for wear. It is less than whole. It exists mainly in our minds as a social goal, not as a realistic description of the American media today. Freedom of expression, of which press freedom is a part, is no settled issue. It is always in play and requires vigilance, not the lazy-mindedness of some who think the battle was fought and won long ago.

ARGUMENT SUMMATION: *Press freedom is not a settled issue.*

Free expression, and specifically press freedom, is a noble social goal, but in reality the United States does not have the unfettered rights implied by freedom of the press. Though not as restricted as in some countries, American press freedoms are conditioned on numerous exceptions. The exceptions are necessary because press rights often must yield to other interests, such as libel, defamation, privacy, and national security—especially in wartime. In addition to legal limits on the press, there are numerous private restrictions, including civil laws such as copyright and contract, concentration of media ownership, public relations manipulation of news, and press policies in editing and publishing news. Although the First Amendment says Congress shall make no law restricting freedom of the press, several restrictive laws exist. The courts have said that only an absolute freedom from prior restraint exists; but papers have been enjoined from printing certain items. These official and private limitations on the press mean that American media may be active in their pursuit of freedom, but they are far from fully free.

RESPONSE

Merrill: *Press freedom is mostly a settled issue.*

When we say that the United States enjoys exceptional freedom of expression and that includes a free press, of course we do not mean that the press is completely, totally, absolutely free of any and all restraints. Anyone who thinks, even minimally, about press freedom—or any kind of freedom, for that matter—knows full well that freedoms require some kind and some degree of restriction and responsibility. It may well be that press freedom is a romantic notion and that it really doesn't *flourish* in the United States. But that is true with all objectives or goals of a society, and freedom, like truth, law and order, friendship, and loyalty, is relative, incomplete, and hedged with inadequacies. And nobody has maintained that press freedom flourishes in the United States. Dr. Dennis, I feel, exaggerates when he says that the American press is simply not free in any real sense of the word.

The press is indeed free in the commonly understood sense of the word; in a nonabsolutist, pragmatic, reasonable sense it is free and can be referred to as free. This is, of course, with the implicit understanding that it is not absolutely free of all the extra-press and self-imposed restrictions that can easily be brought up by critics.

Even Justice Black and others who have taken basically an absolutist view of First Amendment freedoms have recognized some limitations to press freedom. Obviously, nobody—most of all, the Founding Fathers—has ever considered the press completely free, nor would any responsible and moderate person want that. I am not talking about an anarchistic or nihilistic press; I am referring to a free press—free in the sense of having minimal government restraints placed upon it. I am talking about a press in the real world of social and political frictions and problems; I am not considering some theoretical level of freedom for an unreal press that might exist in the minds of absolutists and sophists. Just as I might say that the United States is a democratic country (knowing full well that it is not really or totally so), I can say with assurance and pragmatic validity that the United States has a free press.

Sidney Hook has been quoted asserting that press freedom must yield on occasion to national security. But note that the term *press freedom* is used; and it is this press freedom that *must yield.* Such freedom must obviously be assumed by Hook in order to be yielded. What American would really want an unyielding concept of press freedom? Reasonable persons, and certainly the framers of the Constitution were reasonable, would not want an unyielding freedom in a nation based on law and social cooperation. Indeed, on this point, my colleague Dennis, although he lives in New York City, seems to express a pre-9/11 view. Terrorism, which in that instance led to war in Afghanistan and later Iraq, has certainly been used to justify limitations on media freedom. But we'll take up this issue in a later chapter.

A number of factors limit freedom of the press. Some are external to the press, such as considerations of national security, court rulings, libel actions, pressures from advertisers and other groups, and subscriber desires. Some are internal, such as professional codes of ethics, the editorial power structure itself, press councils, and the like.

I maintain that the core of press freedom in the United States is editorial autonomy, and that this country's press system can be considered free in the sense that it has editorial autonomy—even in the broadcasting aspects of the press (those concerning news and commentary, at least). The American press can make its own editorial decisions and, as a result, can legitimately be considered free. And certainly in the context of the press systems of other countries—even those like the United Kingdom and Sweden—it is free. Relatively free, of course, but free in a meaningful and realistic sense.

In the United States there is no prior restraint on the press by government. This means that the media are free to publish or broadcast what they want to without government interference or prepublication censorship. The press can criticize the government without fear of being shut down. This is a key factor. Although, as Dr. Dennis has pointed out in his *Challenge*, there have been a few instances in which the courts have instituted some prior restraint on publications, these must be considered exceptions and aberrations; they should not be cited to negate press freedom in the United States. General statements that are valid are not to be invalidated by pointing to occasional exceptions.

As to the argument that newsroom policies restrict freedom of the press, nobody would deny that internal journalistic decision making and management control by the news media's own executives have a restrictive and directive role in journalism. But is this a restriction *on* the press? No. It is, if anything, a restriction *by* the press. And it is an inevitable result of freedom *of* the press. Managers of the press must have the freedom to make their own decisions vis-à-vis editorial content; in making these decisions, they are not restricting press freedom, but are exercising it.

Freedom does not simply mean *free from*. To be free from everything—free from other people, free from laws, free from morality, free from thought, free from emotion—is to be nothing. Unlimited or unrestricted freedom is impossible, in fact, and should not be demanded by reasonable people. The truth is that any freedom that is possible and desirable does and should have some limitation. Realistic freedom must have some base point or ground.

An example of this grounding of freedom can be found in Confucian ethics. Here the ground or limitation to freedom is goodness. A person should choose good, not evil. If evil prevailed, freedom would probably disappear. Hence, from an ethical perspective, we should permit only the freedom to select good and not the freedom to choose evil.

Confucius confirmed this principle in his own life as it related to freedom of speech. He was free to speak as he pleased, and he thus recognized freedom of speech; he would oppose only the speaking of bad words or empty words—that is, words without corresponding *right* actions. Incipient authoritarianism? We have seen rationales for limiting freedom in the writings of Plato, Immanuel Kant, Walter Lippmann, and others who have argued that any freedom that harms others or the foundations of society must be curtailed. One might speak of a degree of authoritarianism in Confucius in the same way, and only in the same way, as one might speak of a degree of authoritarianism in Kant or even Jesus. The Categorical Imperative of Kant or the Golden Rule of Jesus carries authority, but this authority is self-realized and is in no way externally imposed.

So we can talk about self-determined restrictions within an environment of freedom. And still we have freedom—of speech or of the press. A contemporary proponent of ethical restraint, very much Confucianist in this respect, has been

Professor Walter Berns. In *Freedom, Virtue, and the First Amendment* (1957) he issues an articulate call to public virtue. While disassociating himself from intolerance and censorship, he favors certain censorship from a moral perspective. Salacious and pornographic publications, he maintains, can be censored. American Communists have no claim to free expression because they are disloyal. Like Confucius, Berns contends that *bad* speakers and *bad* speeches deserve no protection. Government, he believes, should be engaged in raising the moral quality of the community and therefore must judge and limit public discussion according to the moral quality of the writer or speaker. For Berns and others there is a set of moral principles which, though hard to state with precision, are obligatory on all reasonable persons.

Walter Lippmann (*The Public Philosophy*, 1955) would restrict the concept of freedom also—or, more precisely, would have it restricted voluntarily by the individual. He believes as does Berns: As long as they contribute to forming the public mind, speech and writing should be free. Lippmann believes that the criterion of loyalty is "an indubitable commitment to defend and preserve the order of political and civil rights." To Lippmann and Berns, the disloyal have cut themselves out of the basic agreement that supports the process of public discussion. Lippmann maintains, for example, that there can be no right (freedom) to destroy a liberal democratic state—in this he echoes Plato—and Berns points out that we should limit disloyal speech or writing which would generate an American Lenin or Hitler.

So we can see that there have been, and are, thoughtful persons who recognize the necessity of limiting freedom or placing certain moral restrictions on certain forms of communication—whether it is falsely shouting fire in a crowded theater or advocating something that will do harm to national security, public morality, or the continued environment of responsible freedom.

There is, indeed, some danger of authoritarianism implicit in the ideas of these persons. Like the much-maligned Commission on Freedom of the Press (Hutchins Commission) of the 1940s, they often seem to pose a threat to freedom by stressing responsibility or virtue. And perhaps they do. The debate still rages as to the relative benefits of virtue, responsibility, and social stability against the benefits of freedom.

I certainly will not get into that at this point, but you might like to reassess the pronouncements of John Stuart Mill and others (Locke, Milton, Burke, Jefferson, and Voltaire), who base their belief in free expression largely on utilitarian principles. Press freedom is indeed relative and incomplete, but I believe that such qualifications are implicit in the term itself. By and large, the American press is free to be about as free as it wishes—recognizing, of course, that along with this exercise of freedom come certain responsibilities and obligations to the society that permits it to exist.

In a realistic sense, there is press freedom in the United States. The U.S. Constitution protects freedom of the press; so there must be something to protect. Journalists think they have press freedom and what they *think* they have, they have. They are speaking of media self-determinism; they are not thinking about limitations and restrictions imposed on them by the press hierarchy itself.

When I say that the United States has a free press, I am saying that it has a relatively free press, a freer press than almost any other country. I am not saying that it has a completely free press, nor is anyone else who talks about freedom of the press in the United States. In addition, I am not saying that the media in the United States use their freedom to the degree they might. The freedom is there, but it is not always used. I agree with Philip Wylie, who said:

> The image of our media turns out . . . to be cowardly and unfree in a very great though not inclusive degree. . . . The media, in their mass-circulation or mass-viewed forms, either foster industry's synthetic image, or remain silent about the rot, mess, lies, human debasement, and the rest of the unfavorable truth hid behind the idol. They go along, too, with the support at least by silence, of pious interference with liberty. (Wylie, 1969, 212)

Wylie is right in implying that the American press could do better and be freer, if it wanted to be. The freedom is there; the fact is that the press often chooses not to use it. Such self-imposed restriction by the press on its freedom does not negate this freedom. It simply sets it aside temporarily until a stronger will, coupled with more courage, chooses to project the press toward a more forceful and responsible utilization of the freedom that it has.

Freedom of expression, of which freedom of the press is an essential and integral part, is mostly a settled issue in the United States as it is not in other parts of the world. The true test lies in the beliefs of the people and their support for press freedom, which is a deeply felt part of the American constitutional faith, even though one might be momentarily angry at a given newscast or Internet reporter who demonstrates irresponsible behavior. A doctrine that is solidly based in constitutional law and in media practice is occasionally challenged, but that does not diminish its force and purpose. Freedom of expression as a construct and as a matter of daily practice is mostly agreed upon, whether or not Professor Dennis thinks so.

ARGUMENT SUMMATION: *Press freedom is mostly a settled issue.*

The American media are free in the ordinary sense of that term. This does not mean license or anarchism, but legally controlled, socially responsible freedom. It is a socially moderated freedom permitted by the First Amendment to the Constitution. Naturally, journalistic freedom is not total because there are various social pressures on media managers. But press directors can publish what they wish—without prior restraint by government. And this is what is meant by press freedom in the United States. The core meaning has come to approximate journalistic autonomy. Newsroom policies and directives are not relevant to press freedom, although they do apply to the freedom of individual journalists. The First Amendment protects press freedom (the press's freedom); therefore, there must be press freedom in the United States to be thus protected.

SEARCH ONLINE!

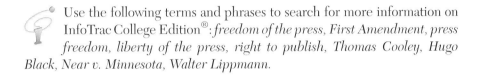 Use the following terms and phrases to search for more information on InfoTrac College Edition®: *freedom of the press, First Amendment, press freedom, liberty of the press, right to publish, Thomas Cooley, Hugo Black, Near v. Minnesota, Walter Lippmann.*

TOPICS FOR DISCUSSION

1. Discuss *freedom*, giving all the possible meanings for the term relevant to the freedom of the press. Now do the same thing with the term *press*. Has interactivity changed the definition of press freedom, given the greater involvement of the online reader and viewer?
2. Should the media be able to publish or broadcast anything they wish? If not, what should be forbidden? Where should the press freedom line be drawn? Who should draw it?
3. What is the problem with the concept of *a responsible use of freedom*? For example: Who—or what entity—should define responsibility?
4. Why do many people believe that press freedom is to be preferred over responsibility or virtue?
5. If there is press freedom in the United States, does it belong only to media managers and owners, or to all journalists? Many say that it belongs to the people. How could it?

TOPICS FOR RESEARCH

1. Thomas Jefferson and other American presidents have typically made positive and negative statements about press freedom. Write an essay indicating why this is the case. Find examples of idealistic pro–press freedom statements from Jefferson or another president. Also find a negative statement. From studies of this topic or biographies of the president, see if you can find public controversies that might have made the given president go sour on the press.

2. Find an example of a media freedom issue either in this country or else-where. Put the issue in some historical context and use appropriate sources to explain why the issue is still unsettled. This might involve book or film censorship, freedom of information, or libel.

3. Do a short paper on your personal freedom of the press. Do you have First Amendment press and speech rights? How can you exercise them? Does the present structure of American media help or hinder you in your exercise of press rights? What, if anything, does the Internet do to alter that structure?

4. Read a biography or autobiography of someone who has helped extend and expand freedom of the press. Assess this person's contribution and indicate how it is relevant to modern media issues.

5. Using the material in this chapter, critique the authors' arguments and their use of the sources they quote to document and defend these arguments. If you could question those sources (or the authors) about the downside of the cited material, what would you ask? Prepare your own inquiry into the authors' approach and conclusions. Pretend that you are their adversary and you are trying to find coherent middle ground in fashioning a sensible argument.

FURTHER READING

Altschull, J. Herbert. *From Milton to McLuhan: Ideas and American Journalism.* White Plains, NY: Longman, 1990.

Becker, Carl. *Freedom and Responsibility in the American Way of Life.* New York: Vintage Books, 1960.

Berns, Walter. *Freedom, Virtue, and the First Amendment.* Baton Rouge: Louisiana State University Press, 1957.

Boaz, David. *Libertarianism: A Primer.* New York: Free Press, 1997.

Bodenhamer, David J., and James W. Ely, Jr., eds. *The Bill of Rights in Modern America After 200 Years.* Bloomington: Indiana University Press, 1993.

Borjesson, Kristina, ed. *Into the Buzzsaw: Leading Journalists Expose the Myth of a Free Press.* New York: Prometheus Books, 2002.

Cahn, Edmond N. "Dimensions of First Amendment 'Absolutes.'" A public interview in Dennis et al.: 41–53: Also see *New York University Law Review* 37, no. 4 (June 1962): 549–63.

Carey, Alex, et al. *Taking the Risk Out of Democracy: Corporate Propaganda vs. Freedom and Liberty.* Urbana: University of Illinois Press, 1997.

Chafee, Zechariah. *Government and Mass Communication.* Chicago: University of Chicago Press, 1947.

Chamberlin, Bill, and Charlene J. Brown. *The First Amendment Reconsidered.* White Plains, NY: Longman, 1982.

Cohen, Jeremy. *Congress Shall Make No Law: Oliver Wendell Holmes, the First Amendment and Judicial Decisionmaking.* Ames: Iowa State University Press, 1989.

Cooley, Thomas. *A Treatise on Constitutional Limitations.* Vol. 2, 2d ed. Chicago: Callaghan, 1888.

Commission on Freedom of the Press. *A Free and Responsible Press.* Chicago: University of Chicago Press, 1947.

Dennis, Everette E., Donald M. Gillmor, and David Grey, eds. *Justice Hugo Black and the First Amendment.* Ames: Iowa State University Press, 1978.

Dennis, Everette E., et al. *The Media at War: The Press and the Persian Gulf Conflict.* New York: Gannett Center for Media Studies, 1991.

Dennis, Everette E., and Robert W. Snyder, eds. *Media and Democracy.* New Brunswick, NJ: Transaction Press, 1998.

Emerson, Thomas I. *The System of Freedom of Expression.* New York: Random House, 1970.

Fallows, James. *Breaking the News: How the Media Undermine American Democracy.* New York: Vantage Books, 1997.

Friendly, Fred. *Minnesota Rag.* New York: Random House, 1981.

Gans, Herbert J. *Democracy and the News.* New York: Oxford University Press, 2003.

Gillmor, Donald M. *Power, Publicity and the Abuse of Libel Law.* New York: Oxford University Press, 1992.

Haiman, Franklyn S. *Speech and Law in a Free Society.* Chicago: University of Chicago Press, 1981.

Hocking, William E. *Freedom of the Press.* Chicago: University of Chicago Press, 1947.

Lewis, Anthony. *The Sullivan Case and the First Amendment.* New York: Random House, 1991.

Lippmann, Walter. *The Public Philosophy.* Boston: Little, Brown, 1955.

MacArthur, John R. *Second Front: Censorship and Propaganda in the Gulf War.* New York: Hill and Wang, 1995.

Meiklejohn, Alexander. *Political Freedom: The Constitutional Powers of the People.* New York: Harper, 1960.

Merrill, John C., Peter Gade, and F. Blevens. *Twilight of Press Freedom.* Mahwah, NJ: Erlbaum, 2001.

Sanford, Bruce. *Don't Shoot the Messenger: How Our Growing Hatred Threatens Free Speech for Us All.* New York: Free Press, 1999.

Soloski, John, and Randall P. Bezanson, eds. *Reforming Libel Law.* New York: Guilford Press, 1992.

Stevens, John D. *Shaping the First Amendment.* Beverly Hills, CA: Sage, 1982.

Tribe, Lawrence. *American Constitutional Law* (Vol. 1). 3rd ed. Mineola, NY: Foundation Press, 2000. See especially Chapter 7.

Wylie, Philip. *The Magic Animal.* New York: Pocket Books, 1969.

Media–Government Relationship

Name any American president from George Washington to George W. Bush, and you can find an instance in which he got angry at the press, even though he steadfastly affirmed his belief in freedom of the press. The fact is that governments and the media do not always see eye to eye. Governments and government leaders want public support for their policies and the press is often the prickly critic and irritant.

As we saw in Chapter 1, the role of government in relation to the media is most often stated negatively. For example, government is commanded by the First Amendment not to intrude on press freedom. It is also relevant to note that the press is regarded as a fourth branch of government or as a fourth estate, which serves as a check on government.

The media, especially those involved in public affairs, are said to play a watchdog role and thus keep the government under surveillance. One of the primary purposes of a free press in a democratic system is to keep the public informed about government activities. However, because the media often run into a resistant government, not eager to disclose all, a natural conflict results.

Press probing and revealing of government secrecy and other restraints lead to what has been called, generally by press people, an adversarial relationship between government and the press. Some critics say this adversarial relationship has a checking value, wherein the press checks on government and makes certain that it is performing properly. This leads to a related question: Who checks on the press and sees that it is performing properly? Whether such an adversarial relationship actually exists—or should exist—is open to debate, but it is widely believed that the job of the media in American and other democratic societies is to monitor and assess the behavior and performance of government. Whether this involves gross corruption or more subtle conflicts of interest, outright lies or misrepresentation, most people will readily agree that the job of the media is to be a vigilant observer and analyst for the public—and often this requires conflict and an adversarial relationship. Although this is a gentler process in the United States than it is elsewhere, a look around the world illustrates the record well: Scores of journalists are killed each year, mostly in countries with little press freedom and zero tolerance for criticism. In other places (China comes to mind) it is not uncommon for a journalist or other media person to be jailed for unpopular opinions that are often equated with treason. Whatever its flaws, the media–government relationship of the United States and other democracies is accepted as a linchpin of modern society and is critical to the so-called digital economy of the 21st century.

CHALLENGE

Merrill: The media and government should not be adversaries.

It is commonly assumed in the United States that we have an adversarial media or press system. The media and government exist as adversaries and that's usually perceived as a proper and necessary relationship. The concept is embraced especially in the rhetoric of journalists.

This assumption is one that needs to be challenged. Granted, many of the hackneyed expressions of American journalism—the press is a fourth branch of government, or a check on government, or a watchdog—suggest the validity of the notion of a press–government adversary relationship, but is it really justified? I believe not. In the argument that follows, I shall try to explain, first, why there is no adversarial relationship under American libertarian theory and, second, why the communications media would not want such a relationship to exist.

Why should the news media and government be adversaries? Why not friends? Why not foes at times and friends at times? Why, then, should not the relationship be ambivalent—especially in a free and pluralistic press system? These are questions that it would seem unnecessary to ask in the United States. But evidently it is necessary, because the press has taken unto itself the role of an adversary to government, and boasts about it. I maintain that, theoretically, the relationship is not really adversarial (the laws are on the side of the press) and should not be adversarial—any more than it should be cooperative and harmonious. It should be an ambiguous relationship, a freewheeling one, and a changing one. That relationship would be in line with the nature of independent editorial determination, with the spirit of pluralism, and with press freedom.

Beyond this theoretical problem with the adversarial relationship, I maintain that the press does not really want such a pragmatic relationship. The press wants to be the sole adversary; it basically desires a helpless and law-bound government forced to provide the press with anything it wants, with no secrecy on the part of the government, no attempts to influence or control any activities of the press, no criticism of the press. What kind of adversarial relationship is this?

Does not press freedom imply, in effect, that any unit of the press system can take any stance it likes toward government? If I am the editor of a newspaper (or

Website), I may want to consistently support all government policies. I am free to do so. Or I may want to oppose some policies or expose some weaknesses. I may want to be ambivalent toward government—sometimes pro and sometimes con. Or I may, indeed, want to determine for my newspaper an adversarial role vis-à-vis government, using my newspaper as a vehicle to fight against government—to check on government, to criticize government, and to make it a policy to root out government excesses and wrongdoing. In short, I may decide to use my newspaper as a watchdog on government or as artillery with which to bombard government.

In a libertarian society the relationship between media and government is so varied and splintered that it cannot be expressed in any monolithic way. It cannot be called adversarial. To call it that is a travesty of rhetoric and reality. It is utterly ridiculous for the media to cast themselves as adversaries of government: Such a stance would imply that the government is always wrong and the press is always right; it would also imply that the press sees itself as an institution dedicated to portraying for the public their government as flawed and negative, and that it must be constantly watched lest it do great harm to the people.

The government, of course, is really closer to the people than is the press, for at least portions of the government are elected by the people. Not so with the press. The press, largely a profit-making private enterprise, has simply set itself up as a representative of the people and a check on government. Kurt Luedtke, formerly executive editor of the *Detroit Free Press* and screenwriter for the film *Absence of Malice*, courageously aimed strong words at the American press in this regard:

> You [the American press] are forever inventing new rights and privileges for yourselves, the assertion of which is so insolent that you apparently feel compelled—as I certainly would—to wrap them in the robe of some imaginary public duty and claim that you are acting on my behalf. If I am indeed involved, then I would like you to do a little less for me. But of course I'm not. Your claims of privilege have nothing to do with any societal obligation, because you have no societal obligation: That is the essence of what the First Amendment is all about (Luedtke, 1982).

Let me follow up this extremely relevant quotation from Luedtke with a brief statement by Paul H. Weaver of *Fortune* and *The Public Interest:* "The romantic image of the 'adversary press,' then, is a myth: 'functional' for certain purposes, but wholly inaccurate as a model of what newsmen actually do or can hope to achieve" (1974, 95).

U.S. journalism has been rather close to, dependent on, and cooperative with official sources. Undoubtedly this has caused problems, but it has been one of its strengths. Perhaps at times it has led to some press cheerleading for government policies, but it has also maximized the amount of information and disinformation available to the citizens of the country. If I, as a government official, see the press as an adversary, how will I respond to it? With caution, with distrust, with skepticism, with a minimum of openness and frankness, and with a certain hostility. I will turn this caution and hostility into considerable secrecy and distortion of information that I may give out to my adversary. Solid and balanced information, therefore, is often the victim in this adversarial warfare, with the consumer (the public) receiving the distortions and informational shreds from the battle.

It seems strange that journalists find any comfort in the concept of an adversarial press. They should know that they are dependent to a very large extent on government for their news. Virtually all the information published by journalists about government is derived from (and often validated by) some government-related person. Newspeople know almost nothing about public events and issues except what they obtain from external sources and authorities. If the media want to limit or cut off access to such sources, then they will stress their adversarial role; if they want to expand their sources and their information, then they will stress their cooperative and friendly role. Adversaries are not friendly. There is the wonderful irony, as sociologist Herbert Gans has pointed out, that government officials see themselves as proxies for the public with some legal authority while the news media also think of themselves as proxies for the public. Both claim to represent the people (Gans, 2003).

An adversarial role is often not even a responsible—or ethical—role. There is nothing sacred or intrinsically good about being an adversary. In fact, adversaries are more likely than not to deal in propaganda—to play games of disinformation and misinformation. Adversaries like to win; they are not comfortable with evenhanded information, with attempts to inform thoroughly and fairly.

In a real adversarial relationship, government would have the same right to fight as the press. The government could, in such a relationship, try to withhold information, to have secret meetings, to distort information for its advantage, to have its favorite reporters and reward them in various ways, to deal in disinformation and other propagandistic techniques, to subpoena journalists, and restrict their activities in various ways. The government would be a true adversary.

The press, no doubt, does have—or would have—the upper hand in a real adversarial relationship, unless the Constitution were changed. The press has the last word in any controversy with government. It not only has the last word, it has the first word. The government really has no word at all—except that provided by the press. Any government official's voice reaching the public through the media is immediately thereafter subjected to analysis and interpretation by media figures—telling the American people who have just heard the official what the person really said, or really meant. Instant analysis, as it is often called, might better be referred to as instant bias, by which the media make sure they have the last word.

The government's hands are largely tied. About the only way it can be an adversary of the press is through occasional verbal blasts at media practices. And these blasts themselves are subject to media control and management and to instant analyses and the *final word* technique. The government does have one other weapon, a purely defensive one—secrecy in certain deliberations. Without a doubt, it makes use of this weapon. But in the process it opens itself to more problems: the *leak* by disgruntled functionaries, escalated criticism by the press when it learns of such government operations, the need to justify government activities at every turn, and the helpless feeling of government people when the press fires its unanswerable barrages at them.

In a true adversarial relationship, there is one thing the government could do (and should do) to help its position: It should involve itself more in the media business. It should cease permitting the press to be the informer of the people; it should itself actively inform the people, circumventing when possible the commercial press. When the government has no real voice, it is an unequal and almost helpless contender in this press–government fray. Perhaps the Hutchins Commission was correct in 1947 when it suggested that government might indeed have to get into the communications business. It is obvious that in any kind of rhetorical battle, the side without control of internal, public channels of communication is at a distinct disadvantage.

If the people were to know the maximum and be exposed to the widest range of positions and opinions, it would seem logical that government voices would be of help. In fact, the government probably has a responsibility to communicate directly to the people, instead of having its messages filtered through the distorted and often biased lens of the American mass media system. Why should the press, any more than any other institution, be saddled with the awesome responsibility of providing government information to the people? Surely my coauthor will contend—speaking, I am sure, for the great majority of media people—that the government has no right to compete with private media. But why not compete? Is not government competition implicit in an adversarial relationship? Could not the government through its own publications, broadcast outlets, and other resources fill a multitude of gaps with information and viewpoints? Could not the government then have an instrument to compete with the private media? Could not the government then have a chance to set the record straight—or at least to tell in its own way what it has to say to the people? This would be consistent with the concept of pluralism, which free press people pay lip service to. It would also make the adversarial relationship more equal. It would give a virtually voiceless entity (the government) a voice with which it could speak directly to its constituency, the people. It would help make it a real contender in this adversarial relationship, which actually does not exist at present. An example of this is in Britain, where the British Broadcasting Corporation (BBC) competes with independent (private enterprise) networks and stands for quality, while still government controlled, however loosely.

But the press would not like this. In spite of its talk, the press does not really want an adversarial relationship. It cannot really tolerate the thought of the government being its adversary.

The fact that the press views itself as an adversary of government is not only theoretically questionable, but leads to problems with ethics. The belief that the press must be a check on government, a critic of government, or a watch-dog on government results in a hyperactive and contentious journalism. The adversarial role causes the press to dig and probe, snipe and snoop; it causes the press to speculate, to deal in gossip and innuendo in its attempt to unearth corruption in high and low places. This press concept is responsible for the press's accentuating the negative in governmental matters, of seldom revealing positive activities. It fosters the idea—or is the creature of the idea—that the government is necessarily and inherently evil and must be checked. And in this little game that the press sees itself playing, the press has appointed itself to keep the government honest.

Today, as an increasing number of voices are asking who checks the checker, the press falls back on its constitutional freedom guarantee, and when all the rhetoric is done, the answer from the press is essentially this: Nobody checks the checker. The press is nearly free from being checked. Is this answer consistent with the contention that the press and government are adversaries?

In conclusion, listen to a legendary American journalist, James Reston, who ends his discussion in *The Artillery of the Press* by contradicting his *artillery fire* title: "Clever officials," he says, "cannot 'manipulate' reporters, and clever reporters cannot really 'best' the government. From both sides, they have more to gain by cooperating with one another, and with the rising minority of thoughtful people, than by regarding one another as 'the enemy'" (1967, 108). So Reston recognizes the mythology implicit in his book's title and in the whole concept of the adversary relationship of the press and government.

In a practical sense most of what the media cover is not adversarial at all. From the workings of government (mostly routine and quite proper) to the conduct of elections (a model of democracy at work most of the time) to the conduct of foreign policy or war, the media are mostly uncritical conduits for information. The same is true in the private sector, where coverage of business can be downright promotional and rarely critical.

ARGUMENT SUMMATION: *The media and government should not be adversaries.*

The media and government are not adversaries—or at least they shouldn't be. Such a situation would assign a role to the press that would be in conflict with editorial self-determination. An adversarial relationship may well exist from time to time, but in a free and open press system such a relationship should be strictly ad hoc. Why should a free press feel it must be an adversary to government?

*Why not just as well be a friend? Some media at some times and in some cir-
cumstances may want to oppose the government in certain particular matters,
but a generally assumed opposition to government is not only irrational, but
contrary to the basic tenets of a free and self-determining press.*

RESPONSE

Dennis: The media and government should be adversaries.

Granted, *adversarial* may be an overly dramatic term to describe the ideal relationship between press and government, but the concept has come to have
legitimate meaning and, in fact, as it is commonly understood, it is quite desirable. Adversarial simply means that when warranted the media should be critical, argumentative, and contentious in their relationship with government.
The media may be the only institution that has what Justice Potter Stewart
called *structural rights*, or rights that belong mostly to institutions—such as the
press—as opposed to rights like religious freedom that are both personal and
institutional or structural under the Constitution. The primary function of the
press under this legal arrangement is to provide the people with a free flow of
information. And that process must be critical, and often adversarial. If there
were a tough-minded adversarial attitude in the media, I would argue that
there would be less secrecy and potential for corruption. In a sense the media
function for society the way an accountant and auditor function for a business.
They check the books looking for accurate balances, but if they find discrep-
ancies they report them with dispatch. A system of auditing and accepted
accounting procedures keeps the unscrupulous businessperson from cooking
the books. The same is true of government. Where there is no scrutiny by the
media and no potential for active, adversarial conflict, there is no guarantee
that democracy is working. In other words, the democratic state is not audited.

Governments try to perpetuate themselves by managing and manipulating
information. The press is one of the very few social forces that can challenge
them. From the time of the divine right of kings to the present, government has
realized that information is power and the control of information (at least to
some degree) is essential to public support for its policies and mandates. This
was the reason for the original press licensing and sedition laws in Britain that
American colonists and patriots such as John Peter Zenger rebelled against. He
took after a corrupt governor involved in secret land deals, which could just as
well be a contemporary issue. In modern times government secrecy, carried to
the extreme, has sometimes deprived the American people of information they
needed to be fully knowledgeable citizens. The White House often tries to delay
or actually cover up scandal or embarrassing revelations. That was certainly true

with the Clinton White House and the Monica Lewinsky scandal in the 1990s and with the Bush White House and the Iraqi and Guantanamo prison torture cases in 2004. Virtually every administration in Washington has denied the media access to information about its decision-making process that the media argued it deserved to have—for the benefit of the public. Illegal domestic spying and wiretapping by the Central Intelligence Agency and the Federal Bureau of Investigation have also been uncovered by a vigilant media, wary of government in the best adversarial tradition.

Several of my coauthor's arguments deserve close scrutiny. He maintains, for example, that under a libertarian theory of the press, there is no adversary relationship between press and government. Indeed, the libertarian idea (not to be confused with the Libertarian Party) allows multiple voices in the marketplace and keeps the press as free as possible from government involvement. He is correct in saying that this is strictly up to the editor or broadcaster. Although we do not live under a libertarian system today, when we did in the late 18th and early 19th centuries, the press fought hard against government strictures on information and helped establish the present adversary relationship. At the dawn of the 19th century, which journalism historians call "The Dark Ages of American Journalism," the government passed the Alien and Sedition Acts which the press opposed with great fervor. Libertarian journalism brought us highly opinionated, partisan publications. Some were adversaries of government; others were *kept cats*, not independent journals, but house organs for political parties. All this ended with the rise of a mass press, which was brought about by a happy mixture of technology, education, advertising, and other factors.

Today some critics argue that we are returning to the spirit of the "dark ages" of American journalism—or at least a robust, opinionated, and volatile journalism and media output. The Fox network, for example, offers its viewers a strident conservative bias to offset what they say is a liberal press. Internet bloggers now drive the news with fierce opinions and assumptions about the motivations of leaders and other concerns. Increasingly, a combative debating style is commonplace on cable television and on talk radio.

Today, although we no longer have a libertarian press system as such, the noisy partisans mentioned above come close at times. We do have a media system that shares a common value—a critical (or adversarial) posture toward government. We have a system of social responsibility, wherein the news media assume certain rights and corresponding responsibilities or duties. One is the full and robust coverage of government. An adversarial posture is helpful if not essential to this arrangement. One American newspaper that exemplifies the libertarian tradition is the conservative *Washington Times*, a newspaper that often frames the news in a politically conservative light. Clearly, such figures as radio talkmeister Rush Limbaugh and Fox TV's Bill O'Reilly or Air America's Al Franken are libertarian in their outlooks. There is probably no better example of a working adversary relationship than the one between government and the media in wartime. This issue we take up later.

No discussion of the typically American media–government relationship is complete without international comparisons. In many countries the press is controlled—not just in North Korea, China, and Cuba, but also in many developing and industrialized states. In some places, government ownership of the media is not uncommon. And a good many of the democratic states of Europe offer their media various kinds of press subsidies, presumably to preserve diversity.

Government press councils and laws also limit press freedom. Even in Britain, the mother of democracies, harsh laws, perpetrated by government, keep the media on a short leash. French journalists rightly complain that they cannot always do vigorous investigative reporting for fear of government reprisal.

A call for greater freedom linked to an ambiguous relationship with government is really quite dangerous, even if well intentioned. It is evident from such recurrent issues as book censorship by school boards, wherein freedom to read controversial works is challenged, that freedom of expression is not something established on marble tablets and enshrined for all time. It must be defended repeatedly and continuously or it will cease to exist. Reporters who cover local government often lament their continuing battles with public officials over open meeting and open records practices. The laws regarding public access to meetings and records are on the books, but many government officials will ignore and thwart them unless challenged by the press. Without an adversarial press, it is unlikely that our *sunshine* laws would be used at all. When it comes to such basic rights as press freedom, we must "use 'em or lose 'em."

Within the framework of an adversary relationship, a whole range of strategies and tactics can be employed by the press and, yes, by government. Washington correspondents, for example, are engaged in an adversarial process. They try to get information about a particular policy or agency. Some of the information is freely provided by helpful information officers; some that might be embarrassing to the agency is withheld or not volunteered. The reporter then develops a strategy to get the missing information. This is done through the use of leaks, alternate sources, or jealous politicians. In this adversary posture the press is suspicious of the actions of government, and vice versa. One sees this system in play on Sunday news and public affairs shows such as *Meet the Press*, where government officials spar with news interviewers and commentators.

Who, in fact, really represents the public interest? Both press and government claim to do so. The government makes a strong claim because it operates by the consent of the governed. The news media, on the other hand, have some basis for asserting that they are also representative of the public. At least the press makes this claim in many lawsuits when its motives are challenged. Thus, through court decisions, terms such as the *fourth branch of government* and the *fourth estate* have gained real meaning with legal teeth. When the courts, for example, allow the press to enter a prison to interview inmates even while denying that this is a First Amendment right, a special privilege is extended to the press as a trustee of the people because we all cannot wander at will within prison walls to find out for ourselves what is happening there. The press does this for us and, therefore, is our representative. Writing in *Saxbe v. Washington Post*, Justice Lewis Powell agreed, saying:

> The people must therefore depend on the press for information concerning public institutions. . . .The underlying right is the right of the public generally. The press is the necessary representative of the public's interest . . . and the instrumentality which effects the public's right (1974, 417 United States, 843 and 864).

In another case, however, a film producer, Fred Wiseman, was denied access to an institution for the mentally ill. It is common for schools and colleges to have stringent rules about who can and cannot film or report on a school campus, arguing that they are protecting the rights of children or students. This sometimes involves privacy. In reality, this is usually worked out through compromise.

Professor William L. Rivers of Stanford University documented the extent of the adversary relationship between press and government in two books, *The Adversaries* and *The Other Government*. He argued forcefully that the press is truly an adversary of government. We need to remember that government is not a single entity, but federal, state, and local units of executive, legislative, and judicial bodies. Columbia University law professor Vince Blasi argues that the press has a checking value in its relationship with government. Famed First Amendment lawyer Floyd Abrams has spent much of his career defending media and other First Amendment interests against government restraint.

The virtues of an adversary relationship between press and government are vividly demonstrated when one compares the news coverage of public affairs with, say, business or sports. Although the coverage of government is by no means exhaustive (and it assuredly has many flaws), there is a conscious effort by the press, both nationally and in local communities, to cover important events—happenings and issues in legislative bodies, the courts, and public agencies. At the federal level the presidency is watched by a legion of several hundred reporters. A large contingent is assigned to Capitol Hill, whereas very few cover the Supreme Court and the federal bureaucracy. Look at any local community and you will see the local press carefully watching the city council, the courts, and public agencies. This coverage includes some that is purely descriptive, some that is analytical, and some that tries to ferret out wrongdoing. All of it contributes to an adversary relationship. Generally, relationships between government sources and reporters are quite cordial. This cooperation is fine when government is running smoothly and the press is simply doing routine, descriptive coverage. The more contentious, adversarial stance is appropriate when things are not going so well and when the public ought to know about it.

Compare media coverage of government with that of business or sports. Business coverage has improved markedly in recent years, but for a long time it was a tedious and cheerleading treatment of commercial activity. Much of it was little more than printing or airing publicity releases that various businesses and industries provided. The press took little interest in internal conflicts and controversies or in corporate strategies that led to a particular product line. In recent years, many news organizations have expanded and improved their coverage of business because the private sector has such a profound impact on individuals and their communities.

Another area where the news media have traditionally cooperated with sources to the extent of becoming boosters and promoters is sports. Local papers typically support local teams and coaches are lionized by reporters and columnists. Under such coverage many fundamental yet changing assumptions about sports in American life went undetected. Conflicts within sports teams and organizations were ignored. Sports reporters often acted not like journalists, but more like advocates for teams or players. They ignored embarrassing facts and helped make heroes of abusive coaches or misbehaving athletes. Today, the adversarial approach is making inroads on sports pages, but progress has been slow.

Critics the world over agree that the adversarial relationship makes the U.S. media distinctive. For the most part, the press in the United States is low key, but on occasion it can rise to greatness by taking on government with a ferocity that can only come when news sources are treated like enemies of full disclosure and free-flowing information. Of course, most of the time this extreme posture is not necessary, but most reporters would argue in favor of a fundamental distrust of government. They might not go as far as I. F. Stone did when he declared that "government always lies," but would agree that it can obscure, distort, and mislead. Michael Janeway of Columbia University agrees but offers a more subtle view in his book *Republic of Denial* (2000). The public needs an advocate to challenge, cajole, needle, and inquire. In the United States this is the job of an adversarial press.

ARGUMENT SUMMATION: *The media and government should be adversaries.*

The fluctuating government–media relationship can be characterized either as disagreement between friends or as occasional agreement between adversaries. The latter relationship is preferable in order to preserve a healthy, fundamental distrust of government among the media that is essential to preserve the checking function of the press. American experience during the libertarian period of the media, when the press became spokesmen for biased views, confirms the power of the press to be used for partisan objectives. A nonadversarial relationship would lead to erosion of press rights by governmental involvement. Although government and media both represent the public interest and can cooperate, an adversary posture is needed to assure a fundamental distrust of government that is critical to democratic society.

SEARCH ONLINE!

Use the following terms and phrases to search for more information on InfoTrac College Edition: *adversarial relationship, checking value, fourth branch of government, watchdog role, pluralism, public interest, concept of representation, Hutchins Commission.*

TOPICS FOR DISCUSSION

1. Should citizens have more trust in their press than in their government? Why? Discuss.
2. In what ways can the government have an adversarial role against the media? Which of the adversaries (government or press) has the advantage? Discuss the reasons for your answer.
3. It is argued that governments manipulate information. Could you say the same thing about the press? Give some examples from actual news stories.
4. Many persons assume that out of an adversarial relationship will emerge truth. Discuss. If the adversarial press makes the U.S. press distinctive in the eyes of the world's journalists, would you consider this to be approbation or a criticism? Why do you think there are not more nations with such an adversarial press?
5. Discuss the advantages and disadvantages that are likely to accrue in a country from having a press that is an adversary to government.

TOPICS FOR RESEARCH

1. Do a study of a local governmental agency—police, mayor, environmental protection or health department, or some other agency—and how it relates to the press. How much of the agency's press relations work is reactive? How much is proactive? What barriers do the media construct

for the agency in getting its message to the people? What problems does the agency cause for the press in trying to get information? Is the resulting relationship characterized by conflict or consensus?

2. Find a public official or politician—locally or on the national scene—and research his or her relationship with the press. Is the relationship organized in a systematic fashion? How does the press treat the individual? If you were giving that person advice about improving or changing his or her image, what would it be?

3. Is there domestic censorship in the United States today? Who, if anyone, are the censors? What is the legacy of censorship of newspapers, books, films, the Internet, and so forth from the past? How much was the result of laws? What is their status today? In assessing who cares about censorship today, you might want to consult library journals and information science publications as well as press and media studies and periodicals.

4. Prepare a comparative analysis of press–government relations in the United States and those of another country, preferably one where the press system is radically different.

5. What does press freedom mean in the United Kingdom, Russia, China, Libya, or Cuba? How is the concept defined by laws there? What does government do to impair or enhance press freedom?

FURTHER READING

Baker, C. Edwin. "Scope of First Amendment Freedom of Speech." *UCLA Law Review* 25, no. 5 (June 1978): 964–1040.

Blasi, Vince. "The Checking Value in First Amendment Theory." In *Samuel Pool Weaver Constitutional Law Series.* Chicago: American Bar Foundation, 1977.

Cater, Douglass. *The Fourth Branch of Government.* Boston: Houghton Mifflin, 1959.

DeFleur, Melvin L., and Everette E. Dennis. *Understanding Mass Communication.* 7th ed. Boston: Houghton Mifflin, 2002.

Dennis, Everette E., and Robert W. Snyder, eds. *Media and Democracy.* New Brunswick, NJ: Transaction Press, 1998.

Friendly, Fred. *Minnesota Rag.* New York: Random House, 1981.

Gans, Herbert J. *Democracy and the News.* New York: Oxford University Press, 2003.

Hertsgaard, Mark. *On Bended Knee: The Press and the Reagan Presidency.* New York: Farrar, Strauss & Giroux, 1989.

Janeway, Michael. *Republic of Denial: Press, Politics and Public Life.* New Haven, CT: Yale University Press, 2000.

Luedtke, Kurt. "An Ex-Newsman Hands Down His Indictment of the Press." *The Bulletin of the ASNE,* May–June 1982: 16–18.

Merrill, J. C. *The Imperative of Freedom.* 2nd ed. New York: Freedom House, 1990.

Merrill, J. C. "The Press, the Government, and the Ethics Vacuum." *Communication* 6 (1981): 177–91.

O'Neill, Michael J. *Roar of the Crowd: How Television and People Power Are Changing the World.* New York: Random House, 1993.

"The Presidency in the New Media Age." *Media Studies Journal*, Spring 1994.

Reston, James. *The Artillery of the Press.* New York: Harper & Row, Colophon Books, 1967.

Rivers, William L. *The Adversaries: Politics and the Press.* Boston: Beacon Press, 1970.

Rivers, William L. *Other Government: Power and the Washington Media.* New York: Universe Printing, 1982.

Rourke, F. E. *Secrecy and Publicity: Dilemmas of Democracy.* Baltimore: Johns Hopkins University Press, 1966.

Schudson, Michael. *The Good Citizen: A History of American Civic Life.* Cambridge, MA: Harvard University Press, 1999.

Shane, Peter M., et al. *A Little Knowledge: Privacy, Security and Public Information after September 11.* New York: Century Foundation Press, 2004.

Weaver, Paul H. "The New Journalism and the Old Thoughts after Watergate." *The Public Interest*, 35 (Spring 1974).

DEMOCRACY AND THE MEDIA

Although there is nearly universal agreement that freedom of the press is one of the prerequisites of a democracy, there is much confusion about just how democratic the media themselves should be. Media often claim to speak for the people, but they cannot do so with the same certainty as public officials or governments who, at least, were elected and have some legitimate claim to power. The earliest media in the United States—namely, newspapers, books, and broadsides—were the products of individual printers and their families. They were private businesses that existed to make money while delivering a public service. Over the years, more complex media organizations have evolved, but they still have at least one thing in common with the earliest media—they are governed by strict hierarchies and are quite autocratic in their operations. No one ever accused a television station, magazine publisher, or newspaper of being a little democracy with elected executives and managers. Anything but, though one could make some claim that officers and executives of media companies are elected by their boards of directors and shareholders. There is also an argument that media content must meet some semblance of public acceptance— hence the reliance on broadcast ratings and other metrics to show that the media are giving the public what they want. That's where preferences stop, though, and the table of organization of a media company or individual media outlet is about as freewheeling as the military. Indeed, media organizations often follow a quasi-militaristic model with clear lines of authority and established reporting relationships. The buck stops with the boss. That's not to say that media employees don't have rights. They do, but one of them is not deciding who will govern the organization they work for, though disgruntled staffs have been known to push for change and even urge the sacking of a given executive or manager.

On occasion, thoughtful media owners and other leaders have proposed a more democratic model of operations. In the 19th and 20th centuries a few enlightened owners—for example, Horace Greeley and Lucius Nieman, respectively owners of the *New York Tribune* and the *Milwaukee Journal*—pushed for employee ownership. Early in the 20th century three famous muckraking journalists—Lincoln Steffens, Ida Tarbell, and Ray Stannard Baker—quit *Munsey's Magazine*, where their autocratic boss ruled with an iron hand even as they did stories that fueled populist reform, and started their own employee-owned *American Magazine*. Even later, in the 1970s when *Ms.* magazine was established, it also chose a utopian, democratic model of operations that attempted to implement feminist values in the magazine's staffing and operations. An Iowa newspaper, the *Burlington Hawk-Eye*, also experimented with an elected managing editor for time in the 1960s and 1970s. None of these and other utopian, democratic efforts succeeded for long or spawned many copycats elsewhere. On the world scene, only the great French daily *Le Monde* has a tradition wherein the staff expresses an electoral preference for the top editorial position, something that few media companies elsewhere have chosen to emulate.

The democratization of media might suggest not just elected editors, but rather a populist approach to content in which the audience plays a greater role in validating the media company or its individual properties. That's a fundamental article of faith on the electronic, digital frontier where "every person an editor" is a prevailing ethic. Interactive media mean audience involvement in content selection, for example. It might also be argued that media strongly influenced by audience ratings (television, for example) do engage the public in deciding which shows to cancel as a result of marginal interest in the mass audience. The motion picture industry similarly charts box office receipts as a measure of appeal, and movies that don't do well over their first weekend of distribution are quickly forgotten. The Internet has been called "the people's medium," and certainly more user involvement in content preferences is key. The cultures of many New Media companies and various entrepreneurial start-ups dispute the need for professional staff and a hierarchical organization. A collegial, more democratic style is often urged, though even in the digital media this is now quite rare as large media companies set the standard and govern the enterprises. Thus arises the question, how free should the media be to govern themselves in a democratic fashion, or does that augur against professionalism and quality control? The prevailing view in the news media—with rare exceptions—is clearly that democracy has no place in the newsroom, a position that often pits older media workers and audiences against those younger and more hip. All this relates to questions of media accountability, a notion nearly rejected by traditionalists who opt for nondemocratic media and embraced by those who court more involvement in governance.

CHALLENGE

Dennis: The media should be more democratic.

Naturally, I recognize that any proposition to democratize the media is radical because it would embrace two interrelated ideas—first, that the audience must play a greater role in deciding what content it prefers and, second, that the people working within the media would throw off their chains and create a system of newsroom democracy. I'm not proposing this quite yet for the entertainment media, which seem to thrive creatively and operationally with their present system of calibrated audience ratings that vote up or down given programs, motion pictures, or music. The only caveat here is that these media are terribly biased in favor of a youth audience—preteens for the movies and the vaunted 18–34 age demographic for television and cable. That cuts out a large part of the population, effectively disenfranchising them, but one could argue that they can go elsewhere for entertainment media that do court them, typically in smaller audience segments. But let's not digress. My colleague John Merrill will argue persuasively, I'm sure, that professionalism will deliver the best possible content to people, and thus that we should not worry about greater democratization. In fact, he discounts audience ratings, which he sees as drivers for poor media content. Further, he suggests we should trust the "professionalized" staffs of the news media to do mostly the right thing, allowing for an occasional malfunction that is quickly corrected. In other words, he is really telling the public to "butt out" and let the media do their thing without interference or, God forbid, accountability, which is surely a constraint on freedom.

He's not entirely wrong, but I say, let's think a little deeper about this problem of our democratic media, which really do keep the public at an arm's length. For years there have been proposals for worker participation committees in media companies that would allow greater involvement of media professionals in decision making. Unions have also made an effort to affect the autocratic environment of media companies, but with little effect. Management specialists sometimes recommend a soft glove approach. But as media economist Robert Picard (2002) points out, "every media company operates within its own culture that is created by its values, traditions, methods of operations, relations among management and employees and other factors." He acknowledges that media firms differ in management styles, with various firms favoring:

- An administrative culture
- An entrepreneurial culture
- A creative culture
- A maintenance culture
- A sales culture

- A production culture
- A process culture
- An outcome culture

Without going into the intricacies of each of these approaches, their labels say it all—the bottom line for the effective organization (wherein people are regarded as human capital and required to be productive) is *economic profit*, pure and simple. That's fine, but there is no mention of democratic values or even much thought about the *social compact* that the media have with the larger society. Many studies of media accountability say otherwise, suggesting that the news media are "citizens of their communities" or that they are obligated to "serve the public interest" or "guard the rights of the citizenry against government" or other powerful interests. All well and good, but how is this supposed to happen? By trusting media professionals to do the right thing? Not good enough, as many critics now proclaim. I am bothered by the fact that many of these critics who find the media too liberal or too conservative, too bold or too timid, would in fact constrain freedom, so the answer is not to turn the operations of the media over to external lobbies who negotiate with a class of media professionals who are further and further from the public in terms of their values and worldview. The organizational specialist Chris Argyris, in his now classic study *Behind the Front Page* (1974), a thinly veiled look inside the *New York Times*, observed something true of all news media operations—that they are quick to investigate the rest of society and reluctant to unveil or discuss their own internal problems, which they regard as "private, not public." Indeed this newspaper and most of its brethren—and even more so, the electronic media—have simply refused to engage in any efforts to assure media accountability, whether through an ombudsman to deal with reader/viewer complaints, news councils, or other citizen-involvement groups. At one time the electronic media were required to engage in community ascertainment—a process whereby local citizens and organizations were asked to assess and critique a given television or radio station's performance in serving the public interest. That was phased out as the electronic media became increasingly deregulated and with the rise of cable and the Internet, on the assumption that all interests would somehow be met by more diverse and fragmented media. A handful of news organizations have ombudsmen; even the *New York Times*, long a vigorous opponent of public feedback, hired one in 2004 after suffering a major scandal that shook public confidence. To suggest that the person selected, a first-class professional appointed for a limited term, will seriously affect the culture of that autocratic institution, however, flies in the face of its long and storied history.

It is my guess that old media organizations will resist any form of democratization, other than market research, a dubious metric. However, technology might just change all that. As late as 2005, the Internet, which is about 10 years old as a serious, public medium, still yields old-fashioned communication as it hosts digital newspapers, magazines, and other traditional media platforms. There is little use of the interactive feature of this new medium and thus little impetus for more democratic media—yet. But wait, new media forms don't come into their own for a considerable period of time as they begin to find their own voice. Early TV was just radio with pictures, but now no one would seriously argue that TV and cable aren't distinct media forms of their own, doing what other platforms cannot. Thus, I believe that true, integrated digital communication will harness the feedback loop, creating what Lawrence K. Grossman has called "The Electronic Republic," making all media more populist—and responsive to their audiences. As I've written elsewhere, even the slow-moving newspaper medium can with fully digitized operations select its topics more effectively and encourage viewer feedback and true involvement both in the editorial process and in a continuing dialogue that would democratize all content operations. Truly, media could be responsive to every and all interests, given the enormous channel capacity and room in cyberspace for content of all kinds. With more effective means of artificial intelligence, the media need not be an endless plebiscite wherein readers and viewers simply make their preferences known, but audiences can also be involved in the public/private conversation that "manufactures" content that is desired, needed, and valued. Constant adjustments are possible and truly personal media can evolve within the great resources of what are now mass media.

That takes care of content, but what of the leadership and management structure of media companies? I don't see many alternatives to the present "election" of the leadership class of the media by the boards of their privately held companies, though there can certainly be more vigorous shareholder involvement and information about the public's response to various activities of the corporation. For example, the radio giant Clear Channel in 2003 became the center of public opposition to new ownership rules at the Federal Communications Commission, something that might not have happened had their management been more public spirited. Clearly, media leaders can do more to involve their employees in the selection of top managers, not necessarily by direct election but through some formal mechanism for expression of employee preferences and a sense of who can work effectively with employees—and show a modicum of respect for the publics being served. After all, the media serve different audiences, taste publics, and demographic groups. That's fine. There need not be national plebiscites on media content and leadership, but there should be at least a respectful effort to truly meet the needs and desires of the audience. Hopefully, that will lead to greater quality, rather than succumbing to a lowest common denominator. Courting the largest possible audience, no matter what, might be appropriate for some media forms—say, popular entertainment sit-coms or reality TV—but presumably not for intelligent public affairs programming, news, high-culture magazines, and the like. All these forms and more will increasingly be digitized and part of a converged media world—and that will help assure more democratic media.

Yes, the media should be more democratic, but in the fashion I have laid out here with the involvement of media organizations themselves, other social interests, the various relevant publics, and when necessary, the government—which after all is the only instrument of society truly charged with representing the people—though this role should be carefully monitored by an independent judiciary and by citizens themselves.

ARGUMENT SUMMATION: *The media should be more democratic.*

The media should be more democratic in their content offerings to both the general public and specialized sub-publics, as well as more democratic in their selection and promotion of leadership and management. Media organizations, especially the news media, cannot continue to hypocritically investigate and assess other aspects of society and its institutions while making their own activities private. Thus, the news media need to be more transparent in the way they select news, cover it, and discuss its consequences. This can be accomplished by making greater use of digital means of feedback and account-ability with the public at large and with specific publics, including those with different cultural backgrounds, interests, geographic locations, demography, and other factors. The media need not be all things to all people, but they should serve the public interest of the specific groups they address. Cumulatively, they can serve the public interest overall as each voice and channel becomes part of the whole. More connection between media organizations, societal interests, and even the government are proposed in a system that accepts accountability as a linchpin of more democratic media.

RESPONSE

Merrill: The media need not be more democratic.

I'm amused that my colleague Dennis, while calling on the news media to be more democratic and offering what I must say is a visionary if utopian scheme, would exempt the entertainment media, including the current wave of bottom-feeding reality TV programs, from any such obligation. I think it is well established that the entertainment media have enormous influence on society in every sense, possibly more than the news media, but let's accept his restrictions for the sake of argument here. There is plenty to debate on the news media side of the house.

Dr. Dennis is right in suggesting that I favor a voluntary system of professionalism as a mechanism to make the media both more representative and, possibly, more democratic. However, I don't think the news media themselves need be models of democracy to promote democratic values and public communication. The role of the media under our constitutional scheme is, after all, that of providing for the free flow of information and the dispersal of opinions. In such a system, democracy can flourish, or so the theory goes.

Professionalism, which we deal with in other chapters in this book, means that the news media need to adopt a systematic approach to the gathering, processing, and dissemination of information. That means making considered, intelligent judgments at all levels of the so-called "manufacturing" process of creating a news product, to use the modern parlance. If the news media do this in an ethical manner that inspires public confidence, from their top leadership through middle management and operational work forces, they will yield better-quality content for everyone. Therefore, I believe that the education, training, and proper development of media professionals, managers, and ultimately leaders is an essential ingredient. This will happen, as it does now, in our journalism and communication schools, in the liberal arts colleges and other educational institutions, and in schools of business. As my colleague, himself a business school professor, knows well, much of the top leadership of the media comes from these educational institutions, and thus we must take care that they too prepare a generation of ethical leaders, not like those who have presided over the corporate scandals in companies from Enron to big pharmaceutical companies in recent years. Given the range of educational options and background from which media personnel come, it is the obligation of individual media companies—and the industry as a whole—to weld them together into well led and managed enterprises. In that regard the media industries could do a great deal more to foster continuing education among their employees—or engage journalism and business schools to work with them in the process. As Dennis has written elsewhere, we are often prisoners of our own education and the generational bias it reflects, unless we keep pace with change.

True professionalism is concerned not only with corporate cultures, management theories, or techniques for producing a newscast, magazine, or Website, but also with public communication, meaning how we effectively communicate with and serve the public. That involves feedback, of course, but also more vigorous market testing of media products. In that regard, one has to admire the Gannett Company, which did that quite effectively in the creation of *USA Today* back in the 1980s. Armed with market research and a driven CEO who had a vision for a national newspaper, the company produced a quite risky paper that was aimed at satisfying people's need for national news—about public affairs, finance, sports, and lifestyles—not always available in other venues. They crafted a product with appeal to youth and then, with the benefits of satellite communication, geographically diverse printing plants, abundant staffing, and deep corporate pockets, created the country's first national newspaper. Hundreds of millions of dollars were spent in its development and it was years before the paper achieved profitability. Over the years it also moved from a paper whose "depth was in its superficiality" to a respected news medium, now much quoted by its competition on the national scene. What I'm endorsing here is the process that involves the public to a greater degree than most media start-ups do—and also the commitment of the company to stay the course, which also rarely happens. Truly we need more media experiments like this one that test out ideas and try to capitalize on a format and content that respond to expressed public needs.

So, yes, more market research, but let it be tempered by intelligent professionalism, not just a process that served up poor-quality, quick and dirty news media. There are standards of quality that can be led and guided by professionals and that's what I propose.

Now, about making the leadership and management of the news media more democratic? This is not likely, I think, for a number of reasons. First, one can hardly have a different standard for the news media than for entertainment, opinion, and advertising media, for example. Why? Because they are owned by the same people. Can you imagine the Time-Life magazines having a different system of governance and accountability (namely, the bottom line) than the rest of Time Warner media? Hardly. At one time the news divisions of television networks did operate as loss leaders for the rest of the organization, but that day passed when cable took on such an important role and every aspect of TV must now return a profit to survive within the company and in the market at large. I think we already have somewhat democratic media in that most media companies are publicly traded with shareholders voting in the management— namely, the CEOs and their teams who select other leaders and managers. Of course, one must recognize that shareholder votes at the annual meetings of media companies involve some pretty big entities, such as giant pension funds and others who are not exactly democratic, with very few small voices at those gatherings. Although there are some tyrannical bosses in media companies at all levels, few of them last very long, nor do they inspire confidence or get the best employees. Abusive, unresponsive management is just not the way to go, as any intelligent executive realizes.

As we've learned in this chapter, there have been efforts to make the media more democratic from the get-go and few have succeeded. The media best serve democracy by hiring high-caliber people to produce the best possible content for the audiences they are serving. That will mean some great variations depending on what people want—and are willing to pay for. The marketplace isn't democratic and neither are the media.

ARGUMENT SUMMATION: *The media need not be more democratic.*

There is no need for the media to be more democratic either in the way they select their leaders and managers or in the way they deliver content. Both are a function of the economic marketplace and that is assuredly not democratic. Media can be more responsive to their audiences through polls, market research, and other means, but the best antidote to undemocratic media is professionalism—professionalism at all levels and across both content production functions (the editorial and programming process) and business operations. Because media must perform for their owners, including shareholders, they need to serve the public interest as it is expressed in the market demands of their audiences. Professionalism, properly instituted and carried out, will produce better and more responsive journalism and other content for the public. No utopian reforms are necessary to make this happen, though continued professional vigilance is critical.

SEARCH ONLINE!

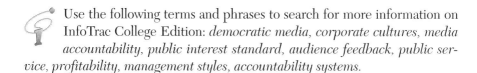 Use the following terms and phrases to search for more information on InfoTrac College Edition: *democratic media, corporate cultures, media accountability, public interest standard, audience feedback, public service, profitability, management styles, accountability systems.*

TOPICS FOR DISCUSSION

1. Why should the public care at all about whether the media are democratic or not? How would democratic or undemocratic media actually differ in the American context? Overseas?
2. To what extent do opinion studies of people's attitudes toward the media, such as those carried out by the Pew Center for People and the Press, differ from market research on media, if they do?
3. How would the process of selecting media leaders differ if either of our two debaters were in charge of a large media company? Would one approach be preferable to the other? Why?
4. For the media, what does "democratic" actually mean? Operating as a democracy with every citizen having a voice—or some other formulation?
5. Can an autocratically organized and run media company—or individual medium—actually benefit democracy and promote democratic values?

TOPICS FOR RESEARCH

1. Write an essay positing that more democratic media do, in fact, promote democracy more effectively than those that follow traditional management structures.
2. Compare and contrast two different news organizations, a traditional newspaper and an Internet news service. Does either purport to be more democratic than the other? Why?
3. Research models of newsroom democracy in the United States and abroad. Do they actually work well? How do you know?
4. Consider methods by which the media can determine whether they are serving the public interest.
5. Do an analysis of media accountability methods internal to a given news organization (e.g., ombudsman) versus those associated with a whole industry (e.g., codes of ethics, news councils) and try to determine which are preferable for a more democratic media.

FURTHER READING

Argyris, Chris. *Behind the Front Page: Organizational Renewal in a Metropolitan Newspaper.* San Francisco: Jossey-Bass, 1974.

Arnold, R. Douglas. *Congress, the Press and Political Accountability.* Princeton, NJ: Princeton University Press, 2004.

Bertrand, Claude-Jean. *Media Ethics and Accountability Systems.* Cresskill, NJ: Hampton Press, 2003.

Briggs, Asa, and Peter Burke. *A Social History of the Media from Gutenberg to the Internet.* Cambridge, UK: Polity Press, 2002.

Dennis, Everette E., and Robert W. Snyder, eds. *Media and Democracy.* New Brunswick, NJ: Transaction Publishers, 1998.

Grossman, Lawrence K. *The Electronic Republic: Reshaping Democracy in the Information Age.* New York: Viking, 1995.

Grossman, Lawrence K., and Newton W. Minow. *A Digital Gift to the Nation.* New York: Century Foundation, 2001.

Harper, Christopher L. *And That's the Way It Will Be . . . News and Information in a Digital World.* New York: New York University Press, 1999.

McQuail, Denis. *Media Accountability and Freedom of Publication.* New York: Oxford University Press, 2003.

Picard, Robert G. *The Economics and Financing of Media Companies.* New York: Fordham University Press, 2002.

CONCENTRATION
OF MEDIA OWNERSHIP

Big media transactions in which major media firms buy up, merge with, and swallow smaller publications and media outlets are frequently in the news. The business news media such as the *Wall Street Journal, Business Week,* and CNBC report these developments rather routinely as media analysts and other commentators discuss the inevitability of larger and larger media corporations taking over smaller ones. In recent years, the world's largest media company, Time Warner, was acquired by the Internet firm America Online (AOL) only to experience a shake-up after the dot-com crash. Rupert Murdoch's News Corporation, another giant, acquired the satellite firm Direct TV in 2003, and most of the 25 largest media firms have gotten bigger and bigger as a result of acquisitions, mergers, and the development of news business, some of it on the Internet. The family tree of media companies is intriguing to follow as many firms, such as broadcast networks, have become part of larger enterprises. For example, CBS merged with Westinghouse, which was subsequently bought up by Viacom, once a small cable offshoot of CBS; Disney, once known only for family-oriented films, acquired CapCities/ABC, itself a combination of newspaper and television properties. These and scores of other financial transactions of the media are part of the concentration of almost everything in a society in which the market economy is the dominant standard and government regulation that once policed bigness and blocked monopolies has declined. Throughout the 1990s and into the first years of the 21st century, the deregulation of most industries, including the media (as well as airlines and banks), conferred society's blessing on growing concentration of ownership. Still there were persistent warnings about the dangers of this trend.

For years media critics such as Ben Bagdikian and Robert McChesney warned about the negative effects of media concentration, especially on newspapers and broadcasting, when independent, family owned papers and broadcast stations fell into the hands of big chains like Gannett, Thompson, and Newhouse. Although these admonitions seem almost quaint compared to today's *really big deals*, as one critic called them, they nevertheless reflect deeply held American values that bigness is bad and diversity is good. People often equate freedom of expression and individualism with small-scale social institutions that are close to the people and accessible to all. Among the fears expressed by media critics is that large companies such as General Electric, which owns NBC, can and will eventually take over media companies once firmly in the hands of media people—editors, publishers, broadcasters, and the like. The prevailing belief is that if and when ordinary businesses take over media companies, they will be dedicated less to editorial independence and integrity and more to the bottom line of profits and, some say, greed. Most Americans, when polled on the matter, believe that media concentration is a bad thing—that it is better to have local ownership and control rather than orders from a distant and often disinterested boardroom in Manhattan or Los Angeles. With the possible exception of the most extreme circumstances, in which lax new ownership rules are proposed by the Federal Communications Commission or a big company, such as the radio conglomerate Clear Channel, wields enormous influence, however, there is generally little sustained public support for government intervention that would prevent big firms from getting bigger. Thus, though there is occasionally a public backlash about media ownership, for the most part there is little will to do anything about it. Exceptions occur when media violence or other issues involving children force the leaders of corporate media to the bargaining table—or to a White House conference—where the summoning power of the president brings them to heel, if only briefly. In the face of the reality of media concentration that intensifies with each passing year, there is a widespread belief that there ought to be a better way.

CHALLENGE

Dennis: The new concentration of media ownership ultimately benefits the public.

For as long as I can remember, media critics, politicians, and community activists have complained about concentration of media ownership. I've heard warnings about the demise of democracy and the closing off of communication for ordinary citizens. Of course, there is little doubt that media concentration is on the rise. A tiny number of corporate giants control most of mass communication—the movie industry, cable, broadcasting, and magazine and book publishing, as well as newspapers. But the same can be said for other industries such as steel mills and computer companies. This has happened for a variety of reasons, including economies of scale, marketing efficiencies, and cost controls. The modern economy seems to push business toward larger and larger units. Whether this is ultimately desirable in a social or moral sense is not necessarily the point.

Concentration whereby a few owners either control or have influence over whole industries is commonplace, not only in the United States but in Europe, Asia, and other places as well. It is strongly reinforced by what is now an almost worldwide devotion to capitalism and market economies. Since the fall of Communism and the end of the Cold War, all but a tiny few nations say they are democracies with market economies, though some are hardly good examples of either. Only in a few isolated places, such as North Korea and Cuba, does another system prevail and even there concentration exists, but in the form of state or government owned and operated industries.

Thus the question is whether the media industries should follow different economic rules than other industries. True, they do have more of a social obligation and get some unique protections under the First Amendment beyond those afforded other businesses, but in the end most of U.S. media are capitalistic institutions dependent on profits to survive. They do so in the economy that exists and that is an economy where big players prevail. Is this a bad deal for the public and for society itself? I don't think so. We have more media and more media content than ever before in human history. It ranges from bottom-feeding supermarket tabloids and TV game and reality shows to highbrow books, magazines, and movies. There is something that appeals to every imaginable taste, though critics complain that many of the mass circulation media, notably television news and drama, have been dumbed down to serve a society that seems coarser than it was a few years ago. In other words, the media mostly respond to public taste in order to make a profit.

It is sad that some of the most critically acclaimed television shows and quality magazines have died for lack of audience to sustain them. But at the same time, others that do honor creative work and quality content come along and succeed. Some media companies are so greedy and slavish to profits that they cheat the public by producing shallow news and poor-quality entertainment. That may be the practice of some influential companies—and it is—but this was also the case with some greedy local owners who were less than professional and only too eager to make large profits. In reality, the main effect of media concentration has been more media and choices for readers and viewers. Instead of a handful of television channels, people now choose from scores and soon from hundreds of cable channels. And though there are fewer daily newspapers in the United States in 2005 than in 1900 or even in 1990, there are hundreds of online news sites, tens of thousands of bloggers, and other alternative media. One true test of the impact of concentration on choice is that public radio and television (such as PBS and NPR), once seen as rare bastions of quality, are having a tough time against cable choices such as the A&E Network, the History Channel, and Discovery, for example. All this has occurred in an age of big media and plenty of content. The big media companies have been promoting the wonders of the Internet and broadband communication with their infinite expansion of Websites and cable channels. These firms make major use of the Internet and have championed Internet advertising that pays for better-quality content. The result is a larger audience for the Web and more opportunities for the smaller players, ranging from ordinary individuals to professionally produced electronic newsletters and information services.

Big media, as represented by media concentration in the United States and other countries, are fostering an accessible global dialogue, e-commerce, and thousands of new media outlets that can only benefit the public. And big companies that produce the various Web browsers and portal services have created tools for any one of us to communicate with almost anyone else. The real test of whether media concentration represents a threat ought to be reflected in the views of political parties and candidates. But there too we come up short. In the 1990s, Eli Noam, a distinguished media and telecommunication scholar at Columbia Business School, could say, "There is very little difference between Democrats and Republicans when it comes to communication policy." That changed somewhat in the first years of George W. Bush's presidency when FCC chairman Michael Powell proposed a major loosening of ownership rules that clearly went too far and ignited a storm of public criticism. Organizations as diverse as liberal media watchdogs and the National Rifle Association squawked, and Congress eventually stepped in to prevent the changes. This was an exception to the usual rule, however, because communication policy—and the control of media by conglomerates—rarely rises to the level of public angst. In reality, few people are clamoring for government regulation, stronger antitrust enforcement, or the end of policies that allow big players to buy small ones or encourage collaboration between and among various media. Where once there were strictly enforced lines between and among some industries, now movie and TV companies collaborate with cable and Internet firms. Phone companies work with traditional publishers or broadcasters and few complain. Those who do, such as Andrew Jay Schwartzman, who monitors electronic media, or Noam Chomsky of MIT, raise alarms, but rarely have adequate answers. Less strident and more thoughtful opposition comes from academics such as Robert McChesney of the University of Illinois and Todd Gitlin of Columbia University, but they too lack persuasive solutions for the inevitability of concentration. Responsible leaders in the media community, represented in a group called the Committee of Concerned Journalists, also grumble about the negative impact of greedy owners on content, but they readily admit that the First Amendment presents a barrier to doing much about it, other than voluntary criticism, which to date has led nowhere.

Unless the world economy changes radically and soon, it seems to me that media concentration is here to stay and that it probably does more good than harm. The idea that cultural products (such as media and media content) can't be bought and sold like lumber, steel, and computers is a lovely romantic notion that belies the truth. Increasingly there is an information economy and media products of all kinds are part of it, like it or not. To date those developments have stimulated diversity of messages overall, as witness the massive bombardment of Internet sites, rather than stymied them. As Columbia's Noam has said, "assumptions about concentration are often plain wrong—first it isn't as simple a picture as the critics suggest—some industries are concentrated, others are not—and there are many considerations such as localism that are assuring new and often diverse content" (Noam, 2004).

ARGUMENT SUMMATION: *The new concentration of media ownership ultimately benefits the public.*

Concentration of media ownership ultimately benefits the public. It is a kind of trickle-down theory not of benevolent owners doing good for the public, but self-serving, often greedy owners eager to make a profit. In order to remain in business, they are required by audience expectations and demands to provide popular and useful content to willing readers, listeners, and viewers. Concentration of the media is simply a case of the media and communication industries following general economic trends in order to survive in the national and world economy. What is happening today is inevitable. The public ultimately benefits because successful media enterprises must serve and please their audiences and customers to survive.

RESPONSE

Merrill: Concentration of ownership is dangerous for people and society.

Professor Dennis notes that corporate giants are growing all through society, not only in mass communication, and concludes that because this is happening it must be all right—even good. Tiny merchants may be disappearing, as Professor Dennis says, and this has not been a bad thing. But one might ask if a diversity of grocery stores is the same as a diversity of information and opinion. Pluralistic media are essential for a democracy that depends on a knowledgeable citizenry. Democracy can, on the other hand, exist with a limited number of banks and steel mills.

It is true, as Dr. Dennis says, that American media are capitalistic institutions that depend on profits to survive. He notes that media exist in an economy today where big players prevail, and he believes that this is a good deal for the public at large. I'm not so sure about that. Certainly it is a good deal for the fewer and fewer big media owners and corporate players who share exorbitant profits. But what of the average citizen? Does he or she get a better newspaper from the absentee publisher, for instance, than from the hometown publisher? I think not. Of course, we may get a superior technological product, but the substance of the paper becomes more corporate conformist and nonlocalized. The amount of advertising grows, the news and views become more formalized and impersonal, and the sense of identification with the community dissipates. Perhaps this is why all surveys show that the public is becoming increasingly passive, even antagonistic, toward the press and losing trust and respect for its contents. Of course, one of the most outrageous cases is that of Clear Channel, which my colleague passes over too quickly. Clear Channel has a stranglehold on local radio, most of which is programmed from afar, thus denying people local news and other localized content. And on top of that this arrogant company has had a profound effect on the music industry, commanding selections and thus influencing public taste. The local outrage over Clear Channel was so great that the U.S. Senate called hearings and heard from a variety of people, including some pretty defensive broadcasters. One result was that even Chairman Powell didn't include radio in his sweeping new ownership reforms.

My opponent notes that the media respond to public taste so as to make a profit. But here is that question again: Do the media respond to public taste, or do they form it? Perhaps both. It seems to me, however, that media today are enslaved to profit making, raking in ever larger profits. It is true that American media have always wanted to make a profit, but their public service function and their multiple-perspective nature in earlier days made the media more responsible and vital.

It is hard to argue that media monopoly and concentration of ownership alone are responsible for the generally sorry state of the media. Many other factors enter in—for instance, basic greediness, a lack of ethical sensibility, and vulgarization of content in order to expand the audience. Dennis contends that people now have scores and soon will have hundreds of cable channels to choose from; and this is due to concentration, he says. And he mentions the Internet and broadband communication as flourishing and providing citizens with ever-increasing sources of information. True. But there is no reason to believe that the Internet, however individualistic it might be at present, will not fall into the grasping hands of the big, profit-hungry corporate communications giants. The trend has already begun. Giants are even swallowing giants. The jury is out on the effect of giants swallowing local newspapers, for example, but I believe there is clear evidence that they are ultimately less responsive to their local communities and more concerned about corporate directives that drive the bottom line. One big newspaper chain I can think of is known for making good papers mediocre and bad papers mediocre too. Is that a net gain? I don't think so.

Global dialogue is being fostered by the corporate giants, says Dennis, and this can only benefit the public, he contends. Certainly CNN and other major organizations are thrusting ideas and culture (mainly American) into the far-flung areas of the world. But to what degree is this helping the citizens? One might ask a simple question: Just how much has American-type media content helped the citizens of Russia and Eastern Europe? It has poured in a plethora of rock music, sensational material, pornography, advertising, and other titillating junk material that stresses sex and criminal activities. It can be argued, I think, that efforts to bombard the Middle East with U.S. messages have largely failed and along with government policies have stimulated more indigenous media in the Arab world because the United States is so reviled. Sure, the big media enterprises like the globalization trend; they see larger audiences, greater profits, and increased power. It is doubtful that their motivation is to help the ordinary citizens of these countries. What they want is a bigger pool of audience members to sell to their advertisers. The way to expand the pool is to provide increasing infotainment and glitz and not to expand the serious core of moral and intellectual dialogue or to foster a respect for the important concepts of life.

Critic Ben Bagdikian has called the leaders of the big conglomerates "Lords of the Global Village." And many years ago, George Seldes wrote a book called *Lords of the Press.* These "lords" have in their grasp the power to transform cultures and to create little Americas around the world. They have their own political agenda, and it is largely to protect the status quo. "All resist economic changes that do not support their financial interests," according to Bagdikian. These "lords" together exert a homogenizing power over commerce, culture, and ideas that affects citizens to a degree never before seen, Bagdikian continues. Perhaps Bagdikian exaggerates the power of the conglomerates, but it is obvious that he is largely correct. Rupert Murdoch, one of the top media moguls, has admitted that he intervenes frequently in the editorial stands of his papers. Some moguls, mostly public corporations owned by pension funds and other shareholders, contend that they are not interested in their papers' contents and policies, only in the money they make, but Bagdikian has called this no more than "a parochial myth that permeates all the media."

Should anything be done about this capitalistic tendency to gobble up competition and expand? Many, like Professor Dennis, might say no. Let the market rule. Let big groups grow until perhaps there are two or three. And then, only one? Could not one big global communication giant provide even better service than many? Probably so, to extend Dennis's earlier argument. It is his feeling that the First Amendment would prevent us doing much about it. But we do have antitrust laws, which in the past have not been enforced. It is my contention that something must be done to stop this global spread of powerful communication giants. They have gotten out of hand and many of them have more money than many of the world's nations. Somewhere, sometime, we need to realize that the market is not sacred and that there are values in the world other than bigness and profits.

ARGUMENT SUMMATION: *Concentration of ownership is dangerous for people and society.*

Media ownership concentration provides the citizen with the viewpoints of a decreasing number of information providers and places undue power in the hands of a minority of very wealthy persons. It delocalizes further and shifts the emphasis from the community to the amorphous mass. Such concentration shifts the emphasis from journalism and other forms of communication to business. Synergy, borrowed from medicine, has come to rule communications. In the media world synergy allows the use of various media controlled by the same corporation to promote similar ideas, products, celebrities, and politicians. The global giants attempt to control as many media as possible, including newspapers, magazines, news agencies, syndicates, radio and TV stations, networks, book publishers, motion picture companies, cable outlets, satellite channels, recordings, and theater chains. They enjoy almost total power to influence the citizens on almost every front from clothing styles to politics and public policy.

SEARCH ONLINE!

Use the following terms and phrases to search for more information on InfoTrac College Edition: *economics of media ownership, concentration, competition, cross-media ownership, synergy, media mergers, conglomerate, newspaper chain, foreign ownership, media monopoly.*

TOPICS FOR DISCUSSION

1. Consider the different patterns of concentration in at least two industries (say, newspapers and television or magazines and book publishing). Is there more or less diversity of content? Are people's information and entertainment needs served better (or worse), in your opinion?
2. The First Amendment says, "Congress shall make no law" with regard to speech and press, but antitrust law and broadcast regulation govern how media companies can do business. What is the rationale for this inconsistency?
3. In some countries communication policy with regard to ownership is the law of the land and hotly debated by the political parties. Why have media ownership issues in the United States attracted relatively little public discussion while inciting much heat among academics and media critics?

4. The greedy-owners-who-must-serve-or-satisfy-the-public-to-make-profits theory of Dennis is based on the assumption that the media are simply following economic trends and that they must do so to survive. Reconcile this with pluralism and the quality of information.

TOPICS FOR RESEARCH

1. Do a content analysis of a newspaper, magazine, or radio station in your area (or on the Web) that is family or locally owned and compare its news coverage to one that is group owned. An analysis for a week should be sufficient. How does the news analysis in the two media outlets compare or contrast?
2. Write a paper linking the claims of media critics that concentration of ownership impairs democracy with actual evidence that would hold up in a debate, or better yet, in court.
3. Compare the communication policies with regard to ownership in any other country in the world with those in the United States. How do U.S. views about *foreign* ownership compare with those of most European or Asian countries?
4. Develop a strategy for an independent media outlet that you think could survive and prosper in spite of the concentration trend. Write either a business plan or a paper.

FURTHER READING

Albarran, Alan B. *Media Economics: Understanding Markets, Industries and Concepts.* Ames: Iowa State University Press, 1996.

Alger, Dean. *Mega Media: How Giant Corporations Dominate Mass Media, Distort Competition and Endanger Democracy.* Lanham, MD: Rowman & Littlefield, 1998.

Bagdikian, Ben. *Media Monopoly,* 7th ed. Boston: Houghton Mifflin, 2004.

Barnouw, Erik, ed. *Conglomerates and the Media.* New York: New Press, 1998.

Bogart, Leo. *Commercial Culture: The Media System and the Public Interest.* New York: Oxford University Press, 1995.

Demers, David. *The Menace of the Corporate Newspaper: Fact or Fiction?* Ames: Iowa State University Press, 1996.

Doyle, Gillian. *Media Ownership: Concentration, Convergence and Public Policy.* London: Sage, 2002.

Hamilton, James T. *All the News That's Fit to Sell: How the Market Transforms Information into News.* Princeton, NJ: Princeton University Press, 2004.

Hoskins, Colin, et al. *Media Economics: Applying Economics to New and Traditional Media.* Thousand Oaks, CA: Sage, 2004.

Low, Linda. *The Economy of Information Technology and the Media.* River Edge, NJ: World Scientific, 2000.

Noam, Eli. Interview with Eli M. Noam, April 10, 2004.

Owen, Bruce M. *The Internet Challenge to Television.* Cambridge, MA: Harvard University Press, 1999.

Turow, Joseph. *Breaking Up America: Advertisers and the New Media World.* Chicago: University of Chicago Press, 1997.

Weaver, Paul H. *News and the Culture of Lying.* New York: Free Press, 1994.

Wolf, Michael J. *The Entertainment Economy: How Mega Media Forces Are Transforming Our Lives.* New York: Random House, 1999.

MEDIA AND THE PUBLIC TRUST

As one encounters the procession of speakers in London's famous Hyde Park, it is clear that some know what they are talking about while others are fanciful, unreliable, even disturbed. We trust and believe some of them but we are wary of others. The same is true in the myriad chatrooms or blogs on the Internet, where knowledgeable people and those who profess nonsense exist side by side. This is also true of our media, whether on paper or online. Unsupported and often abrasive views of some talk show hosts on radio and cable, lurid headlines in supermarket tabloids, and unsupported claims on some Websites may not immediately (or ever) inspire our confidence, whereas network news, major newspapers, and other reliable media usually make an effort to gain public trust.

Discussions of the media and the public trust usually center on the relationship between the media (both individually and collectively) and their audiences. The nature of that relationship is summed up in the term *vox populi*, or voice of the people. In a democracy the news media are said to function as the people's voice—expressing their concerns, providing the information they need, and providing channels for discussion and debate. Humorist Will Rogers once said that a good newspaper was "a nation talking to itself," which expresses very well the idea of public trust. Public trust means that the public trusts, believes, and relies upon the media, which are the necessary representative of the people in much of the public discourse of the nation. In recent years the concept of public trust has often been equated with credibility, believability, and trustworthiness. It is said that a news organization, such as a newspaper or a television news program, cannot survive and succeed unless it achieves public trust. This means that most of its audience trusts and believes what they read, hear, or see in the content delivered by the newspaper or television station. An idealistic view of the media suggests that this is the main reason why media organizations exist and why people choose to work for them rather than for someone else. In this formulation, the media mainly perform a public service in delivering news and information, opinion, and entertainment, and they also serve as a useful marketplace for goods and services. There is another view that says the commercial media, in the United States at least, are capitalistic enterprises whose main concern is profits. In such a scheme, any public service rendered in establishing a public trust relationship is done strictly for self-serving ends. But whatever the view, the media and the public trust are a much-discussed topic and one that applies in one way or another to virtually all the instruments of communication—the news and information media especially, but also opinion media (such as talk radio and opinion magazines), entertainment media (TV, motion pictures, and recorded music), and even such supporting players in the media family as advertising, marketing, and public relations. A relationship of trust, understanding, and ultimately support accompanies all of these media if they are to survive in a market economy. The standard view is that media are glue for the global village, whether for selfless or self-serving reasons—or somewhere in between. The debate continues.

CHALLENGE

Merrill: The media exist mainly to make profits.

Tradition, conventional American wisdom, and oft-expressed idealism combine to suggest that U.S. media are primarily in the business of communication to provide a public service. Certainly, it is said, if the media want to get and retain the public trust they will provide such public service. It is not easy to challenge such a sonorous and idealistic contention, but with profit making and competition being such strong inclinations in a capitalist society and supporting the basic American ideology, such a contention must be challenged. In the United States, regardless of flowery rhetoric at media conventions, the bottom line is the machine that drives media policy and is the main concern of media directors and owners.

All we have to do is to consider the volume and cost of advertising prevalent in our media, spotted here and there with bits and pieces of editorial material, to get a panoramic view of the media's drive toward profit making. Surely the media moguls don't seriously think they're serving the public interest when 65–75 percent of the average publication space is given over to advertising. Such exorbitant attention to commercialism that fills the coffers of the media makes a very weak argument for providing the public with a substantial and healthy diet of nonpropagandistic content.

Let us agree that, under our media philosophy, profits are desired and necessary. The question, however, is whether the media need to make the exceedingly large profits that they do, while sometimes skimping on the number of staff members and their salaries.

Where is the great concern for the public when ever more media units are gobbled up by big media corporations, multimedia conglomerates proliferate, and national media spew forth the same low-level, common denominator pabulum? Where is concern for the public when media owners and executives make salaries well into six digits, many in the millions, while editors, reporters, and writers grind out their days with salaries of $40,000 to $80,000—with some getting even less? One study had the average earnings of new master's graduates in journalism in the mid-$30,000s while MBAs earn on average in the mid-$80,000s—and more.

Where is the concern of the media for public service when even small weekly newspapers in this country are on the selling block for tens of millions of dollars? Where is the concern for the public when family-owned media, which have served their communities for years, are increasingly bought out for fantastic prices by absentee owners who care little or nothing about the communities? Is it the public these media people are concerned about—or lining their own pockets?

Journalism educator Shirley Biagi presents some interesting facts about media ownership: The top 10 newspaper groups own one-third of the nation's dailies; 20 corporations control about 60 percent of annual magazine revenue; 20 corporations account for more than 50 percent of radio revenue; 70 percent of all TV stations are network affiliates; and six book publishers receive 30 percent of all book revenue yearly (Biagi, 2000). Admittedly these figures by themselves do not prove that media have no public concern (sense of responsibility). But they do prove that money and the increase of money through concentration of media power are very powerful in American communications. And they show that growth is what fascinates big media moguls in the United States.

Many critics of the frailties of the news media (among them, Robert McChesney, Todd Gitlin, and Norman Solomon) admit that making money is a goal usually supported by the American people, but it is the way these big media companies make this money that is debatable, Biagi says. And she poses three interesting questions:

> Does the legacy of First Amendment protection for news-gathering organizations mean that they have a special responsibility to provide the information people need in a democracy? Should entertainment-producing companies provide a diversity of cultural outlets for creativity? Will the adoption of corporate values benefit or harm the mass media industries? (Biagi, 2000, 177)

Ben Bagdikian, a longstanding critic, argues that even with increased interest in public affairs, newspapers have reduced their average space devoted to news. He also questions the media's concern for public service: Political coverage is poor; most papers are mediocre and many are wretched; most cities are dominated by one newspaper; advertisements increasingly eat into former news space; live news is decreasing; only about 3 percent of American cities have competing newspapers (in 1910 a majority did); and increasing amounts (probably one-third) of news are supplied by public relations outlets (Bagdikian, 1974, 8–17 passim). In the world of newspapers the control of content is narrowing. Successful companies are growing bigger and more powerful.

Media scholar Ray Hiebert has posited that the media, in general, have become more competitive in trying to capture the largest, most valuable audience available, instead of attempting to meet the special needs of all segments of society. Even a journal that supports the commercial purposes of the media, *Media Week*, admits that money usually talks and drives media decisions. The public interest, accurate information, balance, and ethics clearly take a back seat. Scores of Websites now cover media industries and point up a variety of greedy sins by media people and media companies that hardly serve the public interest. It is therefore awfully hard to argue that the media are much concerned about the public interest. Hiebert et al. and other commentators also say that broadcasters are struggling to reach a mass audience and that specialized audiences are being neglected. When specialized audiences are considered at all, can they be reached profitably? These and other critics also note that media investors are prone to take only mild positions on sensitive issues, and that they seem sensitive only to demands of the marketplace. Perhaps it is not the *public be damned* attitude of a former time, but most publishers and editors seem to care little about the real informational or intellectual health of the people who read their paper. Editorial prerogative is the watchword. "We will make the decisions we want to make. That's our job. You readers will take what we give you. After all, if you don't read us, who will you read?"

When asked about responsibility for finding out what the readers want and trying to provide it, the typical editor responds: "We are journalists, and journalists develop the instinct to know what the readers want. In a real sense, what we want is what you want." So what do readers and television viewers generally get? Endless coverage of sensational trials—from Scott Peterson and Michael Jackson forward—with snippets of gossip and speculation. Pictures of whales trapped in ice. Stories and pictures of congressional malfeasance. A rundown on the brutal rape-murder in small town America, with the grieving mother being asked by the reporter how she feels about her daughter's death. A picture of thousands of university students nihilistically awash in Beijing's main square. And as smoke is shown billowing from a U.S. city, the deep funereal voice of the TV anchor takes us "now to the scene of the devastating explosion that shakes man's faith in technology." Worse yet is the 24-hour news cycle on cable, which is buttressed with mindless screaming heads putting everything into simplistic black-and-white terms—or more accurately, conservative and liberal terms—as if that were the only way to explain the world.

It should be obvious to the American media consumer that most of the messages are trivial, superficial, titillating, sensational, negative, crisis-oriented, and often flippant. Except in certain elite journals such as the *New York Review of Books, Foreign Affairs, New Yorker,* and *Commentary,* the reader seldom gets any thoughtful, substantive information and analysis. And the TV viewer drifts about in a desert of crime, sex, and shallow situation comedies. Programs with depth and insight, such as those found on the Public Broadcasting System, are rare.

But business-oriented media managers will be quick to say: "Such material and such programming aimed at the thoughtful and the educated are not profitable. The readership and viewership would be too small. Our nets must be cast wide and into shallow waters in order to catch as many fish as possible." This is public service? Perhaps. But it is a special kind—providing desserts and pap for idle minds and lazy souls that undoubtedly inhabit vast expanses of the general public. So the motto of the media manager is generally "Give them pap, not what they really need," or perhaps even better, "Give them what we hope they will accept because of its easy assimilation so our circulations will increase and our ratings will rise—along with our profits, of course."

In 1947 the Commission on Freedom of the Press in its report, *A Free and Responsible Press*, rendered the first large-scale indictment of the American press for not taking the public trust seriously. According to the commission, one of the three main dangers facing the press was that the few people who ran the press had not provided a service adequate to the needs of society. Such a criticism, taken seriously even today by many critics, indicates that media are not primarily concerned with public service—but with private interest.

Jerome Barron, lawyer and media critic, has emphasized in *Freedom of the Press for Whom?* that because of their arrogant exclusiveness, the media do not serve the public interest. Barron cites sources that indict the American media for normally accentuating the false and the irrational and for excluding small and powerless minorities from a media voice (Barron, 1973, 78–79).

Media in the United States are businesses, and businesses are profit-making enterprises, with exclusionary privileges, and with financial growth and the bottom line as primary objectives. J. Herbert Altschull notes that in a commercial media system, "the content reflects the views of the advertisers and their commercial allies, who are usually found among the owners and publishers." On the public interest question, he asserts that "no newspaper, magazine, or broadcasting outlet exceeds the boundaries of autonomy acceptable to the paymasters" (Altschull, 1995, 254–55).

Media dealmaker Michael Wolf goes even further in his 1999 book, *The Entertainment Economy: How Mega Media Forces Are Transforming Our Lives*, as does former publisher Nancy Maynard in a volume called *Mega Media: How Market Forces Are Transforming the News* (2000). These two matter-of-fact assessments report that both the entertainment and information industries are creatures of the market economy and everything they do serves its imperatives. That does not necessarily mean that professional quality always suffers, but in my opinion and experience, it usually does. This is something that students can easily test by looking closely at any medium and connecting its content and presumed purposes with its revenue sources, usually advertising. Don't take my word for it or that of churlish critics. Instead, look for yourselves.

Marketplace theory is usually invoked to justify the American profit-making system, as a comprehensive volume on media freedom and accountability indicates (Dennis, Gillmor, and Glasser, 1989). In theory the system is supposed to increase message pluralism—as well as owner pluralism and unit pluralism—because of the natural desire of free people to compete and to make money. But is it working that way? Many would argue—many do argue—that pluralism is really shrinking and fewer and fewer voices are being heard throughout the land. Is not the desire to make bigger profits actually causing media directors to take fewer chances, to play it safe, to lower their sights and aim for the lowest common denominator? How does this adequately serve the public interest? It is obvious how it serves the personal financial interest of the media owners. Trust and respect for the media are deteriorating in the United States, and the high-sounding shibboleths about the media "recognizing a public trust" ring ever more hollow. Perhaps it is time to stop this kind of rhetoric and honestly admit that the main purpose of the media is to make a profit—and that public service comes into the picture only to the degree that it fosters this primary media objective.

ARGUMENT SUMMATION: *The media exist mainly to make profits.*

The American media mainly desire to make profits. Any thought of public service is secondary. Advertising, dominating all the media, is a key to this emphasis—permitting media to make excessively high profits. Where is the public concern when media corporations are gobbling up increasing numbers of smaller media units? Where is the public concern when media executives earn salaries in the six digits, some in the millions, while staffers who actually produce the product earn generally low salaries by comparison? Where is the public concern when the media aim for the lowest common denominator and local, family-owned, grassroots papers are disappearing? Political coverage on TV and cable is poor, most papers are mediocre, most cities have only one newspaper owner, live and hard news is decreasing, and public relations is supplying about one-third of the news we do get.

RESPONSE

Dennis: The media must serve the public interest to maintain credibility and make profits.

In recent years no issue has proved more captivating to the leadership of the American media than credibility and public trust. The terms have often been used interchangeably, although *public trust* is the broader and more inclusive formulation. Beginning in 2001, if not before, such organizations as the Committee of Concerned Journalists and the Project for Excellence in Journalism as well as critics of the media on the left and the right have expressed a common passion for improving the relationship between the media and the public. Concurrently, survey researchers from the Pew Research Center, the Annenberg Center for Public Policy, and the Gallup Organization have tracked and measured public confidence in the media as well as esteem and trust. Why? In response to an increasingly polarized United States evident after the presidential elections of 2000 and more recently 2004, when Americans seem split down the middle on almost everything. And importantly, during this period the news media themselves have experienced scandals—at the *New York Times, USA Today*, CBS News, and elsewhere—involving plagiarism, misrepresentation, and other media sins. In the midst of culture wars wherein the media themselves have become an issue and a polarizing influence, thoughtful commentators and the public worry about the role of the news media in a democracy—and their ability to inspire confidence and trust. With limited access to information from the military during the Iraq War and from the White House on all manner of issues, some critics carped, but there was no evident outcry from the public.

But as Daniel Henninger wrote in the *Wall Street Journal*, "In the Information Age, authority is a priceless franchise." Amid charges that media scandals, political bias, and excessive coverage of missteps in the Iraq War have greatly weakened many large media institutions, including CBS and the *New York Times*, and with evidence from respected pollsters that the public's belief in the media's ability to accurately report the news is declining rapidly, as well as other indicators that citizen trust in political information from mainstream media is also on the wane, a worrisome credibility gap has emerged.

Years earlier, credibility and public trust studies were conducted by respected academic organizations and pollsters such as the Pew Center for People and the Press, the Public Agenda Foundation, and the American Society of Newspaper Editors. There had been such studies before—indeed there is a 60-year legacy of media–public attitude research. These studies provided good news and bad news. In studies cited in *Of People and Media* (1993), I showed that most of the public found the media credible and believable, though a sizable minority did not. A majority also found the press generally accurate and impartial, though again a worrisome minority had grave doubts. Most Americans did want their media to be government watchdogs, although there was precious little understanding of the First Amendment and of press freedom. Studies in 2004 by the Pew Research Center for the People and the Press continued to confirm these sentiments.

The reason for all this consternation about the media and the public trust goes to the heart of John Merrill's arguments regarding profits. I believe that it is difficult to have significant media profits or any kind of economic success under our system unless there is first a climate of public trust. After all, the public is buying a communication system, they are paying for public communication, and it stands to reason that they want the resulting information to be competently gathered, accurate, and useful to them. This is public trust at its best. The public also wants access to differing opinions and interpretations of public affairs, as well as entertainment, sports, and advertising. Some will argue about advertising, but many people do find it both entertaining and useful. Those who do not can press the mute button and silence the commercials.

I believe there is ample evidence to support the idea that a passion for journalism and a desire to serve the public come first for most people and organizations that make up the media business in the United States. This is clear both from many studies of American journalists and from personal experience. That is why press people react so strongly when their lifeline—the public trust—is challenged or threatened by libel suits or by the misbehavior of reporters such as Jayson Blair of the *New York Times* or Jack Kelley of *USA Today*, both of whom misused their positions and betrayed the public. One particularly egregious case was that of Charles Glass of the *New Republic*, a serial fabricator and fictionalizer about whom a movie, *Shattered Glass*, was made. Reactions to these cases were severe—all lost their jobs, and in two instances (the *New York Times* and *USA Today*) their editors did too. During the 2004 presidential campaign, a story on *Sixty Minutes* about George Bush's National Guard service that drew on faked documents also sparked controversy. In all these instances the issue of contaminated content was widely discussed. Whether these media and others that have been the subject of scandal—Rush Limbaugh for allegedly buying illicit drugs and Bill O'Reilly for alleged sexual harassment—have had any direct economic effect on the media is not known, but sustained problems such as these would surely weaken the media's franchise for accurate, reliable, and believable information, its stock-in-trade. The media may be defensive at times, but they have shown that they will act with dispatch to correct situations and mistakes that challenge credibility and believability. In these instances, the media all performed in a more public-spirited way than have corrupt corporations such as Enron. Television journalist and author Robert MacNeil earlier imagined scenarios like these when he suggested "there is plenty of evidence that [the crisis] is grave, evidence that the public trust at least at the moment, is an ebbing tide" (MacNeil, 1985, 4). MacNeil was one of many leading journalists who joined in a constructive critique of such topics as the blending of news and entertainment, biased reporting, and factual inaccuracies. His concern and that of his colleagues is that public trust is essential if media are to command loyal audiences who find public communication both fair and useful. Many of MacNeil's concerns are echoed in pronouncements from the late 1990s forward by the Committee of Concerned Journalists and other groups promoting better media fare for children and less violence and sexually explicit content, whether in movies, comic books, or on the Internet.

It is clear that media people care deeply about the public trust and that they will take steps to see that the quality of their work warrants public support.

In recent years, for some of the reasons Professor Merrill mentions, they have been pushed to do this with even more vigor by economic trends. Today more media outlets are seeking public attention and advertiser support than ever before. Cable television has opened up scores of new, competing channels such as CNN, Fox, and CNBC; we have successful national newspapers, new magazines (and online 'zines), and a growing legion of bloggers who range from thoughtful commentators and experts to adolescent opinionizers emerging faster than we can count them; circulations of once declining newspapers have stabilized and in some instances grown. In this mix there is enormous competition—in spite of ownership considerations that will be discussed later—and with such competition the need for a credible and respected product is more vital than ever.

The issue raised by Professor Merrill is directed toward motivation of media people—both the employees and the owners. He thinks the worst of them: They are all money-grubbing individuals whose only concern is the bottom line. Certainly this is not true of most journalists, who are far removed from profit-making considerations. They are driven more by a love of public affairs, writing, and expression, as well as the ego gratification of bylines and recognition. A similar case can be made for people who make television entertainment programs, edit magazines or books, or draw cartoons. And most media people I know see themselves as engaged in a public service or in producing a product that benefits the public. Many could do other things, pursue other careers, but they do not because they find working for the media a compelling challenge.

Many media owners do make large profits, but for the most part their investments are in media rather than other enterprises. For most (not all) media companies, information and entertainment are the principal concerns. This generally means that they are not investing in other high-yield enterprises or trying to diversify their holdings. They are, in short, committed to the media business, producing a product that will find a receptive public. Any argument blaming the owners—people like Donald Graham of the *Washington Post*, Arthur Sulzberger Jr. of the *New York Times*, Michael Bloomberg of Bloomberg Media, and Rupert Murdoch of the News Corporation—for taking advantage (or accepting the risks) of general economic trends needs to be carefully examined. Most of the criticism of the growing concentration of ownership in U.S. media, with fewer companies owning the means of communication, suggests that this is somehow a unique condition caused by excessive greed. Not at all. Throughout American business there are fewer small firms and more larger companies. It is a fact of life and the media businesses are following the same trend. Of course, even the so-called family media are usually publicly held companies with shareholders.

The media, once believed to be capable of only marginal profits, have really become big business extraordinaire at the dawn of the 21st century, playing an enormous role in the New Economy, a name for the information society forged by an alliance between technology and new media. Although people rightly worry about the motives of firms more driven by the temperature of Wall Street than by immediate concern for their readers and viewers, one does not work without the other. In the end, these firms—whether big media companies such Time Warner, News Corp., Disney, and others or little start-ups in people's garages—produce content that must meet public scrutiny and demand. Thus, the boom economy of the 1990s gave us more media—more quality and competitive media as well as more dumbed down trash media. In the end, though, I believe that diversity is the winner and that people have more choices and better choices.

In 2003 and 2004, along with two research assistants, I visited corporate executives in 23 of the nation's top 25 companies—ranging from CEOs at companies such as Tribune to vice presidents for strategic planning and development at Time Warner, Hearst, Gannett, Cox, Disney, and other companies—to learn something of their concerns about their firms' futures. The values I heard expressed were profit oriented, of course, but also included a commitment to the public interest through information and information services for the public. These people are not the village pornographers or venal profiteers, but rather sophisticated and thoughtful professionals in a creative environment. I was reassured without being naive. I worry that they are too risk averse and, having experienced loss of shareholder value after the dot-com crash in the early part of the decade, lacking in creativity in imagining new content and digital solutions.

Ken Auletta, media critic for the *New Yorker,* has produced several books that offer behind-the-scenes views of media moguls and their executives, which also document a textured mix of motivations ranging from pure economic profit to a public-spirited entrepreneurialism. Few are in the tradition of the robber barons of earlier times or even of earlier press lords, some of whom denied any obligation to public accountability.

To me there are two important questions that we ought to ask about big and little media trends, both relating to the consequences of ownership. First, have the number of voices in the marketplace seriously decreased in a fashion that threatens diversity in communication? And second, has the quality of media fare suffered? To the first question: There are more accessible channels of information today than ever before. Until the 1980s, most American households received only four or five television channels. Today, they get scores of them, all offering diverse fare. Other media enterprises are also prospering. Although there are more big companies, there are also thousands of newsletters published by individual entrepreneurs, courtesy of desktop publishing and the electronic revolution. And don't forget the almost infinite scope and reach of cyberspace thanks to the Internet and World Wide Web, where information galore exists for anyone who wants to download it. The idea that there is no diversity in our media marketplace is questionable. Naturally, it is always healthy to watch these economic trends to see that diversity is not seriously threatened. For this we need thoughtful critics of the media economy today, although they join a longstanding chorus of commentators, including Oswald Garrison Villard and Upton Sinclair, who since the 1920s have predicted that a handful of greedy owners would someday control all U.S. media. To date that has not happened and I do not think it is likely. Even in the midst of considerable government deregulation affecting broadcasting and other electronic media, the government monitors media mergers and other trends, as witness the antitrust case against Microsoft and the prosecution of Martha Stewart.

As to the second point—quality—the quality of American journalism has been on the rise. There is always plenty of room for improvement, but the quality of American journalism and entertainment is far better today than it was 10 or 20 years ago, let alone at the turn of the century when there were 7,000 daily newspapers, compared with about 1,500 today. News coverage has improved enormously, partly helped by technology; writing quality is also better by most accounts; and design and graphics have improved a thousandfold in all media. There is more specialist coverage both in the print and electronic media and in databases. There has been, in fact, a communication revolution in the world, something Professor Merrill and his favorite media-bashing sources seem not to know.

The growth of media and the increased development and use of market research have made the media more responsive to their audiences. Media people know what their readers and viewers say they want. They receive almost continuous feedback in the form of readership studies, television ratings, and other measures of the relationship between the media and the public. These forms of feedback, made possible by market forces and reinvested profits, keep the public trust vigorous and healthy. Without a trusting relationship between media and public and opportunities for feedback, the tendency would be for media consumers, both individually and collectively, to stop watching some TV programs, cancel the newspaper, and fail to renew the magazine. This is not happening and for good reason—the public trust comes first, the profits follow. Though media people may not be saints, their motivations are not as venal as has been suggested.

ARGUMENT SUMMATION: *The media must serve the public interest to maintain credibility and make profits.*

Media professionals, including journalists, seek to serve the public interest, which is why they react adversely when their credibility is threatened. Because the public trust is necessary to sell papers, profit motive takes a secondary role. The vast majority of journalists are far removed from the ranks in which profits are shared. Owners' profits stem mainly from advertising and user fees. Thus, owners seek to diversify media outlets and increase profits under a single ownership of the means of communication, not the message. As a result, centralization has not decreased the number of voices in the marketplace, while the quality of news has improved.

SEARCH ONLINE!

Use the following terms and phrases to search for more information on InfoTrac College Edition: *believability, credibility, trust, vox populi, media moguls, public service, responsibility, media access, accountability, profitability, Committee of Concerned Journalists, Pew Center for People and the Press.*

TOPICS FOR DISCUSSION

1. Is the desire for profit a sign that media evade public service? How would you define *public service* and the *public trust*?
2. Groups and organizations such as the Radio and Television News Directors Association, the Pew Foundation, and the Poynter Institute are doing much to improve the media–public relationship. What do you think is their prime motivation in doing this?
3. Assuming the argument that we have enormous competition in our media system is true, do you think that competition implies public service and concern for the public trust?
4. Are the arguments of Merrill and Dennis, in which they give statistics on media and their audience sizes, in any way related to the question about the public trust and public service? If they are, how do they prove or disprove the contention that profits are the media's main concern?
5. Do you think that most citizens have faith in and admire the media? What leads you to have your opinion? What have surveys said about this?

TOPICS FOR RESEARCH

1. Document the public service activities and programming of a local broadcast station. Interview an official at the station to determine how he or she tries to carry out the FCC's mandate of "public interest, convenience and necessity." Have these activities changed over the past decade? Have they

increased or decreased? Has deregulation of broadcasting effectively abolished the public interest standard?

2. Discuss media ratings, including radio, TV, cable, and the Internet. Do they provide an index for the idea of public trust or not? What about newspaper readership studies? What do these kinds of studies tell news decision makers about the public and its attitude toward local media?

3. Do an analysis of media available to you in your community. What part of their content deals with matters of public service and public trust? How does the content seem to reconcile the difference between journalistic work that informs the public and content aimed more at generating a profit? Can both occur? If so, how?

4. Study the editorial policy of any newspaper, magazine, or cable news operation—traditional or online. From the published editorials, determine how many are truly public service statements and how many are more self-serving, perhaps even pandering to a particular audience or group, such as politicians and sports fans. Characterize the media outlet's editorial policy in terms of (1) issues covered; (2) positions taken (pro, con, or neutral); and (3) audience to whom editorials seem directed (e.g., policy makers, the public, specific interest groups).

5. Examine public service advertising—messages that do not advertise specific products or firms but promote public issues such as the Community Chest, AIDS research, and the environment. To whom do these ads appeal? What is the motivation of the media in running them? Do you discern issues or causes that do not get public service support? Is product placement ever used to advance the public interest? Document carefully, studying a specific magazine or broadcast organization.

FURTHER READING

Altschull, J. Herbert. *Agents of Power: The Media and Public Policy.* White Plains, NY: Longman, 1995.

American Society of Newspaper Editors. *Newspaper Credibility: 206 Practical Approaches to Heighten Reader Trust.* Washington, DC: Author, 1986.

Auletta, Ken. *Backstory: Inside the Business of News.* New York: Penguin Press, 2004.

Bagdikian, Ben H. *The Effete Conspiracy and Other Crimes by the Press.* New York: Harper & Row, 1974.

Barron, Jerome A. *Freedom of the Press for Whom?* Bloomington: Indiana University Press, 1973.

Biagi, Shirley. *Media Impact: An Introduction to Mass Media.* Belmont, CA: Wadsworth, 2000.

Commission on Freedom of the Press. *A Free and Responsible Press.* Chicago: University of Chicago Press, 1947.

DeFleur, Melvin, and Everette E. Dennis. *Understanding Mass Communication,* 7th ed. Boston: Houghton Mifflin, 2002.

Dennis, Everette E. *Of Media and People.* Newbury Park, CA: Sage, 1993.

Dennis, Everette E., Donald M. Gillmor, and Theodore Glasser, eds. *Media Freedom and Accountability.* Westport, CT: Greenwood Press, 1989.

Ghiglione, Loren. *The American Journalist: Paradox of the Press.* Washington, DC: Library of Congress, 1990.

Harwood, Richard C. *News Media and Society: How to Restore the Public Trust.* Dubuque, IA: Kendall-Hunt, 2002.

Henniger, Daniel. "How Dan Rather and Media's Kings Lost Their Crowns." *Wall Street Journal*, November 12, 2004, p. A12.

Hiebert, Ray, Donald Ungurait, and Thomas Bohn. *Mass Media.* White Plains, NY: Longman, 1988.

Lichter, S. Robert, Stanley Rothman, and Linda Lichter. *The Media Elite: America's Powerbrokers.* Bethesda, MD: Adler & Adler, 1986.

MacNeil, Robert. *The Mass Media and the Public Trust.* New York: Gannett Center for Media Studies, Occasional Paper No. 1, 1985.

MacNeil, Robert. *Media and Public Life.* New Brunswick, NJ: Transaction Publishers, 1998.

Maynard, Nancy. *Mega Media: How Market Forces Are Transforming Our Lives.* New York: Maynard Partners, 2000.

McChesney, Robert. *Rich Media, Poor Democracy: Communication Politics in Dubious Times.* Urbana: University of Illinois Press, 1999.

McQuail, Denis, ed. *McQuail's Reader in Mass Communication Theory.* London: Sage, 2002.

Sanders, Karen. *Ethics and Journalism.* Thousand Oaks, CA: Sage, 2003.

Weaver, David H., and G. Cleveland Wilhoit. *The American Journalist in the 1990s and the End of an Era.* Mahwah, NJ: Erlbaum, 1996.

Wolf, Michael. *The Entertainment Economy: How Mega Media Forces Are Transforming Our Lives.* New York: Random House, 1999.

THE RIGHT TO KNOW

Members of a local school board exclude journalists while they discuss a motion to dismiss a teacher and void her contract. Later, the board chairman urges a newspaper editor not to print the story. Here are two related instances blocking what is often called *the people's right to know*. In the first instance, there is an effort to stop the *gathering* of information; in the second, its *publication* and *dissemination*. As defined by many journalists and some legal scholars, the right to know is the right of the listener to information of public interest and importance. In order for this *right* to be functional, however, information must be acquired and published.

Although it is not specifically stated in the Constitution, there is a widely held belief among journalists and other media personnel that there is a right to know. This right is usually defined as the right of the public to have access to information about government policy and decision making. The press sees itself as the conduit for such information because the average citizen has neither the capacity nor the resources to gather continuing and detailed intelligence about what the government is doing. The people, the argument goes, must have full and robust information about what their government is doing in order to be knowledgeable voters and good citizens. Government secrecy leads to suspicion and a lack of confidence in public officials and their policies. The people's right to know is transformed, however imperfectly, from an abstract principle to a concrete reality in *sunshine acts* that require government bodies to hold open meetings and to have their records open for public inspection. Theoretically, government should operate in the open and should be accountable to the people and the right to know would make that possible. Rights— strong, fundamental rights—almost always trump legislation and privileges. For example, the constitutional right to speak usually overrules a community's concern about protecting the peace in instances of controversial marches by unpopular groups. The media's access to information has traditionally been a *privilege* rather than a *right*. Still the belief persists that the public has a right to know, one that the media happily trumpets whether it is constitutionally guaranteed or not.

CHALLENGE

Dennis: There is no right to know.

The right to know is not an inalienable right guaranteed by the Constitution, but is instead something that was invented by journalists and citizens interested in getting information held by government or the private sector. For a number of years journalistic organizations have been badgering the courts and the legislatures in the hope of establishing their right of access to various confidential sources of information. This so-called right now has some modest basis in law, in that on occasion courts have said that under certain circumstances and in very specific areas there is a right to know. But this is something so conditional that it is not a right at all, but a quite limited privilege that depends on the disposition of judges. What they give today they can take away tomorrow. I believe that the right to know is a badly flawed concept that actually interferes with other rights and may do more to impair than to advance First Amendment freedoms. Still, it is important to note that the right to know is frequently a privilege created by the legislature rather than something that someone finds by name in the Constitution. In fact, 31 states as of 2004 had such a journalist's privilege statute, some constructed quite narrowly and others giving journalists considerable latitude not to reveal their confidential sources. Technically, the media and the public do not have a strong right of access to information for one simple reason: The Supreme Court has not seen fit to recognize a constitutional right of access except to the courts. The press and the public do have a constitutional right of access to attend open court proceedings and some other public meetings.

The right to know is most often invoked when media people are asking for rights and privileges that the rest of us do not have. It is a justification for a vague category of corporate rights because the right to know is not put forth as an *individual* right but as an *institutional* right, and here is where the argument gets hazy. The First Amendment guarantees a right to speak that belongs to individuals. Advocates of the right to know say that this new right is derived from the right to listen. Listeners (or anyone receiving the messages of free speech and press) are entitled to a flow of information—hence the right to know. It is notable that most of the rights enumerated in the Bill of Rights are for individuals, but the media would change this by adding a little corporate institutional appendage.

According to Harvard law professor Lawrence Tribe, a leading constitutional scholar, right-to-know advocates would differentiate between the "focused right of an individual to speak" and "the undifferentiated right of the public to know" (Tribe, 1988, 674). People who take this position, he notes, argue that the First Amendment does not confer individual rights but protects a system of freedom of expression. "This view," he says, "unduly flattens the First Amendment's complex role" (Tribe, 1988, 675). Another leading scholar, Edwin Baker, agrees. A right to know, he says, is never more than a right to have the government not interfere with a willing speaker's liberty.

The right to know is something of a journalistic invention. It began in the early 1950s when the press felt increasingly thwarted by bureaucrats who were standing between them and government information. It began as a quest for access to records and meetings, the so-called sunshine laws, short for government operations *in the sunshine* or open. These journalists wanted access to government records, documents, and proceedings at both the state and federal levels. This was called the Freedom of Information (FOI) movement. The bible for this activist effort was a thoughtful, weighty tome called *The People's Right to Know: Legal Access to Public Records and Proceedings* by Harold L. Cross (1953). The FOI movement had many positive consequences. It brought sunshine laws (open-meeting and open-record legislation) in most of the states, fostered the federal Freedom of Information Act, and opened up many government meetings from which the press and public had previously been barred. The FOI movement was both necessary and desirable, but the journalists did not stop there. Many excesses followed. The press claimed that it should have access to many classified government records and files, including some dealing with national defense and national security. Journalists also asked for greater immunity from libel suits, whether brought by public officials or private citizens. Some reporters asked for a right to rummage through the private papers of individuals to pursue the truth and frequently claimed that the right of privacy was an undue hindrance on the press and public.

Over the years the media and some legal scholars have rightly pressed for the free flow of information, including access to judicial proceedings, open records, and open meetings, all essential to a functioning democracy. But they've also gone further, arguing that a vague right to know, often linked with gossip and curiosity, trumps the right of privacy. Additionally, the media community has been joined by various health crusaders, the environmental movement, and people associated with emergency preparedness, who also argue for a right to know. This has led free press advocates such as Jane Kirtley of the University of Minnesota to assert that "it is generally acknowledged that Americans enjoy this right" (Kirtley, 2003). She invokes a broad interpretation of the First Amendment to justify almost any intrusion of the media into private matters.

In 2004 there were a number of high-profile cases in which journalists were threatened with contempt of court and jail sentences for refusing to reveal confidential sources. Judith Miller of the *New York Times*, for example, got caught up in a bizarre conflict with the courts for refusing to reveal a source related to information about White House aides who allegedly leaked the name of a CIA agent who was married to an administration critic. In this instance, Ms. Miller had not even published the information, but this didn't stop the courts from insisting that she lift the veil of confidentiality. She truly believes that what she was doing was right, but only on the basis of civil disobedience, not settled law. That's always a journalist's "privilege," of course.

So what if journalists argue for their position? If it were merely the mutterings of media people at the press club, there would be no problem. But all of these claims and many more have been brought to the Supreme Court of the United States. In each case the rationale has been the people's right to know. This approach is what Anthony Lewis calls "press exceptionalism": special rights for the press that are not available for the rest of the public. This approach also introduces a conceptual problem because the rest of the Bill of Rights applies to individuals but the right to know is advanced as an *institutional* right. Efforts have been made to establish a broad constitutional right. And, as good lawyers will tell you, there is always *authoritative support* for any position if lawyers look hard enough. In this instance authoritative support was found in the writings of James Madison, who once said, "A popular government without popular information, or the means of acquiring it, is but a Prologue to a Farce or a Tragedy; or perhaps, both. Knowledge will forever govern ignorance; and a people who mean to be their own Governors, must arm themselves with the power which knowledge gives." As Justice William O. Douglas once wrote:

> The press has a preferred position in our constitutional scheme, not to enable it to make money, not to set newsmen aside as a favored class, but to bring fulfillment to the public's right to know. The right to know is crucial to the governing powers of the people. (Douglas, 1972, *Branzburg v. Hayes*, 408, U.S. Reports, 665 at 713)

This has a bittersweet ring for a number of publishers, broadcasters, and Internet entrepreneurs who are clearly in the communications business to make money and who have only the vaguest passing interest in the people's right to know, even though their rhetoric sometimes suggests otherwise.

Although the right-to-know leaders appreciated the support of Justice Douglas, they hankered for something more than mere rhetoric. They thought they had it when Justice Potter Stewart gave a notable speech at Yale Law School. In that now famous speech Justice Stewart said that the "Free Press Clause extends protection to an institution" (Stewart, 1975, 631). This is what the right-to-know advocates were waiting for: the First Amendment as an institutional right, and mighty support for the idea of a people's right to know. But alas, the word according to Stewart seemed to have currency only at Yale. It was not a majority position of the Court (or even a minority view) and thus not the law of the land. The people's right to know was still in the realm of grand theory. Although it has been repeatedly pointed out that the Stewart speech had no standing in the developing law of the First Amendment, it is often invoked as though it were chiseled in stone and blessed by the framers. This position of structural freedom of the press based on a right to know was and remains one person's opinion and has not become law. The Stewart speech nevertheless gave much fuel to hungry legal and journalistic minds seeking support for the right to know.

The next turn in the debate was a position put eloquently by federal judge Irving Kauffman, who said that freedom of the press was dependent on protection for three aspects of the communication process: acquiring, processing, and disseminating information. This makes perfect sense, and journalists argued vehemently that it is virtually impossible to disseminate information without acquiring it (through news-gathering methods) and processing it (by editing and preparing it for publication). This is logical, of course, but once again journalistic fancy was light-years ahead of legal reality. What Judge Kauffman posited was a theory of freedom of expression and from my point of view a very desirable one, but one without a solid legal foundation.

Most legal scholars agree that there is powerful constitutional support for the dissemination of information; most First Amendment law centers on the right of people to speak and to publish. There is much less legal basis for acquisition of information and, in fact, much of the press's claim in this area is tied to a case that *denied* the press any special privilege to withhold names of news sources in court proceedings. In that case Justice Byron White offered a less than reassuring statement with a double negative construction, that "news gathering is not without its First Amendment protections" (White, 1972, in *Branzburg v. Hayes,* 406 U.S. Reports, 655 at 707). He did not say what they were. On the matter of processing news or editing it, the law is quite thin. Rarely have courts been asked to give special protection to this aspect of media work, and not surprisingly they have not initiated it themselves. In a few instances when they been asked to grant news-processing rights, they have generally declined to do so. An exception was in May 2001 when the Supreme Court said the press was not liable for ill-gotten tapes and opted for the public's right to know over personal privacy (Greenhouse, 2001).

The press has been inventive and resourceful in trying to establish the right to know as a provision of constitutional law, but to date it has not done so; and from all appearances this idea will have to percolate for a long time before it is allowed to raise conceptual havoc with the rather specific language of the First Amendment. Justice Stewart aside, the right to speak and publish is both an individual right and an institutional right. However, for many years the ability to publish and broadcast really was limited to media owners. This has changed somewhat, first with the advent of desktop publishing allowing cheap and easy communication for ordinary people and even more so with the coming of the Internet and the World Wide Web enabling people to create Websites that can theoretically reach millions. The tension between the little media made possible in a digital age and the still large organizational presence of big media means that controversies over the so-called right to know are usually associated with the economic motives of media companies. In reality, however, media are mostly large-scale enterprises and getting an individual message through for the ordinary person is pretty difficult.

The right to know is a very limited privilege with many important exceptions, so many that to call it a right is misleading. One of the strongest advocates of the right to know is communication law scholar Franklyn S. Haiman, who says the public's right to know is a vital element of the First Amendment "because much essential knowledge is in the hands of agencies and officials of government who can thwart the democratic process by keeping relevant material secret" (Haiman, 1981, 368). Haiman says the right to know is based on the need of the public for information to exercise its responsibilities of citizenship. "In a fundamental sense, data in the hands of government belongs to the public, having been collected through the use of taxpayers' money and for the exercise of authority derived from the people as a whole" (368–69). All well and good, but then come the exceptions (which Haiman acknowledges and supports) to government disclosures that seriously undermine any right to know:

- The need to protect the privacy and other legitimate personal interests of those about whom information is gathered
- The need to insure candid deliberative processes
- The need to safeguard the public's economic interests
- The need to preserve the physical safety of society and its institutions (Haiman, 1981, 369)

These broad and compelling exceptions blow a hole in the people's right to know, which need not be absolute, but certainly must have a broader reach than Haiman and other scholars envision if it is to be a fundamental right and have real meaning. Rights are not "now you see them, now you don't" propositions.

The right to know has a flimsy legal foundation, which is reason enough to question whether it should be accorded the kind of status journalists want to confer upon it. But there are even more compelling reasons for viewing this so-called right with real trepidation. Journalist and screenwriter Kurt Luedtke, quoted elsewhere in this book, put it succinctly when he told the Newspaper Association of America:

> There is no such thing as the public's right to know. You made that up, taking care not to specify what it was the public had a right to know. The public knows whatever you choose to tell it, no more, no less. If the public did have a right to know, it would then have something to say about what it is you choose to call news. (Luedtke, 1982, 4–5)

Luedtke got it right. If the public really does have a right to know, it surely has a right to determine what information it truly needs to know and to demand that the press (as its surrogate) deliver that information forthwith. Out the window goes the right of the editor and broadcaster to edit and to decide what is news. And here the nightmare begins. If the press is to become the legal representative of the people under a general principle of a right to know, then it will certainly be told by the courts and legislatures that it has a duty to provide particular information to the public. This definitely would be a shocking intrusion on freedom of the press and is something that I would hope no thinking journalist would advocate. New rights bring new duties, and I have serious doubts that the press will want the baggage that will come with the public's right to know, if such a right should be given full and complete constitutional protection. I say let well enough alone, stop making self-serving claims in the name of this public *need*.

ARGUMENT SUMMATION: *There is no right to know.*

The right to know is not to be found in the Constitution, which preserves individual rights—not institutional rights. The right to know is, rather, a creation of courts and is therefore a privilege that can be taken away. Before rising to constitutional importance it must take on more breadth than is presently recognizable. Originally the freedom of information movement achieved legitimacy by focusing on the need for access to government records, but it has since expanded its aims to include a general right to know. However, even the right of access to government records is severely limited by exceptions such as privacy, economic interests, social stability, and national security.

RESPONSE

Merrill: There is a right to know.

My coauthor contends that the right to know is not an inalienable right guaranteed by the Constitution but is, rather, something invented by journalists or granted to us by benevolent legislative bodies. It is difficult to dispute either of these contentions. Such a right is not overtly in the Bill of Rights, and it does seem that only journalists and public interest advocates have made much, if anything, of such a right.

Nevertheless, even after saying this, I must insist that a right to know for the citizenry of a libertarian (free and open) society does indeed exist—even if such a right is a philosophical right and not spelled out literally in the First Amendment. In my mind a fundamental or natural right exists whether or not there is any provision at the moment for constitutional enforcement. That often comes in due time. Rights, I believe, do eventually emerge and gain legitimacy in the law, even if the government at the moment (here or elsewhere in the world) temporarily balks at what is really a right.

It may well be that a people's right to know is not explicitly stated constitutionally, but journalists did more than invent it: They inferred from the freedom of the press clause that a people's right to know existed. I suppose that by making such an inference, which seems quite logical to me, they did in a sense invent this right to know. But instead of feeling guilty for such an invention, if such it was, journalists should be proud that they have seen this public right standing in the philosophical shadows supporting a free press.

Why, we should ask, did the Founding Fathers provide for a free press? Simply for the sake of having a free press? Just so future citizens could brag about such a provision? Obviously there was a pragmatic reason for the free press (as well as the free speech) provision in the Bill of Rights. And this reason revolves around what we now call the people's right to know. (If the people (the sovereign rulers of the republic) do not know about public affairs and government business, they surely cannot be good sovereigns; they cannot govern themselves well.) In the philosophical framework in which they find themselves, they *must* know. Their government is built upon the assumption that they will know; therefore, certainly it is their right to know. They need to know; they have a philosophical mandate to know in order to be consistent with their political purpose. The very reason for a free press is so that the people can know.

Someone will ask: If the people have a right to know, then does not the press share responsibility with government for letting them know? My answer is yes. If the press argues for such a right (and I maintain that the press in a free society, with its press freedom, *must* believe in such a fundamental right), then it must take very seriously its responsibility of providing knowledge about public affairs to the people.) If there is such a public right to know, and I believe there is, then the press has an important responsibility to fulfill this right—to see to it that the people are able to know.

At this point the government enters the picture, for the press cannot let the people know what the press cannot get from the government. So, I maintain that the people do have a right to know public business and that both the press and the government have the responsibility to let the people know. Certainly the people cannot know about their government without the cooperation of both press and government. But the fact that the press and government both fail from time to time to let the people know does not eliminate that right.

The concept of the people's right to know has mainly been promoted since World War II, with books such as Harold Cross's (1953) *The People's Right to Know*, Kent Cooper's (1956) *The Right to Know*, Althan Theoharis's edited collection, *A Culture of Secrecy: The Government vs. the People's Right to Know* (1998), and numerous articles declaring such a right and castigating government for infringing on it. No adherent to a libertarian theory of the press can help admiring and applauding such antigovernment broadsides, but the problem is larger than this. Two other important factors are involved in this business of letting the people know: the people and the press. Too often they are left out of the discussion of this topic.

Frankly, the people either don't know they have a right to know or they don't take it seriously. It appears that they simply don't care. Such a right to know is certainly of great importance—a civil right if ever there was one. Such a right is at the very foundation of American government, of public discussion, of intelligent voting, of public opinion, of the very fabric and essence of democracy. And yet the people appear to have little or no concern for this right. But unconcern does not do away with the right. The only segment of our society that seems really concerned about the people's right to know is the press. Journalists criticize, agitate, and fret about government infringing on the people's right to know. They justify—rightly—their own press freedom by appealing to the public's right to know.

A problem with the press is that it places all the blame on government for denying the people their right to know. This, of course, is not true. The news media themselves participate in the denial of this right. Persons familiar with the typical news operation must recognize that only a very small portion of government-related information gets to the average citizen's eyes or ears. So, in effect, the news media are guilty of the same sins of omission and commission that they point to in government.

 Editors and news directors, while promoting the idea of a people's right to know, are busy selecting and rejecting government information. They leave out this story, that picture, this viewpoint. They are, in effect, censors—perhaps with the best of motives, but censors nevertheless. They manage the news just as government officials do. They also play their part in the restriction of the people's right to know. Editors call this practice "exercising their editorial prerogative." They see themselves as editing; they see the government as managing and restricting public information. But the people's exercise of the right to know is being limited regardless of these semantic games.

One who observes the editing operations of a newspaper or magazine is struck by the swiftness with which government news is discarded. While wastebaskets fill with information that the people presumably should be reading, one sees few tears and little gnashing of teeth in journalistic ranks. It is as if these practitioners of journalism obscure their own coverage of government without even realizing that they, like the government officials they criticize, are keeping back information that, in their own words, "the public has a right to know." And though it can be argued that virtually all government agencies have Websites with voluminous material available to the public, I worry about what's not there in that sea of information, the very facts and information that are much needed to make personal and institutional decisions. And all the while press people are hailing the right to know as indispensable for the country.

Media people are correct, of course. The public does have a right to know. This right has always been embedded in the American journalistic context, even though it has not been traditionally as popular as it has been since World War II. Now the emphasis is shifting from the press to the people, from journalistic freedom to journalistic responsibility, from institutional rights of the press to social rights of the citizenry. It is all part of the shift from negative freedom to positive freedom. Part of the social responsibility theory of the press is an emphasis on what the press does positively rather than what the press might be kept from doing by government. The people's right to know is a logical outgrowth of this trend. I maintain that the philosophical rationale for press freedom (interpreted until recently as the press's freedom) all along has been that the people need to know. This need is translated philosophically into a right in our type of pluralistic, open, libertarian society where the people theoretically are the sovereigns.

Professor Kirtley, who is cited by my colleague Dennis, has written persuasively that the right to know is crucial to democracy itself—and I agree. As she puts it, "In any democracy, an informed public is vital. The public votes to elect officials who draft and execute their laws. Without information, citizens would risk being alienated from a government that becomes less and less accountable to them" (Kirtley, 2003). She goes on to quote one of Dr. Dennis's favorites, Justice William O. Douglas, who wrote, "Secrecy in government is fundamentally anti-democratic, perpetuating bureaucratic errors. Open debate and discussion of public issues are vital to our national health. On public questions there should be 'uninhibited, robust, and wide open' debate."

Outrageous cases of courts' and judges' effectively blocking the right to know do exist, of course. In 2004, in addition to the Judith Miller–Valerie Plume case involving revelations about a CIA agent that could have put her life in danger, a more typical case of "notebook and shield" occurred in Providence, Rhode Island, where a TV reporter was put on trial for criminal contempt for doing his job. His "crime" was accepting a videotape from a confidential source that showed a city official accepting a bribe. As NBC News president Neal Shapiro wrote of the case, "This is precisely what news organizations are supposed to do. The footage gave the citizens of Providence information they deserved to have about city officials who, since the story broke, have been charged, tried and convicted of criminal activity" (Shapiro, 2004). He adds that "it is high time journalists were added to the list" of shield laws that protect psychotherapists, doctors, lawyers, and the clergy.

In conclusion, despite the sophisticated arguments put forward by Professor Dennis and others who deny this right, I again assert that the people's right to know does exist. However often it is denied—by government and by the press—it is still there, serving as the main underpinning of a democratic society of the American type. It is the justification for press freedom and an absolute requirement for the political viability of the United States.

ARGUMENT SUMMATION: *There is a right to know.*

Certainly there is no explicit constitutional right to know, but there is surely an implied or natural right to know. The concept of press freedom assumes such a right, for obviously the press would not have such freedom for no (or only a selfish) reason. The country's philosophy is based on the people as sovereigns; therefore, there is a need for them to know, and this need is logically translated into a right. Both the press and the government share in the responsibility to let the people know. The people may not think much about such a right, but they instinctively feel they have it, given their type of government. If they do not have such a right, then they see no real reason for a free press.

SEARCH ONLINE!

Use the following terms and phrases to search for more information on InfoTrac College Edition: *rights, duties, responsibility, sunshine laws, access to information, right of access, individual rights, institutional rights, First Amendment law, censorship, positive freedom, negative freedom, right to know.*

TOPICS FOR DISCUSSION

1. Think about the public's need to know, desire to know, curiosity to know—and consider these alongside a *right* to know. What are your conclusions?
2. If a right to know is not in the Bill of Rights, where do we get such a right? Is it any more than a theoretical or idealistic right?
3. If it is a right of the people to know, why do media themselves withhold information? How can a newspaper editor believe in such a people's right while refraining from giving a quote's source, naming a rape victim, or divulging the source of a government leak?
4. Can press freedom, which *is* in the Constitution, be equated with the public's right to know? Explain your answer.
5. If the invention of the right to know came about in the early 1950s, why do you think it developed so late in American history if the principle on which it rests is valid?

TOPICS FOR RESEARCH

1. Write a paper about forces for and against the right to know. Who have the right-to-know spokespersons been over the years? Who have been their opponents?
2. Prepare a study of the origins, present status, and probable future of the federal Freedom of Information Act.
3. Write a review essay about three or four major books or articles about privacy from the perspective of the right to know. When do privacy rights take precedence over the media's desire to know something?
4. What is intellectual property? How is it connected to the law of copyright? Why is copyright law a part of U.S. federal code? How do copyright and protection of an individual author's rights impair the people's right to know? Should anyone care?
5. Why is there a debate over the right to know? Why is it that media people believe it exists and lawyers say "no way"?

FURTHER READING

Anderson, Jack. "We the People: Do We Have a Right to Know?" *Parade* (January 30, 1966): 4–5.

Boyer, John H. "Supreme Court and the Right to Know." FOI Center Report 272. Columbia: University of Missouri, November 1971.

Cooper, Kent. *The Right to Know.* New York: Farrar, Strauss & Giroux, 1956.

Cross, Harold L. *The People's Right to Know: Legal Access to Public Records and Proceedings.* New York: Columbia University Press, 1953.

Davis, Charles N., and Sigman L. Splichal. *Access Denied: Freedom of Information in the Information Age.* Ames: Iowa State University Press, 2000.

Dennis, Everette E., D. M. Gillmor, and David Grey, eds. *Justice Hugo Black and the First Amendment.* Ames: Iowa State University Press, 1978.

Douglas, William O. *The Right of the People.* New York: Doubleday, 1958.

Greenhouse, Linda. "Court Says Press Isn't Liable for Using Ill-Gotten Tapes." *New York Times,* May 22, 2001, A14; also see editorial, "A Victory for Press Freedoms," p. A18.

Haiman, Franklyn S. *Speech and Law in a Free Society.* Chicago: University of Chicago Press, 1981.

Kirtley, Jane E. "Privacy vs. Public Right to Know." *Encyclopedia of International Media and Communications,* Vol. 3, pp. 573–583. Amsterdam: Academic Press, 2003.

Kurtz, Howard. *Media Circus.* New York: Times Books, 1993.

Luedtke, Kurt. "An Ex-Newsman Hands Down His Indictment of the Press." *Bulletin of ASNE* 65 (May–June 1982): 16–17.

"The People's Right to Know: How Much or How Little?" *Time* (January 11, 1971): 16–17.

Rourke, Francis E. *Secrecy and Publicity: Dilemmas of Democracy.* Baltimore: Johns Hopkins University Press, 1966.

Shane, Peter M., ed. *A Little Knowledge: Privacy, Security and Pubic Information after September 11.* New York: Century Foundation Press, 2004.

Shapiro, Neal. "Notebook and Shield." *Wall Street Journal*, November 17, 2004, A16.

Stewart, Potter. "Or of the Press." *Hastings Law Journal* 26 (January 1975): 631–38.

Sunstein, Cass. *Democracy and the Problem of Free Speech.* New York: Free Press, 1993.

Theoharis, Althan G. *A Culture of Secrecy: The Government vs. the People's Right to Know.* Lawrence: University Press of Kansas, 1998.

Tribe, Lawrence H. *American Constitutional Law.* Mineola, NY: Foundation Press, 1988. See especially Chapter 12, "Communication and Expression," 576–736.

Whalen, Charles W., Jr. *Your Right to Know.* New York: Vintage Books, 1973.

Williams, Lord Francis. "The Right to Know." *Twentieth Century* (Spring 1962): 6–17.

MEDIA BIAS
AND POLITICAL LEANINGS

A free and independent press is almost universally regarded as essential to democracy, but there is considerable argument about the political leanings and potential bias of reporters, editors, and others engaged in gathering the news. Political conservatives—from commentators such as analyst Brent Bozell to radio talkmeister Rush Limbaugh and others—strongly argue that the press is liberal, tilted to the left, and often biased and unfair. This view is widely disseminated by various media critics, foundations, and study centers that are tilted to the political right. On the left, commentators and critics using the same terms but different definitions say the press and news media are too conservative and oriented to supporting the status quo and establishment organizations. Critics such as Eric Alterman of *The Nation* and the advocacy group Fairness and Accuracy in Media (FAIR) promote this view. In the middle are journalist-critics who regard themselves as fair-minded, nonideological professionals guided by standards and practices learned in journalism schools and in the nation's newsrooms, which always warn against too much political involvement. Still, some of these people will readily agree that much of the news media does tilt in a political direction, and which way depends on to whom you talk. Fred W. Friendly, the legendary CBS and PBS giant, once said, "Of course the press is liberal," but then admitted that he was talking mostly about the major newspapers and networks that he knew well. Richard Clurman, former chief of correspondents at *Time* magazine and author of several leading media books, agreed, even though he was regarded by many as an establishment figure who is left of center.

Pollsters and various survey organizations and study groups have also weighed in on the matter. The Center for Media and Public Affairs in Washington, D.C., is headed by social scientist Robert Lichter, whose findings often identify a liberal bias in the media, although his critics point out that much of his work is supported by conservative organizations. The Accuracy in Media group, headed by conservative activist Reed Irvine, also documents what Irvine terms "liberal and radical abuses in the media." John Corry, a columnist for the conservative

American Spectator, agrees and says that journalism is sometimes a status game wherein a liberal ideology is required for success. From a more theoretical perspective, media economist James T. Hamilton of Duke University says his data show that the news media do opt for liberally oriented stories, especially on economic, social, and political matters.

Sociologist Herbert Gans and a number of other scholars dismiss the idea of political bias of the media, saying that the media are essentially apolitical, with few reporters playing a direct political role and most jealously guarding their impartiality. Media critic Edwin Diamond once characterized American reporters as "the best and the blandest," noting their essentially neutral role in public life and in the media industries. Journalism educators David Weaver and G. Cleveland Wilhoit, authors of the respected study *The American Journalist*, also document an essentially apolitical press corps; although more journalists identify with the Democratic Party than with the Republicans, they find no evidence of heavy-handed political bias. Students of the international media find the American press to have what Victor Navasky of *The Nation*, a liberal magazine, calls "an ideology of the center," and one of the authors of this book once told an international audience: "Look—forget about political bias and a party press in America. If anything, objectivity is our ideology, even though we really don't believe in any pure form of objectivity." Media critic Jay Rosen of New York University similarly debunks objectivity in his book *What Are Journalists For?*

This debate notwithstanding, when most Americans are asked whether they believe that the press does have a political agenda and ideological leanings, whether liberal or conservative, they answer yes. In a society where the free flow of information and opinion are at the core of democratic values, the integrity of the media is severely challenged by the belief in the notion of political bias in the media.

CHALLENGE

Dennis: The news media are not biased.

This rather stark statement may seem to lead the author on a fool's errand, since so many Americans instantly assume that the news media are filled with political bias and often reflect the personal politics and outlook of its practitioners, whether newspaper reporters, television anchors, or other communicators. Indeed, if one listens in on the liberal versus conservative argument as it plays out in American media, it would seem that, more often than not, critical commentators on both sides of the question stipulate that, yes, the media are liberal (meaning leaning toward Democrats and others who fashion themselves progressives of the left). The shrill cable commentator and author Ann Coulter strongly articulates this view, even suggesting that the "liberal media" hate America and lean toward treason. In more measured tones, Robert J. Barro, an economics professor at Harvard, says "the liberal media—it's not myth" and notes that the news media and talk shows more often feature liberal sources, even though the country is increasingly conservative. As he put it in *Business Week*, "if the opinions of viewers and readers are similar to those of their representatives, the media slant is far to the left of their customers" (Barro, 2004). And, as mentioned earlier, the respected media economist James Hamilton also cites data that suggest the media lean left in their news coverage. On the other side of this argument is Eric Alterman, whose book *What Liberal Media?* (2003) makes a powerful case that consistent disinformation on the right has led many people to believe that the news media are liberal in a robust ideological sense. Adding fuel to the argument in 2004 was the *New York Times* ombudsman Dan Okerant, whose column trumpeted what seemed to many a given, that "*The New York Times* is a liberal newspaper," though he later argued that the paper generally treats the concerns of a metropolitan, urbane audience, which can seem leftist to some but might only reflect establishment views.

In the midst of this confusion, and recalling that the news media are diverse not monolithic, let me begin by removing from the argument opinion journalism and commentary. The views expressed on editorial pages, on op-ed pages, in television commentaries that are clearly so labeled, and on talk radio have a point of view; these are biased in a sense, but not necessarily prejudicial. The best commentary sifts through evidence and offers conclusions. That is its function and, of course, commentators tend to come from a given section of the political spectrum and to reflect their own experience and self-interest. That is opinion journalism, a form practiced by many magazines and newspapers in many countries of the world, especially in Europe.

But what we're really talking about here are the news columns and the news delivered on television, which for better or worse are often more descriptive than interpretative and are laden more with facts than with ideas or opinions. Much of American journalism is simply descriptive, some is analytical, and some gets involved in interpretation. As we argue in Chapter 12, journalistic objectivity is a style of presentation wherein information is organized to answer certain questions: What happened? Who was involved? When did it occur? Did it make any difference? Although surely there will be different answers to some of these questions, the idea that this approach constitutes political bias is nonsense.

A look at history demonstrates how the political bias argument evolved. President Franklin Delano Roosevelt, knowing that more than 80 percent of the nation's newspaper publishers opposed his administration, courted reporters who he knew were younger and more liberal than their conservative bosses. He also made an end run around then traditional media by giving his own *fireside chats* on radio, where he could present his point of view. To Roosevelt the press was both conservative (in its editorial expressions) and occasionally friendlier to him—and apparently more liberal—in its news columns, not because reporters were cheerleaders for his administration but because they played the news straight. Years later Adlai Stevenson, the Democratic candidate for president, called the American media a "one-party press," by which he meant a conservative, anti-liberal press. Since that time virtually every U.S. president has had strong views about the press, which was typically tough on them and their administrations, thus giving rise to charges of bias—either conservative or liberal, depending on the time and the administration. Still later, in the election of 1996, one study reported that 87 percent of the Washington press corps voted for Bill Clinton. In 2000, both George W. Bush and Al Gore complained about press coverage given their campaigns. In the 2004 national election, the media were very much an issue when Dan Rather and the CBS program *Sixty Minutes* got caught up in a controversy over President George W. Bush's service in the National Guard using documents that could not be authenticated. There was a storm of criticism blasting Rather as a predictably liberal journalist. Similarly, the *New York Times* late in the campaign reported on hundreds of tons of missing explosives in Iraq—and was immediately accused by the Republicans of an eleventh-hour attack on the president and his party.

Herbert Gans, in a detailed analysis in *Columbia Journalism Review* (1985), has dissected claims that the press is too liberal, challenging the assumptions of conservative researchers and urging them to make their data available for others to assess. Robert and Linda Lichter and Stanley Rothman, in their book *The Media Elite* (1986), make the case for a biased, left-leaning media but point mostly to major media outlets such as the news magazines, networks, and big-city newspapers. A counterargument is made by Weaver and Wilhoit, who, using a national sample, suggest that journalists are not driven by political ideology and bias nor are they joiners of organizations. And as Gans and others have pointed out, affiliation with a political party—as long as one is not an activist—does not prove that the individual colors the news to suit his or her fancy, any more than one's religion precludes one from writing fair-minded reports on other people's religions.

The reason I side with this view is *professionalism*. The employees of news media organizations are *trained professionals* and there are many checks and balances to keep them from using the news media for their own personal or political ends. Journalists are either trained or initiated into methods of gathering information, sorting out sources, and synthesizing reports and documents into a coherent news report. Although there is less newspaper competition city by city than was once the case, you can bet that a biased report in the *New York Times* would be quickly challenged and savaged by the *Wall Street Journal* or even by network television. Scores of news organizations in television, print, cable, and even cyberspace gather and disseminate information, and these serve to check and balance each other. There are also ways for the public and for sources to respond through letters and by lodging personal complaints; they appeal to other media to tell their story as they see it, and they can and do sue for defamation when they believe their reputations have been unfairly sullied.

The U.S. media system is far from perfect—it has many flaws, from tabloid sensationalism to overemphasis on sex and violence, not to mention lack of continuity in coverage—but it is not a political press in the sense that other nations' media are. That is, we rarely have a pro-government newspaper or network, one that is uncritical of those in power. If anything, we have an antiauthority press that is always suspicious and critical of the status quo and of those in power. The press and other news media are largely, though not entirely, negative in their news judgments, portraying society's warts more often than they do its strength and triumphs. Also, it is clear that our dynamic media are changing, that they rarely adhere to a strict separation of fact and opinion, that interpretative journalism is on the rise, and that sometimes this is confused with bias and political leanings.

Increasingly, too, politicians looking for the friendly reporter who is biased in their favor—whether Democrats or Republicans, liberals or conservatives—are disappointed. Luckily, reporters ready to write up biased reports are rare, and media organizations deal effectively with those who are found to be unethical or prejudicial in their work. Of course, much that is poorly reported, weakly reasoned, and ineptly edited does get into the American media, but not because of bias.

Louis D. Boccardi, who as president and CEO of the Associated Press presided over the world's largest news-gathering organization, refuses to say whether he belongs to a political party and for whom he might have voted. Boccardi is so well regarded as an exemplar of impartial news judgment that he makes a strong case against any kind of deliberate (or accidental) political bias in his organization, which is a major supplier of news to print and electronic media. Indeed, after he retired from the Associated Press in 2003, he was asked to lead an independent investigation of the *New York Times* after a reporter was fired for falsifying stories—and subsequently in 2004 and 2005 was asked by CBS to look into the charges against them.

The media, of course, have a strong vested interest in not succumbing to political bias: credibility, their most valuable asset. Without credibility, which comes with impartial, professionally gathered and edited news, the news media lose their franchise with the public. That's why so many news groups and scholars have regularly studied credibility. The self-correcting nature of the press in regard to deliberate political bias is swift and unforgiving, just as it is for fabrication, uncaring sloppiness, or other behaviors that contaminate what the Hutchins Commission called "fair and accurate presentation of the day's news." I reject the simple-minded idea that the news media, which have so much to lose if they contaminate their own product, can be accused of biasing the news, whether in a leftward or rightward direction. If anything, the American news media often err on the side of blandness, bending over backward to be fair in delivering a truthful account to their readers and viewers, who they hope will return again and often.

ARGUMENT SUMMATION: *The news media are not biased.*

Bias and deliberate distortion are rarely found in the U.S. news media. Forces of professionalism on the one hand and fear of litigation on the other make it highly unlikely that the news media will engage in deliberate bias or allow the political leanings of a reporter to overly distort what he or she is writing about. Some critics are fond of accusing the media of having a liberal or a conservative bias, but in fact the news media in the United States have more of a centrist approach and try very hard to hew a neutral line rather than take sides. Of course opinion media and editorial pages often argue a strong point of view and do have ideological leanings, but the news media for the most part (and compared with the media of other countries) not only are not biased but are often rightly accused of blandness, so cautious is their coverage.

RESPONSE

Merrill: *The news media are biased.*

Dr. Dennis, perhaps tongue-in-cheek, contends that the news media are not biased. He admits that most people believe they are biased, but he seems to put this perception down to a kind of populist ignorance. But to Dennis's credit, he does explain that he is talking not about opinion aspects of the media, but only about news columns and TV news. Editorial pages, op-ed pages, and television and radio commentary, he says, are naturally biased, as is most opinion journalism.

So now we have a focused statement, somewhat different from the debate topic. Dennis is really talking about this proposition: *The news segments of the news media are not biased.*

I must take the position that even the news in the news media is biased. Of course this statement is not easy to prove. Bias is a complex concept, almost impossible to ascertain and measure. Often one sees bias, or the lack of it, through the lens of one's own biased perceptions.

But it seems quite evident to me that a reporter's reality strainer (one's own subjective value system or perception) projects or reflects reality from a personal and biased perspective. A liberal reporter and a conservative reporter will report the same issue or event differently. A black reporter will report the Los Angeles riots differently than a white reporter, other factors being equal. A reporter who is a member of the Branch Davidian religious sect would report the 1993 Waco episode differently than an Episcopalian liberal. A female reporter will report a spousal abuse story differently from a male reporter. An

Arab reporter will report the Israeli–Palestinian confrontation in a manner different from that of a Jewish reporter. A Cuban-American may have a different take on the Elian Gonzalez case than his Anglo counterpart.

Dennis says that journalistic "professionalism" protects the journalist against biased reporting. He speaks of many checks and balances keeping reporters from biasing their stories. And he maintains that one newspaper will savage another quickly if a report is biased. This may all be true in an ideal journalistic world, but the present one falls short of that. Look at any complex and controversial story carried, for instance, by a liberal and a conservative paper. Note who is quoted, which quotes are selected for use, what pictures are used, and so on. It is not too difficult for the reader to tell which is the liberal and which is the conservative paper. Bias is there, all right, even if it gets in through emphasis and de-emphasis of portions of the story or through the sources chosen to be quoted.

In recent years a number of scholars, among them economists, have developed some quite disturbing data about the political bias of the press. For example, Professors Tim Groseclose of UCLA and Jeff Milyo of the University of Chicago have produced a book called *A Measure of Media Bias* (2004), in which they try with empirical precision to create the same kind of bias index that has long been used in assessing U.S. senators and their political leanings. They found a pronounced liberal bias in the news, with spokespeople on the left getting far more coverage—and more sympathetic coverage—than those on the right. Professor Dennis has already mentioned the work of Jay Hamilton at Duke, which draws on other sources to show the economic tendencies of the news media to favor liberal topics and sources. These researchers are not ideologues and their studies—and methods—are made public for anyone to inspect and come to their own conclusions. More than I can say for many blathering commentators who simply pronounce the media liberal—or conservative—on their say-so, nothing more.

Dr. Dennis goes on to support his media-are-not-biased contention by saying that the United States does not have a partisan press, that seldom do we have a pro-government newspaper or network. "If anything," he says, "we have an antiauthority press that is always suspicious and critical of the status quo and of those in power." Well, if this is so, doesn't it indicate a bias? A bias against authority? A bias against the status quo? I agree with Dennis that the media are largely negative in their news judgments. And this, for me, indicates a negative bias, certainly not a balanced or neutral concept of news.

Another point made by Dennis to show a lack of bias is that when stories are poorly reported, weakly reasoned, or ineptly edited, that is the result of ineffective reporting and sloppiness rather than bias. Well, maybe, but how do we know? He also says that bias is lacking in the media's news coverage because the media have credibility; this, he says, is their most valuable asset, and they must keep it. If public faith in the news media is indeed correlated with lack of bias, I propose that this shows only too clearly that the media are biased. Why? Because all surveys show that the media are not very credible with the public.

My opponent says that politicians looking for a reporter to bias stories in their favor will be disappointed. This is another reason, he says, that news stories are not biased. But cannot a reporter bias a story *unintentionally?* And is this not still bias? Maybe what we should be debating is the topic of *intentional* bias. Do reporters intentionally bias stories? Well, maybe and maybe not. But whether bias appears in the news media intentionally or naturally, bias is still there. It would be difficult for any student of the press to conclude that the media's news coverage is bias free. Reporters may not often intentionally contaminate the news one way or another, but we've seen from the Jayson Blair case at the *New York Times* and the Jack Kelley case at *USA Today* that reporters have a great deal of latitude to do what they choose and only when they get caught do we know just what they've done. I too believe that most reporters are ethical professionals, but some are not, and this is where the rub lies.

Finally, Dr. Dennis seems to wish the media were more biased, because he says, "If anything, the American news media often *err* [my emphasis] on the side of blandness, bending over backward to be fair in delivering a truthful account to their readers and viewers." Admittedly much of what is found in the media is bland, but this blandness does not indicate a lack of bias. I worry that the perceptions of a liberal bias greatly compromise the media and that the media do precious little to combat this view. Although I have no doubt that the Fox Network as a matter of finding their market niche have tilted rightward, much of the rest of the media do appear to be leaning left, and even when so charged they rarely "dignify" the criticism with a response. The public is entitled to that. Otherwise we'll devolve into a noisy period in which we can't authenticate the truth of news and information. That this would be bad for democracy is beyond question.

ARGUMENT SUMMATION: *The news media are biased.*

News reporting by the media is largely biased, especially when dealing with political news or other social news of controversy. This bias is natural and stems from the individual reporter's value system and culture. It also is derived from other factors such as the reporter's education, religion, social class, gender, party affiliation, political ideology, and a whole bevy of personal biases. The reporter filters the story through this personal subjective point of view and, although doing so may be largely subconscious, biases the story in some way. Even the reporter who is most concerned about bias will influence the story out of an overcompensating attempt to be balanced, accurate, and fair. So the news media are biased. In fact, they simply represent (or reflect) the bias of their reporters and editors. The bias may be unintentional, but it is still bias; it may be subconsciously woven into the fabric of the story, but it is still bias. Bias is natural. It permeates the media—even the news stories.

SEARCH ONLINE!

Use the following terms and phrases to search for more information on InfoTrac College Edition: *bias, media bias, ideology, conservative, liberal, centrist, moderate, one-party press, media elites, subjectivity, value system, vested interests, fairness, Fairness and Accuracy in Reporting (FAIR), Accuracy in Media (AIM), Media Research Center, media power.*

TOPICS FOR DISCUSSION

1. Take the dictionary definition of *bias*—a preference or inclination that inhibits impartial judgment—and consider how this might apply to the news media. How would you recognize bias in the news? How would you offer evidence of bias from your own viewing and reading?
2. Delving into journalism history, consider the differences between the biased party press of the early republic and the corporatized news media today. Do the media have a political agenda? Can they?
3. Compare and contrast the opinion magazines' view of the world and that of major newspapers and news magazines. For example, how is the president of the United States portrayed in the news columns of *Time, Newsweek,* and the *Wall Street Journal* versus an essay in *The Nation, Weekly Standard,* or *National Review*?
4. How can a news medium best make the case with the public that it is unbiased and impartial with regard to politics and elections?
5. How does political coverage differ on NBC, CBS, or CNN versus Fox TV or the Christian News Network? What about MTV News—what are its politics?

TOPICS FOR RESEARCH

1. Do a study of news coverage of a major state or national political figure in newspaper, magazine, or television sources, assessing each story as positive, neutral, or negative. How did you develop your definitions for each category,

and how well did the medium you picked for study (for example, your local newspaper or a television evening news program) do?

2. Examine the criticisms of the news media by public officials: the president, Speaker of the House of Representatives, minority leaders of the House and Senate, and others. Do they charge bias or unfairness? If so, what are their specific complaints? Act as an investigator and substantiate or discount their claims.

3. Interview a reporter or editor on political bias. What does this person think it is? How does the person guard against it in his or her news organization? What does the person think of the performance of other media, including his or her competitors, regarding bias?

4. Many critics of the media come from fields such as business, education, labor, medicine, and others. They sometimes charge bias and misrepresentation with regard to their fields. Take the argument that the media are anti-business or opposed to some other institution or group. What are your own conclusions?

FURTHER READING

Alterman, Eric. *What Liberal Media? The Truth about Bias and the News*. New York: Basic Books, 2003.

Barro, Robert J. "The Liberal Media: It's No Myth." *Business Week*, June 14, 2004.

Benjamin, Burton. *Fair Play: CBS, Westmoreland and How a Television Documentary Went Wrong*. New York: Harper & Row, 1988.

Bozell, L. Brent. *Weapons of Mass Distortion: The Coming Meltdown of Liberal Media*. New York: Crown, 2004.

Commission on Freedom of the Press. *A Free and Responsible Press*. Chicago: University of Chicago Press, 1947.

Dennis, Everette E. *Of Media and People*. Newbury Park, CA: Sage, 1992.

Dennis, Everette E., ed. *Media Studies Journal: The Fairness Factor* (Fall). New York: Freedom Forum Media Studies Center, 1992.

Fallows, James. *Breaking the News: How the Media Undermine American Democracy*. New York: Vintage Books, 1997.

Gans, Herbert. "Are U.S. Journalists Dangerously Liberal?" *Columbia Journalism Review* (November/December 1985): 29–37.

Goldberg, Bernard. *Bias: A CBS Insider Exposes How the Media Distort the News*. New York: Regnery, 2001.

Goldstein, Tom, ed. *Killing the Messenger: 100 Years of Media Criticism*. New York: Columbia University Press, 1989.

Groseclose, Tim, and Jeff Milyo. *A Measure of Media Bias*. Chicago: University of Chicago Press, 2004.

Henry, William A., III. "Are the Media Too Liberal?" *Time* (October 19, 1992): 46–47.

Lichter, Robert S., Stanley Rothman, and Linda S. Lichter. *The Media Elite*. Bethesda, MD: Adler & Adler, 1986.

Manoff, Robert Karl, and Michael Schudson, eds. *Reading the News*. New York: Pantheon, 1986.

McQuail, Denis. *Media Performance: Mass Communication and the Public Interest.* Newbury Park, CA: Sage, 1992.

Protess, David L., et al. *The Journalism of Outrage: Investigative Reporting and Agenda Building in America.* New York: Guilford Press, 1991.

Sabato, Larry J. *Feeding Frenzy: Attack Journalism and American Politics.* New York: Lanahan, 2000.

Schudson, Michael. *The Power of News.* Cambridge, MA: Harvard University Press, 1995.

Weaver, David H., and G. Cleveland Wilhoit. *The American Journalist: A Portrait of U.S. News People and Their Work.* Bloomington: Indiana University Press, 1986.

MEDIA, POLITICS, AND ELECTIONS

In the U.S. presidential election of 2004 it was estimated that total campaign expenditures of all candidates were just under $1 billion. Nearly twice as much was spent on state and congressional elections, making the 2004 election the most expensive in history. Where does the lion's share of that money go, about $4 out of every $10 spent? To the media, of course. Why? Because media, through paid (advertising and sponsored programs) and free (news coverage of candidates, debates, etc.) content, provide the means by which people learn about, get to know, and choose their candidate for president. Candidates for office at all levels of government actively campaign through personal appearances at shopping centers, in public speeches, and by other means, but they reach relatively few people this way and must depend on the media for wide exposure.

Few people believe that the media conspire to control elections, but their influence and power are almost universally recognized by ordinary citizens and political experts. Heavy exposure for a candidate through positive news coverage, strategic use of media endorsements, and effective placement of advertising is deemed important in deciding who wins elections. The power of the press, more often stated in subtler terms as the influence of the media, shows in the spending patterns of candidates and interest groups who favor a particular individual, party, or issue. That influence is also evidenced in the way political candidates and their handlers court the media, nearly begging for attention and approval. Candidates with modest public support and little funding have a difficult time because they fail to win notice in the media and thus from the public. On occasion, candidates for public office have tried to make *end runs*, sometimes successful, around the mainstream media by using alternative media, direct mail advertising, and the Internet. Even successful use of the end run or alternative media suggests the profound impact of the mainstream media—notably, television and radio news, cable and radio talk shows, newspaper treatment, and other outlets. The fact that a candidate has to make an end run underscores and reinforces the perceived power of the media to promote candidates and issues and to swing voters. At times the media even help candidates they might not ultimately favor because they like a good fight, a contest that the audience follows, rather than the inevitable march of a front-running candidate toward victory.

News coverage claims to be neutral and impartial, but talk show hosts make no such claims as they promote candidates they like. This is as true for conservative Sean Hannity as it is for maverick liberal Don Imus. Similarly, the editorial pages of most newspapers and some magazines make definitive endorsements, stating that they favor one candidate over another. Whether those endorsements actually swing elections has been widely debated, but because candidates crave this kind of support, it is reasonable to assume that they see benefit in endorsements. Some political scientists and communication theorists have argued that endorsements do sway elections, even if only by a few percentage points. In a country where elections are often close, endorsements can make all the difference.

Scholars have debated the power of the press to control elections, once thinking them all powerful, then minimally important, and now again significantly influential in helping voters narrow their choices. People in the political process are less ambivalent. The media are powerful, they believe, and they want as much exposure and support as possible. Failing that, they sometimes engage in media bashing, claiming that the press is biased or unfair to their candidate, not so much to win media friends as to demand (and often get) more coverage. The high cost of campaigns is central to arguments for campaign reform. The dominant view of both the general public and the most savvy campaign manager is that the media do make a difference—a powerful difference—and they can and often do swing elections.

CHALLENGE

Merrill: The media cover but don't control elections.

One reason, it is said, that the public is tired of elections is that the media, rather than parties and individual determination, control elections. I contend that this is not true—that the media simply cover elections. The extent to which they do this, of course, does have an impact on the election through the exposure of platforms, principles, and images of the candidates. The media, without a doubt, do have an impact on elections. In a sense they spotlight the candidates; they focus on them and their ideas and rhetoric as well as on their personalities. In fact, they may well present a multifaceted image of the candidates, providing too much information and exposing blemishes beyond their real importance.

Media are important to political campaigns. Nobody is denying that. But controlling elections? I believe not. The decisive factors in an election, as the 2004 presidential election showed, are (1) money and (2) being an incumbent president in the midst of a war. Both George W. Bush and John Kerry had loads of money, each in the $350 million range, or more than any candidate had ever spent before. As a third-party candidate, Ralph Nader had very little and mounted a less impressive campaign than he had in 2000 or certainly than Ross Perot did in 1992, when he drew a large enough vote to prevent either candidate's getting a majority of the votes cast. Sometimes insurgent candidates can garner plenty of publicity, though, and that can feed into the money machine. Witness Howard Dean in 2004 or Bill Bradley in 2000, neither of whom won the nomination. Some candidates rely mostly on free publicity—especially those running well back in the various primary races such as Al Sharpton and others in 2004 when the Democrats had a full field of candidates while President Bush ran unopposed. But as much as the media can expose candidates with limited support and money, they rarely if ever win the all-important primary elections that lead to electoral victory in November. Most of the time, I'd argue, factors other than media power win elections. Political advertising is a driving force for sure, but there are many complex nuances that determine who wins a primary in New Hampshire or a caucus in Iowa or elsewhere to sew up the nomination.

The candidates make their pitches these days not from the stump and in newspapers, but principally through television. In a sense they are simply extending their formal appearances beyond a narrow locality. It is true that the TV *spin doctors*—often frustrated politicians themselves—have an effect on the overall image of the candidates. President Bush has benefited enormously from the services of brilliant political strategist and adviser Karl Rove, who was dissed as *Bush's Brain* in a 2003 documentary film.

It is my contention that *people* (voters) really control the elections, not the media. People generally vote their party line—or their ideological line—regardless of what they may see or hear on TV and radio and what they may read in the press. The staunch conservative Republican will vote for a George W. Bush regardless of an endorsement for John Kerry in the *Washington Post* or pro-Kerry reflections on a television talk show. The media may strengthen a voter's candidate preference, but there is little evidence they change it. And even if the media change a few votes, this is a far cry from controlling the election.

I cannot deny that media can give greater coverage to some candidates than to others. We saw that in the 2004 election. Where was the Libertarian candidate? the Socialist candidate? the Green candidate? We did get a little exposure to the Reform Party candidate, but not much. The media focused on the Democrats and the Republicans. The rationale: The others did not have a chance to win. Another rationale: They did not have as much money for advertising. In his first run for president, Ross Perot got extensive media coverage—even if it was largely through advertising. Talk shows are increasingly popular with candidates. But their biased or freewheeling hosts do not control elections; they simply use the candidates to enhance their own celebrity status. They—the hosts—talk much more than the candidate guests, reveling in their own on-camera sophistication.

It is doubtful if Imus or any of the other hosts cause many voters to change their votes. It is doubtful that Sean Hannity and Rush Limbaugh, for all their bombast and verve, win many converts to conservative causes or candidates. Always remember that there are many drivers in an election—political activists from the two parties for sure, religious groups that get out the vote, political action committees, special interest groups, and so on. To be sure, all of them use the media as a stage or platform to reach voters, though they also make direct "sales pitches" on the phone and with house-to-house calls. In 2004, the Internet with its robust interactive capacity also played a great role. Howard Dean took an early lead in the polls among the Democrats by activating his followers on their medium of choice—online communication. Later, both Kerry and Bush also made heavy use of this new medium.

ARGUMENT SUMMATION: *The media cover but don't control elections.*

The media, although they play a large part in exposing candidates and issues to the public, are mainly concerned with reporting on elections, not with controlling them. The media's objective is to gain big audiences for their advertisers. Individual journalists may prefer one candidate to another, but the media as an institution are neutral to politics if not to profit. There is always one sure winner in every election: the media. They want to play the election as long as possible and to squeeze every dollar possible from the candidates, the parties, and the advertisers. This is why they will never be interested in shorter campaigns or campaign reform that limits money to the advertising coffers.

    Media are powerful, but personal political preferences of the people are stronger, and it is doubtful that the media themselves change many votes. The candidates, through what they say or do on television, may gain or lose some votes. It would be silly to say that media have no influence on elections. Of course they do. But they are only instruments in the hands of the candidates and their handlers. They are, in one sense, controlling the media, not the other way around.

RESPONSE

Dennis: *The media influence and often control elections.*

Professor Merrill is correct, of course, in stating that the media don't conspire or act with any collective mindset about the American people's choices for political offices. There is a good reason for this: People simply wouldn't stand for it. Suspicious of any kind of power, whether in the corporation, the labor union, or the press, American voters would react quite negatively to heavy-handed attempts by the media to control elections. However, the story of media and politics in the United States is not quite as simple as Dr. Merrill would have us believe. No one I know really believes that the media gracefully cover the news on the basis of merit, giving fair and impartial coverage to candidates. It is true that we don't have partisan papers or state broadcasting as some countries do, but the interplay between all of our media and the political process is complicated. I believe there is ample evidence to convict the media of strongly influencing, if not outright controlling, elections. Why do I say this?

Look first at news coverage. Do all candidates for public office—or, for that matter, all ballot initiatives—get equitable, even-handed coverage? No, of course not. Some candidates are deemed more worthy and likely to win than others. Often an incumbent in office will almost automatically command more coverage than someone making a challenge. Take, for example, incumbent President Bush's natural home court advantage over Senator John Kerry in the 2004 election, accentuated by the old political slogan invoked in time of war— "don't change horses in the middle of the stream." The media are powerful not because they necessarily control behavior or even change attitudes and opinions, but because they narrow the choices voters have by emphasizing some candidates over others. In this way the media set the political agenda; they do what political scientist Bernard Cohen described as "not telling people what to think, but what to think about." An attractive insurgent candidate will often get the kind of positive, uplifting coverage a challenger gets in any field. Thus the spirited primary candidacies of Howard Dean in 2004 and Bill Bradley and John McCain in 2000 got lively and largely positive publicity for a while. One could also argue that the media have expectations that, when not met, rebound to negative coverage for those who disappoint them. For example, it was widely anticipated that Democrat Al Gore would be a better debater than plainspoken George W. Bush in 2000. But when Bush failed to collapse at the podium and Gore was less impressive than expected, Bush was perceived as the winner and the press trumpeted this loudly. In 2004, Kerry was believed to be the better debater, but Bush's performance was in the view of many below par and Kerry was perceived to have won all three debates.

Kathleen Hall Jamieson, who directs the Annenberg Public Policy Center, and coauthor Paul Waldman argue that both conservative and liberal critics are wrong—that media coverage does, in fact, determine much of what voters know about politics and elections. They call this "the press effect." As they put it:

> When reporters transform the raw stuff of experience into presumed fact and arrange facts into coherent stories, they create a way of seeing individuals and events as well as a way of making sense out of politics writ large. Because the success of our democracy depends so heavily on journalists' exercise of their constitutionally protected mission, it is important to understand the ways shifting journalistic perspectives alter the facts that are deemed important, the ways in

which fact is framed and frames come to be assumed, and the ways journalism facts and frames become the stories we tell each other and our children about the meaning of our times. (Jamieson and Waldman, 2003)

As for opinion media, candidates eagerly seek the editorial endorsements of newspapers and magazines that give them. Meetings with an editorial board that is considering whom to endorse in an election get the highest priority on any candidate's schedule. And for good reason. In close elections it is clear to many authorities that editorial endorsements do matter. Conventional wisdom says this old-fashioned form of making the newspaper's preference officially known turns off voters as much as it influences them. A study in 2004 looking at endorsements in the toughest 15 battleground states where the race was too close to call found that George W. Bush benefited greatly by having key editorial endorsements, according to Greg Mitchell, editor of *Editor and Publisher* magazine and author of several books on history and politics. His conclusion is that "editorial endorsements do matter" (Mitchell, 2004).

Although the political views of most talk show hosts are widely known, candidates still scramble to get exposure and win converts on the talk show circuit, whether on radio, television, or cable. From the 1990s forward, serious candidates for public office have made a beeline for talk shows, even the daytime television programs where irreverent questions are commonplace. In a country where most media are more opportunistic than political, a lively candidate with a message can win converts through talk show appearances. Even entertainment media get in on the act when it comes to politics and elections. Programs such as *The Tonight Show* or *Late Night with David Letterman* are venues much sought after by candidates. Hillary Clinton as a U.S. Senate candidate in New York, for example, appeared on Letterman after weeks of prodding because her advisers thought it would be advantageous. From the monologues of the talkmeisters to actual appearances by candidates, entertainment media offer exposure and celebrity.

Although the presence of Internet news and commentary sites, such as that of Matt Drudge, have been a factor for several years, 2004 was the year when the Internet bloggers triumphed. The bloggers ranged from single-issue advocates to others who saw themselves as alternative news services. They not only covered campaign events but were more outspoken about who won (or lost) debates, as well as providing insider information from the campaigns or from various supporters. With a less rigorous standard for news and information and a penchant for gossip and name calling, the bloggers played a colorful role in the election as they appealed not only to young voters but to people from various causes and religious preferences. It was the bloggers on election day 2004 who reported what the news networks said they wouldn't—the results of exit polls—which led to an inaccurate perception that Kerry would likely win the election, which at least for a few hours on election day was enough to convince even hardcore conservative commentators that a regime change was in the offing.

Much has been written about the impact and influence of political advertising. It is a part of the political socialization process—teaching people how to be voters as well as a kind of consumer's guide on candidates and issues. Candidates use the ads to get out their essential message of values, platform ideas, and so forth. The amount of advertising also tells how well candidates are funded and the likelihood they can go the full distance in an electoral campaign. People debate how much influence advertising has, whether positive or negative appeals are the most effective, and other issues. These matters aside, advertising is believed to be essential by those who buy it. Other persuasive media also contribute to winning campaigns, such as candidate Websites as well as those moderated by supporters, and various lobbies. The power of the press to drive home winning elections was once downplayed by scholars and critics, but this is no longer the case. Those with the most to gain from strongly positive news coverage actively seek it because they know that it does help win elections.

Who consistently denies the influence of the media? The media. Why? Because they don't want to be seen as too powerful and thus undermine their own power and influence. Watch the media's political mavens as they strut their stuff on Sunday talk and public affairs shows. For all of their disclaimers, they act like political brokers. Some analysts think the media are the new electors of American politics, playing the role that party bosses did in the past, but with a bit more subtlety. So how does the charge that media strongly influence and play a profound role in the electoral process actually fit? Like a glove.

ARGUMENT SUMMATION: *The media influence and often control elections.*

The media pay considerable attention to elections not for impartial or neutral reasons but because they believe that political power achieved through elections is ultimately a vitally important news story. Communication theorists believe that the flow of information about public life and the interplay of opinion are the media's most basic and vital functions. Thus the media set agendas and have a cognitive effect—influencing not what people think but what they think about. This cognitive effect influences what voters think about and how they make their choices at the polls. Media decide which people and what issues will get the most coverage and which candidates will win endorsements. Talk show hosts make their opinions about candidates and their views abundantly clear, and the media court political advertising. Why? The candidates, political operatives, and especially the general public believe that media have a strong influence on elections and thus play a significant role in electing public officials from town hall to the White House.

Search Online!

Use the following terms and phrases to search for more information on InfoTrac College Edition: *political advertising, media influence, election coverage, spin, spin doctors, media power, agenda-setting, attitudes, opinion, behavior, cognitive influence, impartiality, feeding frenzy.*

Topics for Discussion

1. In this debate topic, the words *cover* and *control* are the key terms and they are semantically very difficult. How would you better frame the discussion topic?
2. Do we have any real research evidence that the specific activities of the media influence elections to any degree at all?
3. What might lead us to assume that the media influence elections? How would their possible influence differ from the stump speeches and political conversations of the 19th century?
4. If money is related to media coverage of a candidate and media coverage controls elections, then candidates with little (or less) money would be at an initial disadvantage. What does this mean for the concept of democratic elections?
5. What would you do to change media coverage of elections to mitigate the influence of the media (if you think they have any)?

Topics for Research

1. Write a paper about political advertising. Discuss its historical development and current role in political campaigns.
2. Research and write a paper that evaluates the relative importance of any two media outlets with regard to elections—talk radio, newspaper editorial pages, or opinion magazines. Do any of these truly influence elections? How would you assemble evidence to make your case?

3. Examine the changing role of the Internet in political campaigns. How do candidates use Websites and digital media to promote their campaigns? How do media use their Internet capacity to cover and assess campaigns? Is this new medium making a discernible difference in elections, and how do we know?
4. Make the case for powerful media that try to play a role in election campaigns and contrast this with the position that the media should be impartial observers.

FURTHER READING

Capella, Joseph N., and Kathleen Hall Jamieson. *Spiral of Cynicism: The Press and the Public Good.* New York: Oxford University Press, 1997.

Davis, Richard, and Diana Owen. *New Media and American Politics.* New York: Oxford University Press, 1998.

DeFleur, Melvin L., and Everette E. Dennis. *Understanding Mass Communication,* 7th ed. Boston: Houghton Mifflin, 2002.

Dennis, Everette E., and Ellen A. Wartella. *American Communication Research: The Remembered History.* Mahwah, NJ: Erlbaum, 1997.

Jamieson, Kathleen Hall, and Paul Waldman. *The Press Effect: Politicians, Journalists and the Stories That Shape the Political World.* New York: Oxford University Press, 2003.

Mitchell, Greg. "Editorial Endorsements Do Matter." *Newsday,* November 17, 2004.

Perlmutter, David D. *The Manship School Guide to Political Communication.* Baton Rouge: Louisiana State University Press, 1999.

Plissner, Martin. *The Control Room: How Television Calls the Shots in Presidential Elections.* New York: Free Press, 1999.

Sabato, Larry J. *Feeding Frenzy: Attack Journalism and American Politics.* New York: Lanahan, 2000.

PUBLIC OPINION
AND THE POLLS

When it comes to media coverage of public affairs on topics ranging from elections to people's attitudes about the economy, international affairs, and even sex, surveys and polls are the preferred instrument. The media not only conduct their own polls—sometimes in collaboration with another news organization, such as the USA Today/Gallup poll, the New York Times/CBS poll, or the Washington Post/NBC poll—but also carry various commercial and independent polls such as the Harris, Gallup, or Zogby polls. Some colleges and universities—Marist and Quinnipiac come to mind—conduct polls too. In recent years, the Annenberg Public Policy Institute at the University of Pennsylvania put itself on the map mostly by doing polls that heretofore were the purview of commercial firms. The Pew Center for People and the Press, which is funded by a foundation, is especially attentive to public attitudes toward the media. In addition, scientific sample surveys on all kinds of topics, some of them linked to politics, come from universities, private companies, think tanks, government agencies, even accounting firms and advertising agencies. Each claims to present an accurate picture of public opinion at a particular moment in time—when the poll is actually taken. The most responsible media organizations not only run the results of polls, but also provide information about the methods by which they were conducted, by whom, when, and for what purpose. And most media organizations have standards by which they judge polls, accepting those that meet their criteria and rejecting those that do not.

For decades polls have been used to track politics and elections ranging from likely candidates for the presidency to a governorship or Senate race. Even before a campaign begins in earnest, polls are taken to measure name familiarity, relative popularity, and other factors that might play into a candidate's chances of being elected. Once a campaign begins, especially for the presidency of the United States, polls are plentiful as they report on partisan political differences in terms of geographic region, race, religion, and gender. These polls take the pulse of public opinion. They are, as pollsters say, a *snapshot in time*, providing a portrait of what people say they think or believe in response to particular questions. Measurements of public opinion tell us a president's approval rating, who the most admired people in the nation are, and how given institutions (Congress, business, Supreme Court) rate with the public. Other topics of public polls include attitudes about marriage and divorce, people's health practices, economic views, degrees of prejudice and tolerance, and many more.

Some polls are stories in themselves, complete with data and warnings about the margin of error, thus providing the public with a bit of consumer guidance about the poll and the way it was conducted. Other polls are simply used as content for larger news stories with the summary findings as the starting point for a detailed, fully reported story. Surveys have been used to track views on race, sexual orientation, and other topics, all as part of a larger story. And we should remember that polls have gone from simple house-to-house in-person surveys to those conducted by mail, over the telephone, and now on the Internet as well.

Political candidates often complain about polls—those that portray them running behind their opponents or other negative findings—but polls are part and parcel of American life. Many self-serving polls are conducted by political candidates, lobbies, businesses, and others who load questions to generate favorable answers; but the media usually report these for what they are, giving more attention to independent polls (or their own) whose research methods are clearly known and verified. Polls about campaigns and elections are usually watched closely and when they err, their credibility and that of the media are questioned. Another problem at the dawn of the 21st century is that it is harder to get people to participate in polls and surveys, especially over the phone or in apartments where security systems bar pollsters and other door-to-door solicitors. Still, the polling industry and profession have taken measures to make their work as rigorous as possible because they have a vested interest in accurate results. Polls are generally regarded, by the media as well as the public, as a reliable measure of public opinion.

CHALLENGE

Dennis: The media structure and shape public opinion through polls.

As much as people would like to believe the polls, thinking they measure the pulse of public opinion just as a thermometer reports the temperature, polls are a social construction of reality and report only what the pollsters want them to report. The media do conduct their own polls, but these are relatively few compared with those drawn from other sources ranging from various self-serving manufacturers to lobbies and think tanks. The media select the polls they use and generally try to have rigor and consistency when it comes to politics and elections. These sound-ings are eventually tested at the polls and the media can be greatly embarrassed if they have been forecasting results that prove wrong on election day. Many polls have been wrong, sometimes predicting landslide victories when the result was actually a close election. This is frequently true in presidential primary polls when candidates are not especially well known and public opinion can shift at the last minute. Of course such findings always raise questions about the credibility of pollsters. In the highly contested presidential election in November 2004, poll-sters said it was "too close to call," though they gave a slight edge to President Bush which turned out to be right. However, on the day of the election exit polls con-ducted by leading firms—but not officially released—called a number of battle-ground state elections for Kerry over Bush, which was widely reported first by Internet bloggers and later by television and cable networks. For several hours, even conservative pundits thought that Kerry was the likely winner.

Most political polls are relatively accurate. However, news organizations often track elections using what critics call *the horse race*, with seemingly end-less tracking polls throughout the election. A candidate's place in the polls often becomes the basis for coverage. A candidate who does well gets strong cover-age, whereas a candidate running behind is barely noticed. A candidate's stand-ing in the polls is also crucial to his or her ability to raise money, and those who have the most money tend to get more coverage. Thus, the polls drive cover-age. Early standing in the polls is often flimsy because a person who is already well known almost always runs ahead of a newcomer; therefore, polls are often overvalued, leading to distorted coverage. Sometimes, though, an insurgent candidate such as Vermont Governor Howard Dean in 2004 may run ahead in national polls for months but fail to win any crucial primaries and thus lose the nomination for president. Years before, in the 1992 election, the governor of Arkansas, Bill Clinton, was little known when the primary season started and ran poorly in the polls. Only later did he get what reporters call *traction* or gen-eral recognition that brought substantial and sustained coverage. As president, Clinton made heavy use of polls and often benefited from them, especially dur-ing the impeachment crisis when he had high job approval ratings from the public in spite of sustained criticism in Congress. Media coverage during that period reported polls along with the views of those urging impeachment and removal from office.

There can be little doubt that polls provide a metric for the media that is directly linked to news coverage. This is especially true in election campaigns when candidates running well in the polls almost always get the most coverage. Frontrunners are followed closely while those running well back in a race, espe-cially a presidential primary, are hardly noticed at all. What could be better evi-dence of this than the way that campaign planes and buses carrying the media empty out as once leading candidates falter in the polls. In 2004, for example, the scrappy Vermont Governor Howard Dean mounted an impressive campaign through heavy Internet fundraising and ran first in the national polls for several months before the early primaries. After Iowa and New Hampshire, however, the number of reporters following him immediately dropped and so did their coverage of his campaign. In this way the media front-load the elections in favor of early winners, even in small states like New Hampshire and Iowa, thus setting the stage for what comes later. By the time that big states like New York and California have their primary elections, the nominees of both parties are usually already selected. Do the media, guided by polls, play a large role here? You bet.

Polls provide a report on the questions that are asked, but rarely do the media take up major social issues or other public questions on any consistent basis. News decision makers seem more comfortable tracking politics than delving into the great number of local issues that would benefit from survey research. This disappoints scholars such as Philip Meyer of the University of North Carolina, who has long been a champion of precision journalism, or the application of social science methods to journalistic practices. The advent of civic journalism in the 1990s, however, sometimes encouraged poll taking as a measure of public life, an exception to the general practices of the media. Rather than initiating and carrying out their own surveys, the media more often make liberal use of polls and studies offered by various business and industry associations. For example, soft drink manufacturers will offer survey data about the public's attitude toward their product or the pharmaceutical industry about theirs. *Wall Street Journal* reporter Cynthia Crossen has decried that practice and notes that in their use of industry-provided graphs and charts, the media are often uncritical, accepting the latest poll conducted by a self-serving interest rather than doing their own.

Polls are less and less accurate, given the tendency of many in the public to refuse to participate (the refusal rate), and thus serious questions can be raised about their overall value. The media don't often warn the consumer about the iffy nature of some survey results they present with apparent precision and finality. There is a tendency to believe numbers instead of more impressionistic and possibly more accurate gauges of a community's mood or attitude. Sometimes an insightful reporter's observations are more on the mark than is a community survey. In recent years other problems have arisen. For example, a disproportionate number of young people use cell phones exclusively and they are often not included in survey lists, thus underrepresenting this portion of the population. The national "do not call" law that blocks junk calls from commercial firms is another barrier. Pollsters find it harder and harder to get people to respond to their questions, though they find inventive ways to weight their findings and correct for these deficiencies.

Media organizations come from a tradition of somewhat questionable research. Ask a given media industry association to provide data about the best possible venue for advertising and the newspaper industry will tell you their ads have the best reach, magazines will say the same about themselves, and so will television, radio, and other outlets. It all depends on how you frame the question and how narrowly the answer is interpreted.

Polls are useful as one measure of a larger picture, but should not have a powerful role in driving news coverage. Too often polls are self-fulfilling prophecies either for the organizations conducting them or the media outlets that give them wide exposure. Studies of religious and racial bias, for example, are often done without context. I recall one study of the public's attitudes toward media coverage of Catholicism. The poll conducted by the Center for Media and Public Action found that the public thought the media were anti-Catholic, a finding that would have been more interesting if respondents had been asked about other Christians, Jews, and Muslims, thus providing context about whether the media were simply antireligious or especially biased about Catholics. In my opinion, the media are heavy-handed in their selection and coverage of polls—their own and others—eliciting views artificially from people who don't really care about the subject. One researcher, Alex Edelstein of the University of Washington, made an effort to move beyond the forced-response poll questions in which one must choose from four or five views. This researcher instead tried to find out what people said they and their neighbors really talked about, what politicians they really admired or loathed, and their own personally stated choices regarding public policy. Those results were quite different from those of most media polls and thus raise concerns about overreliance on typical polls as a measure of public sentiment.

ARGUMENT SUMMATION: *The media structure and shape public opinion through polls.*

The media shape their own polls carefully and typically emphasize politics and elections rather than social issues or other aspects of public life. Media also make heavy use of polls conducted by others but do little to distinguish reputable public polls from those provided by lobbyists, business interests, and others with an axe to grind. The media favor horse-race coverage of campaigns and give more attention to people running ahead in the polls even if their advantage is early and artificial. Sometimes this becomes a self-fulfilling prophecy wherein those with the most name recognition get special advantages and a better chance of winning the election. Poll results and media coverage are important factors in a candidate's ability to raise money and thus compete effectively for public office. Graphs, charts, and other quantitative measures of public acceptance are readily provided by self-serving interests and are used somewhat indiscriminately by the media. Flaws in methods and the rising refusal rate also call polls into question. This serious problem is also underplayed in the media.

Response

Merrill: Polls in the media mainly report on public sentiment.

Professor Dennis and I are poles apart on polls. Although it may be impossible to completely and accurately gauge public opinion by any technique, public opinion polling is the best way to ascertain main tendencies in public thinking. Polls are often wrong, as Dennis says, but this does not mean that they are not useful. Medical diagnoses are often wrong, too, but would you want to throw them all out? When George Gallup began his Institute for Public Opinion in 1935, he was certain that polling would be a powerful tool for the presentation of what the people really believed. He never seriously questioned his original belief, although his polls were not always correct. He saw them, as do I, as a means of gaining general trends and even specifics of public thought and opinion.

Critics of polls can cite memorable failures of polls: The *Literary Digest* poll of 1936 predicted that Alf Landon would defeat Franklin D. Roosevelt in his reelection campaign, and in 1948 polling data led some newspapers to predict a victory for Thomas Dewey over Harry Truman. As recently as 1996, the polls underestimated the strength of Senator Bob Dole, though he lost anyway. However, innumerable instances of polls' being correct in describing public opinion can swamp the instances of failure. Professor Dennis maintains that very seldom are controversial local issues commissioned by the media. He is probably right, but this seems beside the point of whether polls shape public opinion.

Polls are less and less accurate, asserts Dennis, because many in the public refuse to participate. Perhaps we should say that our actual elections are less accurate (meaningful?) because many in the public do not vote. Polls should not drive news coverage, believes Dennis, but it is my belief that polls are news. They are news in the same way that weather forecasts are news. Many people may choose not to take either polls or weather forecasts seriously, but it seems unlikely that they will disappear from the media.

Professor Dennis gives the example of one study of the public's attitude about media coverage of Catholicism. The poll found that the public thought media coverage was biased. But Dennis says that because the study did not compare Catholicism with other religions, the findings were flawed. I wonder why that is. If the poll was to find out what the public thought about media coverage of Catholicism, that is what it did. It is quite possible that Catholicism got more or better press than did Islam, for example, or Hinduism. But that was not the question.

It is possibly true, as Dr. Dennis says, that to a certain extent the media shape public opinion through the publicizing of polls. But if I am a Democrat, I'll likely vote for my party's candidate even if a poll says that the Republican candidate is ahead. If I am so influenced by a poll, it is simply an indication of my weakness and not that of the polling procedures.

Dennis might be right about the media and the politicians relying too heavily on polls and thus being too influenced by them, but that doesn't require the public to slavishly believe these reports. And I think there is growing evidence that they pay less and less attention to the mainstream media. Scandals at the *New York Times*, CBS News, and *USA Today* in 2004 were only the tip of the iceberg in what the public suspects about the media and their ability to get things right. Polls predicting an easy victory by a given candidate have often caused that campaign to take too much for granted, assuming an easy victory. Over the years, I can recall many occasions when the polls—and media predications based on them—were dead wrong. There was embarrassment all around. When media use polls or the pernicious exit polls on Election Day to make predictions there is sometimes real disaster. As Tom Brokaw famously said after the 2000 election when several networks declared Al Gore the winner in Florida and thus winner of the election, "we don't just have egg on our face; we have an omelet on our shoulder." The same was nearly true, as Professor Dennis notes, in 2004 when exit polls (not run by the networks this time, their having burned their fingers in 2000) suggested a comfortable Kerry win in several key states. Nevertheless, the news leaked out and even commentator Rush Limbaugh excoriated the public, wondering how, in his view, they could be so dumb. So much for polls and their influence.

Many journalists are rightfully concerned about what they believe is too much emphasis on polling results. The potential for manipulation is indeed recognized, and many of us would wish away polls and await the results of the actual election. But poll-less elections are unlikely. The public should smile at polling data as they do at weather reports and go about their business of voting their consciences.

ARGUMENT SUMMATION: *Polls in the media mainly report on public sentiment.*

Although it is true that media often emphasize candidates rather than issues in elections, there is little or no evidence that they purposely try to influence or control these elections. Polls across the country are consistent in their findings and there seems little indication that the media are trying to put their own people in office. They cannot seem to do it on their editorial pages, so why should they try to undo it with polls? In believing the media do this to a significant extent, Professor Dennis seems to find the media unprofessional and perhaps even unethical. It would be a good thing for polls to lose their important place in the media during elections, because they are certainly a kind of pseudo news, manufactured for public consumption. But, like weather reports, they are considered news by the media and will most likely retain their importance. The problem is not the poll, but the weak-headed member of the public who changes his or her vote on the basis of a poll.

SEARCH ONLINE!

 Use the following terms and phrases to search for more information on InfoTrac College Edition: *polls, survey research, pollsters, public opinion, attitudes, samples, "horse race" coverage, tracking polls, pseudo event, scandal, forced responses, open-ended questions.*

TOPICS FOR DISCUSSION

1. Discuss Dennis's contention that news decision makers seem more comfortable tracking politics then delving into a myriad of local issues that would benefit from survey research.
2. To what degree does the publishing of polls actually influence voters' minds as to the candidate they will vote for? Is there any evidence that polls change votes?
3. It is often said that polls are used uncritically by media and that such polls often reflect the self-serving interest of the pollsters. What should the media do—conduct a methodological examination of the polling organization? Discuss.
4. Polls are considered news by the media. Given that many of them may be inaccurate or biased, does this obviate their news value any more than the media publishing what a candidate says in a speech that is not substantiated by the media?
5. Dennis points out that stories are legion about polls that were wrong. One might as well say that stories are legion about weather experts whose prognostications were wrong. What, if anything, is wrong with this analogy?

TOPICS FOR RESEARCH

1. Write a *consumer's guide* to polls about politics, advising people how to read and evaluate the polls. What criteria are most important? Provide examples of good and bad polls.
2. Examine the largest, most important, or most influential polls in the United States or worldwide. What are they, who operates them, where are they seen by the public, and to what effect?

3. Contrast any poll operated by media outlets (a network/newspaper poll, for example) with a freestanding commercial polling service. What, if any, are the differences and similarities?
4. Write a paper on the people behind the polls, featuring major pollsters or analysts of polls who appear on television. Who have been the influential leaders in polling historically and who are the important ones today?
5. Examine the role of Internet polls. How are they conducted? By whom? Are they as reliable as other methods of polling and survey research?

FURTHER READING

Bardes, Barbara A., and Robert W. Oldendick. *Public Opinion: Measuring the American Mind*. Belmont, CA: Wadsworth, 2002.

Dautrich, Kenneth, and Thomas H. Hartley. *How the News Media Fail American Voters*. New York: Columbia University Press, 1999.

Dennis, Everette E., and Robert W. Snyder, eds. *Media and Democracy*. New Brunswick, NJ: Transaction Press, 1998.

Gallup, George, Jr. *The Gallup Poll: Public Opinion 2003*. Boston: Rowman & Littlefield, 2004.

Genovese, Michael A., and Matthew J. Streb. *Polls and Politics: The Dilemmas of Democracy*. Albany: State University of New York Press, 2004.

Glasser, Theodore, and James Ettema. *Custodians of Conscience: Investigative Journalism and Public Virtue*. New York: Columbia University Press, 1998.

Glynn, Caroll J., et al. *Public Opinion*. New York: HarperCollins, 1999.

Janeway, Michael. *Republic of Denial: Press, Politics and Public Life*. New Haven, CT: Yale University Press, 2000.

Lambeth, Edmund B., Philip E. Meyer, and Esther Thorson. *Assessing Public Journalism*. Columbia: University of Missouri Press, 1998.

Lippmann, Walter. *Public Opinion*. New York: Free Press, 1999 reissue.

Norris, Pippa, et al. *On the Message: Communicating the Campaign*. London: Sage, 1999.

O'Neill, Michael J. *The Roar of the Crowd: How Television and People Power Are Changing the World*. New York: Times Books, 1993.

Rosen, Jay. *What Are Journalists For?* New Haven, CT: Yale University Press, 2000.

Schudson, Michael. *The Good Citizen: A History of American Civic Life*. Cambridge, MA: Harvard University Press, 1999.

Toobin, Jeffrey. *A Vast Conspiracy*. New York: Random House, 1999.

When Should the Watchdogs Bark? Media Coverage of the Clinton Scandals. Washington, DC: Center for Media and Public Affairs, 1995.

DECIDING WHAT IS NEWS

What is sometimes called the *news-making process* is the result of a daily bargaining process among various personnel in newspapers and broadcast stations. Editors look at the world they cover with particular standards and measures. They attempt to direct reporters to cover the most interesting, newsworthy material. There are some generally accepted definitions of news, and these provide the justification for what appears in the newspaper and on the newscasts. But many competing forces want space in the news columns and on newscasts. Some are self-serving, external persons who want their stories told sympathetically and well; others are reporters who want their work in the paper; still others are subtle influences ranging from values and habits to personal preferences.

The nature and definition of news often become a matter of public concern as people object to coverage of particular topics—for example, in time of war when negative accounts of one's own armed forces are revealed or during heated political campaigns when the amount and tone of coverage of a candidate anger that person's supporters. And as new technologies allow all forms of information to flourish—cable channels, Internet Websites, desktop publishing—news takes on a different character and challenges old definitions and assumptions. Some critics deny that news reports in a controversial media outlet are, in fact, news, but argue that the content in question leans more toward opinion and editorial comment than impartial news. Critics of the news almost often have their own ideas about what the news should be—that is, what should be featured and emphasized and what ignored altogether. Other commentators, including one of the authors here, question whether "news can survive the age of information," wondering whether the flow of detailed information and the avalanche of new sources made possible by the Internet might diminish the importance of news gathered in an orderly fashion and presented in a context by professional news gathers and processors—journalists and their kin.

A standard view is that news is determined by editors and that editors' (or other gatekeepers') judgments should, in fact, decide what is news. There can be no mechanical standard, it is said, because the news of the day is dynamic and its results are uncertain. Therefore, the well-trained editor or news director makes judgments reflecting prevailing journalistic practices and the specific needs of the audience as perceived by upper management. This, it is further stated, is the essence of journalistic (and other media) leadership. It is, after all, the job of editors to edit.

CHALLENGE

Dennis: Market forces, not editors' judgments, should decide what is news.

There is a longstanding debate among media professionals and media critics about what news is and who should make decisions about it. Editors and reporters say with much assurance that they and they alone should determine what will and will not appear in the news columns and on newscasts. Some critics of the press—for example, people in business—say that the sources of news, those quoted in stories or covered in some fashion, should have a role in defining and shaping the news. In actuality, news decisions are made by journalistic professionals with little guidance from anyone, no matter how much their detractors may complain. This situation is changing, though, as intuitive judgments are being challenged more and more by market forces, which we learn about most effectively through market research. In my view, this change is good, and I hope that before long many of today's smug, all-knowing editors will replace their seat-of-the-pants (or skirt) decisions with more thoughtful, better-researched, systematic decision making. To such persons, this position is heresy.

For as long as anyone can remember, editors (with the help of various minions) have decided what will grace the pages of newspapers and appear on newscasts. They have engaged in a hard selection process, elevating some items to importance and public exposure while relegating others to the wastebasket. Editors are hired to make these judgments, and for the most part they do so with the best of intentions. But how are these judgments made and are they the right ones? Against what set of criteria are news items and stories selected? On what basis are others deemed unworthy of coverage?

Most editors would tell you that they make their choices from among those news stories that they assign or that flow in from their regular channels (such as wire services) and that they do so with proper regard for their audience. They would also tell you that they rely heavily on the budgets of the wire services (priority lists of stories deemed important or significant) and take cues from such major national media as the *Wall Street Journal*, *USA Today*, and the major television and cable networks or heavily visited Internet sites such as MSNBC, CNN, or ABC. What will interest the audience is of paramount importance, for, after all, if readers and viewers are not attentive, newspaper circulation may drop and broadcast ratings may falter. This situation would push revenues down and the editor might be fired or see the paper die.

It came as a surprise to many editors when in 1947 the Hutchins Commission on Freedom of the Press, a privately funded blue-ribbon group that evaluated the news media, suggested that the media were failing to give readers a representative account of the day's news, let alone present a representative picture of the constituent groups of society. As with most media criticism, however just, editors rejected these ideas wholesale. The issue raised by the commission, however, continues to surface at professional meetings and in scholarly critiques of the media. The definition of news is the subject of much wrangling—and for good reason. I believe that a new approach to news decision making is needed more than ever.

1. News is a highly complex formulation that requires the best intelligence and a thoughtful strategy for professionals to fashion it properly.
2. Editors and reporters are elitists, unrepresentative of their readers and viewers and unable to act effectively on their behalf.
3. A marketing approach to news is the most effective and efficient way to select and present news that is of interest to and pertinent for the audience. In such a system, market research findings, which indicate reader and viewer preferences, are used to decide news.

Ask journalism students if they know what news is and they will tell you, "Yes, of course." Ask them to define it and confusion sets in. News is difficult to define, which explains why so many people continue to debate this issue. All kinds of people—journalists, sociologists, political scientists, news sources, and others—have engaged in this exercise. It is more than a theoretical discussion, because knowing and understanding what news is can have real payoffs. Imagine the political candidate whose idea of news differs radically from that of the local editor. The candidate is likely to be a defeated candidate if that view persists. The same is true for others who want to place something in the news.

In a rather scornful view of news, Henry David Thoreau once wrote:

> I am sure that I have never read any memorable news in a newspaper. If we read of one man robbed, or murdered, or killed by accident, or one house burned, or one vessel wrecked, or one steamboat blown up, or one cow run over on the Western Railroad, or one mad dog killed, or one lot of grasshoppers in the winter—we never need read of another. If you are acquainted with the principle, what do you care for myriad instances and applications? To a philosopher all news, as it is called, is gossip, and they who read it or edit it are old women over their tea. (1854, 148–49)

Thoreau clearly identifies some of the negative characteristics of news. Some commentators have tried to explain the difference between facts, truth, and news with less than full success. Walter Lippmann once wrote that "news is not a mirror of social conditions, but the report of an aspect that has obtruded itself." One famous definition of news is attributed to John Bogart of the *New York Sun*, who famously said in 1880, "When a dog bites a man, that is not news, but if a man bites a dog, that is news!" Former television anchor David Brinkley would seem to agree: "News," he said, "is the unusual, the unexpected. Placidity is not news. If an airplane departs on time, it isn't news. If it crashes, regrettably, it is."

Some of the standard criteria that are said to make up the news are the following:

1. Conflict (tension, surprise)
2. Progress (triumph, achievement)
3. Disaster (defeat, destruction)
4. Consequences (effect upon community)
5. Eminence (prominence)
6. Novelty (the unusual, even the extremely unusual)
7. Human interest (emotional background)
8. Timeliness (freshness and newness)
9. Proximity (local appeal)

Sociologist and distinguished analyst of the news Bernard Roshco says that all news has a dual origin. It is a *social* product that represents an effort to make sense out of what is happening in society, and it is an *organizational* product representing what the news organization decides to do with it.

After reading scores of articles and treatises on news, Melvin DeFleur and I came up with this definition that reflects some of the factors that go into news:

> News is a report that presents a contemporary view of reality with regard to a specific issue, event, or process. It usually monitors change that is important to individuals or society and puts that change in the context of what is common or characteristic. It is shaped by a consensus about what will interest the audience and by constraints from outside and inside the organization. It is the result of a daily bargaining game within the news organization that sorts out the observed human events of a particular time period to create a very perishable product. News is the imperfect result of hurried decisions made under pressure. (DeFleur and Dennis, 1998, 446)

We later modified this definition as follows:

> News is current or fresh knowledge about an event or subject that is gathered, processed, or disseminated via a medium to a significant number of interested people. (DeFleur and Dennis, 2002, 73–74)

This is not to suggest that a definition of news changes daily. There is considerable consistency over time as to what editors deem newsworthy; the similarity (some would say sameness) of our newspapers and newscasts suggests considerable agreement about what news is, under most conditions.

One aspect of what constitutes news is to be found in the external events that await report. In addition, the consideration of what is news depends partly

on the audience to whom it is directed. The journalist and the editor are sup-
posedly acting as and on behalf of *every person* in deciding what is worth
reporting. It is said that they have a built-in understanding of their readers and
viewers if they are any good at their jobs; after all, readers and viewers are the
journalists' next-door neighbors, friends, and companions at sports. Although
this vision of the journalist may be true in very small communities, for the most
part it is not true. Editors and reporters are part of an elite. They simply are not
like most of the citizens of the community. They are better educated, more liberal politically, less religious, and more likely to be single, to live in an apart-
ment (as opposed to a single-family dwelling), and to have social and cultural
values quite distant from those around them. National studies have documented this condition for a number of years, drawing a portrait of journalists
as relatively isolated from and out of touch with their communities. As one
reporter was quoted in a 1982 study:

> It is an inherent problem; inbred newspapers don't trust the people they are writ-
> ing about. . . . Especially the younger reporters are getting removed from society.
> They come from different backgrounds than the average public. [Theirs is] a snob-
> bish view of the world. (Burgoon, Burgoon, and Atkin, 1982, 5)

That study, based on a national survey conducted for the American Society
of Newspaper Editors, went on to say that journalists underestimate reader
intelligence, have a poor understanding of what people will actually read, and
simply do not comprehend the role of television in delivering news to people
who also read newspapers. The report was a stinging indictment of the press
that was not out of line with a more impressionistic speech by Kurt Luedtke,
mentioned earlier in this book. Luedtke charges that his former colleagues in
the media suffer from the twin perils of "arrogance and irrelevance." Arrogance
keeps them unpleasantly off the track with readers; irrelevance could spell
doom in an era when other information sources (data banks provided by cable
systems or the telephone company) can supply much of the factual information
(sports scores, weather reports) that people now gain from newspaper and television news. Editors and reporters can take a number of steps to stay in touch
with their communities, but nothing will change the inevitable: Journalists will
continue to be elitists, continue to be unlike their readers and viewers.

A marketing approach to news makes news decisions less of a guessing
game and more of a thoughtful, systematic process that takes into account the
interests and needs of the audience. The marketing approach to news is nothing new. In the 1970s, when newspaper circulation was sliding downward, a
national Newspaper Readership Project—which has been written about in
many newspapers, news reports, and books such as Leo Bogart's *The Press and
the Public* (1989) and *Preserving the Press* (1991)—collected data about reader
interests, preferences, and reading habits. As a result many American newspapers changed their formats radically, offering special sections on lifestyles,

neighborhoods, and entertainment. News was packaged differently, with livelier design and more vivid writing. For example, a news story on a zoning ordinance would begin by suggesting the consequences of the news story for potential homeowners, rather than simply summarizing the action of the zoning board in a procedural manner. The story would likely be presented with striking photos or line drawings and readable, attractive headlines.

The marketing approach to news depends on a regular and accurate flow of statistical data about the audience. The data are then used as one factor, a central one, in determining what will be offered to the audience and in what manner. News is matched to the interests and potential interests of that audience. Some critics have called this approach "soft and sexy in the afternoon," suggesting that a marketing approach must always emphasize soft news rather than important news of public affairs. The best papers using the marketing approach, however, have an effective blend of editorial leadership, wherein professional journalists make news selections and prepare material with strategies for reaching the reader. Those strategies depend largely on marketing research data. This process is not a mindless one, whereby journalists succumb to cold statistics while ignoring professional ethics and a desire to be complete in their coverage of a community issue or problem. Information is a calibrating tool that, when used by intelligent people, can result in a higher-quality product. Market information gives news organizations a continuous source of feedback from their readers and viewers, something that is lacking in many places today.

Any discussion of the marketing approach to news naturally revives the old debate of whether the press should give readers what they want or provide leadership that gives citizens what they need. I believe that the two are not incompatible, that the public is ultimately better served if market information plays a more important role in guiding editors' decisions. If today's newspapers and television stations guided mainly by intuition are so far out of touch, it is worth making our best effort to bridge the gap. Market information, intelligently used, will do it.

Even beyond the marketing approach to news comes James Hamilton's economic theory of news that posits that "news is a commodity, not a mirror image of reality." He notes that what information actually becomes news depends on a set of questions (a new 5Ws) that are, in fact, answered in the economic marketplace:

1. Who cares about a particular piece of information?
2. What are they willing to pay to find out, or what are others willing to pay to reach them?
3. Where can media outlets or advertisers reach these people?
4. When is it profitable to provide the information?
5. Why is this profitable? (Hamilton, 2004, p. 7)

Another key driver for news that is directly linked to economics is technology and this has inspired much debate since the advent of the Internet. Before the mid-1990s, there was little debate about news as a commodity for sale. It was assumed it had to be paid for and neither the newsstand sales of magazines and newspapers nor other forms of user fees for news were very controversial. Free papers, usually insubstantial tabloids, rarely challenged the economic supremacy of their larger rivals. News on the radio was essentially free to the consumer but funded by advertisers. The Internet, however, raised new questions. Should news delivered online be free or paid for? Many New Media devotees argued that all content on the Internet and World Wide Web should be free to all users, which was after all the theory of the "information highway." However, organizations like Dow Jones, which publishes the *Wall Street Journal,* demurred. Thus, while most newspapers developed free companion Websites to accompany their ink-on-paper products, the *Journal* created a paid WSJ.com online that quickly demonstrated that it could not only be profitable but attract nearly 900,000 exclusive paid online subscribers. Overnight and to the present day, news organizations fashioned a digital strategy tied to economic profit. The role of technology in driving news decisions is linked to the social construction of reality and the economic imperatives that allow such innovation and development.

News organizations are first and foremost businesses, though one would hope businesses that ultimately serve the public interest. They market audiences to advertisers and their consumers (the audience) are served in a fashion that yields economic success or they simply go out of business. This is true at the macro level, of course, and in spite of claims of church–state divisions between the editorial content of media and business operations, media executives and their staffs are always and ever conscious of the bottom line and serve it by offering high-quality news tailored to specific audience interests and needs. In the best of circumstances that means maintaining professional standards, of course, but in others there is clearly a tilting of emphasis and orientation to please (some would say pander to) audience expectations. One only need mention the Fox Network, which has succeeded by offering news with a politically conservative perspective.

ARGUMENT SUMMATION: *Market forces, not editors' judgments, should decide what is news.*

Editors have too much control over selecting what news to present to the public. Selection emphasizes the editors' personal biases and fails to give a representative account of the day's news. Because news is difficult to define and numerous perspectives exist on what actually is news, it is preferable to have news selection determined by market forces, which give a broader account of events, rather than relying on an editor's preferences alone. Research shows that editors tend to be part of an isolated elite and that this lack of interaction with and understanding of the public results in poor decisions about what is news. A marketing approach focuses instead upon a regular and accurate flow of statistical data about the audience. This systematic criterion based on market forces is preferable because it relies on the interests and needs of the audience in defining news. Moreover, new economic theories of news and studies of news and technology demonstrate that news is a commodity, an economic product that requires profits to survive.

RESPONSE

Merrill: Editors' judgments, not market forces, should decide what is news.

Unfortunately perhaps, my coauthor has challenged a proposition that is not contradictory to what he is advocating. What Professor Dennis seems to be saying is that news should be determined by a regular and accurate study of audience desires. In this view, the audience and not the editor determines what is news. The editor, in the Dennis perspective of news, is consigned to a mechanistic role in which he or she serves as a short-order cook preparing only what the customer orders. This is harsh pragmatism, crass capitalism carried too far, in my opinion.

The marketing approach to news relegates the press to a powerless dispenser of desired services. Editors take on a strange role; they do not make decisions but only grant requests. They do not determine what their audiences need or should have; rather they provide the news that the audiences—the real editors in the marketing approach—say they want. In Dennis's concept of editorial leadership, journalism would become a passive and uninspiring vocation.

Now Dennis realizes this danger, and he tries to moderate his advocacy of the marketing approach to news by conceding that the "best papers using the marketing approach, however, have an effective blend of editorial leadership, wherein professional journalists make news selections and prepare material with strategies for reaching the reader." In other words, Dennis would have editorial leadership with editors who follow the dictates of audience research. He wants it both ways.

If this is the case, then I have very little to argue against, because I agree that market forces enter into the editor's decisions about news. Any American journalist who has ever dealt with determining what news is and how to play it has recognized the natural symbiosis between editorial decision making and audience desires. Only the most naive person would think that the editor's judgment and the audience's preferences are mutually exclusive.

The editor (or some journalistic decision maker) should decide what is news. He or she may do this while either taking audience desires into consideration or simply ignoring what he or she believes to be the will of the audience. In other words, market forces may or may not enter into the determination of news. I see news as an editorial matter, not a public matter. This is the main business of the editor: determining what news is and how it shall be played.

No editor has ever ignored the audience, so in that sense at least, editorial determination of news has always taken market forces into consideration. But editors have generally prided themselves on their own ability to recognize and determine news. They have seen themselves as independent decision makers in journalism and not simply reactors to their audiences. I believe that they have been justified in this image of themselves. Anybody who has worked for a news medium knows that the great majority of news decisions are made by journalists without evidence of what the audience wants. News is determined quickly, selected from the many available stories without too much deliberation, and journalists make these determinations almost instinctively. They certainly do not have the luxury of holding various stories in abeyance until they can survey their readers to find out which stories might be desired. The pragmatic aspect of journalism militates against the marketing approach to news.

This approach does not mean that the reasonable news executive does not have some general guidelines for news based on inferences drawn over time from the audience. My coauthor has already presented some of the standard criteria that help determine news and, of course, these criteria did not suddenly leap full-grown from the editor's head. Over the years, journalists came to the conclusion that these criteria were generally agreeable to news consumers. So the editors did have some overall, long-range guidelines for news but on a daily, decision-by-decision basis they made their own determinations as to what would be news in their media.

As Dr. Dennis says in his *challenge,* all of this brings up the old debate of whether the press should give readers what they want or what they need. I believe that the press should give readers what the editors think they want and what they need. This is, really, what the press does. What the people want can also be what they need. What they need may not, however, be what they want— that is, unless they are made somehow to realize that there are some things they need that they have not thought about needing.

A good editor is one who recognizes that it is a journalistic responsibility to provide the reader with some significant, useful news that may or may not be of great immediate interest or appeal; editors know that in order to get the reader exposed to such news, they must also provide news of a shallower—perhaps even sensational—nature. The good editor is a pragmatist, not a one-dimensional person seeking either to entertain or to educate. The good editor wants to do both and other things as well. But in addition to being a realist, the editor is something of an idealist also, believing that readers should get certain information that they might not choose if given the chance. In this sense the editor is much like an educator.

Editors may very well use marketing information for some of their decisions. Certainly they have access to a considerable amount of such information. They may, however, decide not to use marketing data for their news determinations; in fact, they generally do not. They use intuition, instinct, and perceptions of news value stemming from experience and common sense. They often project their own likes and dislikes about news to their readers. This may not be scientific, but it is useful and quick—and it works very well. An editor is a kind of one-person sample, projecting to the newspaper his or her own news values. Therefore, the editor can retain at least the illusion of independent editorial news determination while taking into consideration the assumed interests and desires of the audience.

There is no doubt that the news media need to be economically successful to survive, but they must also succeed substantively by offering a good product. News that is distorted, biased, or generally unreliable has no value except as entertainment, which Jon Stewart's *The Daily Show* has demonstrated. Media controversies involving news often center on an editor's being fired for insisting on rigorous news-gathering standards and refusing to yield to a buttinski publisher who wanted to slant, color, or otherwise spin the news. In most instances when that happens and become controversial, external scrutiny keeps the publisher from pandering and we usually learn that the dispute was all about personalities and egos. The point is that the best thing the news media have to sell is news and it must be uncontaminated to have any value at all. In all but a few bizarre circumstances news people work diligently to produce the best possible reports for their audiences. There are different styles and standards of presentation, of course, but in the end professional judgments validated by peers and competitors drive the news, not marketing considerations. A first-class news report can coexist with an economically successful Webcast, newscast, or newspaper.

Perhaps the philosophical rationale for audience-determined news is the same one that has resulted in a shift in several areas from an emphasis on the press to an emphasis on the public. Examples: increasing talk about "public access to the media" and the "public's right to know." Now we have people talking about the "public's right to determine what is news." Granted, the public (non-journalists) can consider anything it desires to be news. As a member of the general public I have a right to determine what I want to call news, and I can pass this information on to whomever I wish. But in the context of journalism such determination is up to journalists, not members of the public.

As a private citizen I have the right to make home movies and to show them to anyone who will watch. But I do not have a right to determine for a cinema owner or a television director that my home movies will be shown in their facilities. I can indeed determine what I want to consider a movie, but this does not and should not imply that I will determine what is to be shown as a movie through the mass media. Doing this is the prerogative of the media decision makers. Market forces must be taken into consideration, because no medium of mass communication is an island. But news determination, like movie determination, lies with the disseminating medium. And technology really makes no difference. People know the difference between a serious Internet news service like MSNBC, for example, and a blogger who is offering opinions and sensational drivel. I realize that Matt Drudge has been a great success with his unsavory and controversial reports, but he has also been wrong on occasion when his speculations and leaks didn't pay off. Give me a reliable, validated report anytime, though I may enjoy the edgy speculation of the bloggers.

Only a stupid or unrealistic editor would continue providing readers with news that was not wanted or read by these readers. In fact, the newspaper would not exist very long if this were done. In the case of viable newspapers, the editors are taking the news values of their readers seriously. However, they are not being dictated to by the readers; they can and often do go against the wishes of their readers. Admittedly, many journalistic news determiners do bow to the wishes of segments of their readership; this pandering often results in largely sensational material with negative overtones. Some editors do indeed stoop to the lowest common denominator.

But the question is whether this should be the case. Should market forces determine the news? My answer is: No! An editor or any journalist responsible for news judgments should make news decisions. This is the nature of journalism. This is the job of journalists as long as they, not non-journalists, are in the business of news collection, definition, and dissemination.

ARGUMENT SUMMATION: *Editors' judgments, not market forces, should decide what is news.*

In a free-press nation like the United States, market forces, advertisers, government, and other institutions naturally have their impact on news, but the media managers should determine what to publish or broadcast. That is the essence of press freedom in the United States. Obviously editors will take audience desires into consideration (when they know what they are), but these desires should not determine news decisions in a microscopic sense. The daily pragmatic nature of journalism militates against the marketing approach to news. News ebbs and flows rapidly, and only journalists can make decisions as to how it is to be handled.

SEARCH ONLINE!

Use the following terms and phrases to search for more information on InfoTrac College Edition: *newsmaking, news, gatekeeper, news values, news judgment, news editor, readership, audience, soft news, hard news, market values, information, public affairs.*

TOPICS FOR DISCUSSION

1. How can market research be used in the everyday newsroom decisions about news?
2. The marketing approach depends on a regular flow of statistics about the audience. Editorial staffers on a daily newspaper, therefore, would have to get these data constantly. Is accomplishing this possible? If they are successful in doing so, how might a publication's basic editorial policy be affected?
3. If editors gave their news determination right to the audience surveyors, would they lapse into being mere functionaries with no decision-making responsibilities? How would their jobs change?
4. Consider various economic theories of the news. Are they consistent with or at odds with news professionalism?
5. What might be a good compromise position in news determination? How would it work? Is it different from what is presently done?

TOPICS FOR RESEARCH

1. Examine the proposition that editors should be quite conscious of their audience and target their work for the people who read, listen to, or view their reports. What role should the audience play in shaping the news?
2. Write a short paper on audience research (including ratings) in broadcasting or newspapers. What role does it play? How does it measure the relative health of a given medium?
3. What impact do ratings have on television news? Research this question by looking at the discussion in recent years involving people meters. Do the audience data yielded by people meters tell us anything about the demographics of the audience that will likely influence the news on television?
4. Discuss news decision making, consulting major books and studies on this subject. Can editors exercise professional standards and still please the audience?

5. Examine yourself as a consumer of news. If you could design your own paper tailored to your personal tastes and interests, what would it contain? What would it look like? Assume that you can create a Web-based news service from scratch and select bits and pieces from several existing news sources to create your personalized product. Discuss whether your site or blog would appeal to others. To whom would it appeal? Do you think there is enough of a market for it to create a niche?

FURTHER READING

Argyris, Chris. *Behind the Front Page: Organizational Self-Renewal in a Metropolitan Newspaper.* San Francisco: Jossey-Bass, 1974.

Boczkowski, Pablo J. *Digitizing the News: Innovation in Online Newspapers.* Cambridge, MA: MIT Press, 2004.

Bogart, Leo. *Preserving the Press.* New York: Columbia University Press, 1991.

Bogart, Leo. *The Press and the Public: Who Reads What, When, Where and Why in American Newspapers.* Hillsdale, NJ: Erlbaum, 1989.

Burgoon, Judee, Michael Burgoon, and Charles Atkin. *What Is News? Who Decides? And How?* A report of the American Society of Newspaper Editors. East Lansing: Michigan State University, 1982.

Carey, James W. *Communication in Culture: Essays on Media and Society.* Winchester, MA: Unwin Hyman, 1988.

DeFleur, Melvin L., and Everette E. Dennis. *Understanding Mass Communication.* Boston: Houghton Mifflin, 1998.

DeFleur, Melvin L., and Everette E. Dennis. *Understanding Mass Communication,* 7th ed. Boston: Houghton Mifflin, 2002.

Dennis, Everette E. *Of Media and People.* Newbury Park, CA: Sage, 1992.

Dennis, Everette E. *Media and Public Life.* New Brunswick, NJ: Transaction Press, 1997.

Gans, Herbert. *Deciding What's News.* New York: Pantheon, 1979.

Gans, Herbert. *Democracy and the News.* New York: Oxford University Press, 2003.

Gitlin, Todd. *The Whole World Is Watching: Mass Media in the Making and Unmaking of the New Left.* Berkeley: University of California Press, 1980.

Hamilton, James T. *All the News That's Fit to Sell: How the Market Transforms Information into News.* Princeton, NJ: Princeton University Press, 2004.

Sabato, Larry J. *Feeding Frenzy: Attack Journalism and American Politics.* New York: Lanahan, 2000.

Sigal, Leon V. *Officials and Reporters: The Organization and Politics of Newsmaking.* Lexington, MA: D. C. Heath, 1973.

Thoreau, Henry David. *Walden, or Life in the Woods.* Boston: Houghton Mifflin, 1854.

MEDIA ETHICS

Ethics is a branch of philosophy concerned with the general nature of morals and specific moral choices that people make in relationships with others. Media ethics, of which journalistic ethics is a subset, is usually taken to mean the study and application of content standards of conduct and moral choices. Content/journalistic ethics usually links a system of values and principles with choices that must be made in day-to-day media work and assignments. These value choices most often deal with right and wrong choices or degrees of rightness and wrongness, because many journalistic choices are difficult calls. Values refer to an ideal or highly desirable situation. For example, fairness is a value that most news people and other media people would hail. But fairness for whom? To the person being interviewed? To the public? To one's employer? To oneself? Fairness, which seems so obvious and easy from a distance, may be difficult in a given situation. Journalistic ethics most often relates to news decision making, and ethics in journalism has for the most part been a code of conduct expected of news people, especially editorial employees of news organizations.

Until recently, the same ethical guidelines did not apply to media owners, advertising and business personnel, and some special assignments personnel. That is changing, however, as support for general business ethics has been advanced by educators, critics, and the public. Journalistic ethics is always seen in the context of the functions and purposes of the media, which include the delivery of information, opinion, entertainment, and advertising. In order to fulfill their information and news functions, the media quite naturally confront conflicting rights and duties. When the media's desire to publish a story that is important to the public conflicts with someone's right to privacy, for example, an ethical dilemma arises. The dilemma will be solved by determining what the responsible course of action is in this case. Sometimes this means balancing freedom and responsibility, in which case the freest choice—to do what one pleases—is not always the most responsible choice. Journalistic ethics involves making choices in specific situations that are related to general rules and principles. For journalists and other communicators this means making choices that conform with the rules and conventions of the profession, embodied in written codes of ethics. In a practical sense ethical choices suggest freedom in decision making when there might be degrees of rightness and wrongness to consider. There might not be a single right ethical choice in all situations. Some ethical values and standards become codified into law, when the state requires that a person follow a particular rule or convention in making choices. Journalistic ethics is a more voluntary endeavor, however, and the American system of freedom of the press allows considerable latitude not present in other professions where ethical rules have the force of law.

In a field with many standard practices but few absolute rules, the journalist has many independent choices to make in sorting out ethical from unethical conduct. It is not surprising that there is little agreement about what, under all conditions, constitutes ethical conduct for a journalist. Although seeking the truth is an ethical imperative for most civilized people, there are conditions in which highly ethical journalists have lied for what they said was a greater public good. Media ethics proponents usually distinguish between general principles of ethics and the daily application of situational ethics, when ethical choices are made on the spot with little time for analysis or introspection.

CHALLENGE

Merrill: Journalists and other media people are essentially unethical.

Until the early 1960s little thought was given to the ethics of journalists. The history of American journalism had included some famous media hoaxes, periodic wheelings and dealings by media publishers, sensational news and propaganda dissemination by men such as William Randolph Hearst and Joseph Pulitzer, and forays into *yellow journalism*, muckraking, and questionable publishing practices. But, generally, it was assumed that journalists were trustworthy, honest, dependable, just, unbiased, and concerned with uncovering and delivering the truth.

But oh how that has changed! We've already mentioned the sorry case of Jayson Blair at the *New York Times* in 2003, in which a disreputable reporter was allowed to get away with shading the truth and outright fabrication until he was finally caught. And there have been other celebrated cases as well. Although we're dealing mainly with news media and journalism in this debate, examples in which media owners and executives have been unethical are legion. Conrad Black, the Canadian media mogul, was caught in a scandal in which he virtually pillaged his company, the owner of newspapers in the United States, Canada, and Britain. And, hello, does anyone remember why

Martha Stewart went to jail? Of course, the entertainment industry is full of examples too numerous to even mention, so let's stick to news.

Now we are overwhelmed with publications, television roundtable discussions, Socratic dialogues, speeches, conferences, and workshops, all on the subject of journalistic or press ethics. Everybody has discovered that journalists have a big ethical problem. Journalists, who enjoy bashing everything and everybody in sight for ethical lapses, are beginning to get huge doses of their own medicine.

And it's about time. For too long media professionals have been pushing their own ethical problems aside and enthroning their freedom, expediency, and self-interest. Pick up almost any copy of a magazine or journal, especially one dealing with the press, and you will encounter articles detailing some journalistic ethical lapse. The situation is so pervasive in the media that many critics— from cranky politicians to learned philosophers—have come to believe that ethical journalism is an oxymoron.

Some critics, admittedly, seem too extreme in their press condemnation. And don't bother to get me started on the transgressions of bloggers and even some so-called legitimate news Websites that have played fast and loose with the truth. I'm fond of the words of the author Janet Malcolm who lambastes journalists as follows:

> Every journalist who is not too stupid or too full of himself to notice what is going on knows that what he does is morally indefensible. He is a kind of confidence man, preying on people's vanity, ignorance, or loneliness, gaining their trust and betraying them without remorse. (Malcolm, 1989)

She goes on to say that journalists "justify their treachery in various ways according to their temperaments." The "more pompous," she notes, talk about their freedom and the "public's right to know"; the "least talented" talk about art; the "seamiest" refer to earning a living (Malcolm, 1989, 38).

Naturally many journalists took Malcolm to task for her critical words, but not all. Jonathan Yardley, in a *Washington Post* column (March 27, 1989, C2), regrets the fact that Malcolm does not distinguish between the separate crafts of nonfiction and journalism, but contends that journalists should take her criticism seriously. He concludes: "People who write nonfiction, whether books or journalism, are not responsible solely to themselves, which is a lesson all of us can learn to our profit."

John L. Hess, in *The Quill* (May 1989, 29), rebuts Malcolm's charges by saying that "the sins of journalists are more imagined than real." He dismisses Malcolm as an "apostate Freudian" who is "full of herself," as she relies on a "single case history" to make her point that journalists have little respect for the truth.

Hess represents the typical defensive reaction of journalists to criticism of their ethics. But in spite of their efforts, they are viewed (in public surveys) as arrogant, self-righteous, and power hungry—never willing to accept responsibility for mistakes, always anxious (and able) to get the last word.

Some journalistic ethical codes (such as that of the Society of Professional Journalists) insist that journalists "take nothing of value," that they refrain from political "involvement," that they serve the truth, and that they show respect "for the dignity, privacy, rights, and well-being of people encountered in the course of gathering and presenting the news." Compare this rhetoric with the actual daily practices of journalists and you will quickly see that ethical *practice* has a long way to go.

And, what is more interesting, journalists seem to have a difficult time accepting a major code admonition: that they "be free of obligation to any interest other than the public's right to know the truth." Truth, truth, truth. The gentlemen and women of the press enshrine the word, but go about their daily business as if they were not bound by the truth. Half-truths, distortions, and outright censorship are the main game played by journalists. In fact, they even purposely omit or distort the truth when they feel it is necessary.

Many journalists will tell you that, despite what their ethical codes say, there are some things more important than reporting the truth. So they fill their days with bits and snippets of the truth; they hide certain truths—often, strangely, because they feel it would be unethical to tell them. At least these journalists have an ethical motivation. Others, however, because of personal biases, withhold information and names, selectively quote sources, distort their stories, and tamper with the truth.

Press people, by and large, conceive of ethics as prudential actions that will achieve some preconceived plan, whether this is to get information from a source or to keep certain bits of knowledge from the public. Journalists often obtain their ends and then rationalize the means they used. If most journalists today have any ethics it is a kind of Machiavellian ethics—the ethics of power and expediency.

Reporters have posed as mental patients in order to write exposés of mental hospitals; slanted stories in favor of preferred candidates; fictionalized to make lifelike points (as in the famed Janet Cooke case, in which a *Washington Post* reporter fabricated a story and subsequently won a Pulitzer Prize for it; the prize was later withdrawn); and surreptitiously recorded conversations or interviews. In a discussion of "Machiavellian Ethics in Journalism," Ralph Lowenstein and I raise the question of American journalistic expediency ethics and note manifestations of Machiavellianism (1990, Chap. 17).

Machiavellianism appeals to American pragmatic journalists. It appeals to the desire for power, for success. It appeals to individualism, dedication, and pride. Machiavelli (1469–1527) said all there is to say about a sizable slice of hard-nosed American journalists and their desire to "get the story at any price." Machiavelli might well be called the father of American journalism, setting its tradition for competitive, bottom-line, winner-take-all, success-oriented media practice. The name of the game in this pragmatic media world is "using other people to achieve desired ends," as I elaborated in the British journal *Encounter* (April 1987, 80).

Certainly I am not maintaining that *all* journalists are unethical, but that *generally* the press and its practitioners indulge in unethical practices. Even the journalists themselves must recognize their general unethical status (or at least *image*) in American society, because they are extremely uptight and defensive about the subject. If they have no ethics problem, as many of them insist, then why don't they just get on with their work and stop all their ethics dialogue, conventions, workshops, and speeches?

ARGUMENT SUMMATION: *Journalists and other media people are essentially unethical.*

Journalists and other media professionals are generally not concerned with acting properly, informing and enlightening the people, telling the truth, and having standards that guide them. Self-interest and a kind of Machiavellianism guide their basic actions. Pragmatism, power, and success are their key motivations. Ethical journalism is an oxymoron. Ethical codes are useless and are mainly for public relations purposes. Journalists enthrone truth, but deviate from it for a multitude of reasons. They talk of the people's right to know, and impinge on it regularly. They invade privacy, tamper with quotes, select only certain stories and information that conform with their biases, and are basically arrogant, defensive, and self-righteous.

RESPONSE

Dennis: Journalists and other media people are essentially ethical.

Because professional journalists and other media people deal in the currency of information and news or even competently developed entertainment, their work is closely watched and often disputed. The reason, of course, is that they are (or ought to be) writing for their audience. While the best of them fairly represent their sources with accurate descriptions of events, situations, and quotations, there is often conflict because the source wants to be seen in the best possible light, even when his or her actions are reprehensible. This puts the journalist in an uncomfortable situation. One can serve the interests of the source, avoid conflict, and mislead the public or one can pursue the truth, cover the news, and accept the consequences.

This is essentially the dilemma described, though somewhat unkindly, by Janet Malcolm. She was hardly the first person to suggest that writers always sell out their sources. An eloquent statement to that effect is found in Joan Didion's *Slouching Towards Bethlehem.* When it comes to dealing with and representing the views of news sources, there are many complicated factors to consider in determining what is right. In *The Social Responsibility of the Press* (1963), J. Edward Gerald identified several factors in the ground rules that ought to govern reporters' conduct. First, he asks, "What are the conventions journalists are taught to respect?" Second, "What are the rules of their trade?" To this he adds, "What skills in communication entitle a journalist to the acclaim (of colleagues)?" And, "What errors bring loss of face?" Scores of books have been written exploring the points Professor Gerald introduced in these four questions, which travel over uncharted ground, but also over much settled territory. Not incidentally, Professor Gerald also suggested that publishing executives should have professional standards and subscribe to a code of ethics. He even thought it might be useful for media people of all kinds to have advanced degrees, a suggestion that the *Chicago Tribune* found outrageous enough to inspire a stinging rebuke.

While recognizing the foibles of individual journalists and other communicators such as public relations personnel, I believe that there is a great body of evidence, including books describing how journalists uncovered corruption from Teapot Dome to Watergate and Monica Lewinsky, that suggests journalists are essentially ethical.

The media both suffers and benefits from its enormous freedom. Freedom of the press allows enormous latitude in communication: No law can command a journalist to be responsible or fair or just. A journalist can be a highly ethical, moral individual who makes fair-minded choices, or a mean-spirited polemicist who is out to get people. That is what freedom of the press guarantees, and through history there have been plenty of journalists who have not been nice people. But we are not talking here about eccentric exceptions, but rather about the norm, the typical journalist who is increasingly driven toward responsibility and fair play—in other words, ethical conduct. Why do I say this is so?

The large plurality of media professionals today are the products of communication, journalism, or media studies program or have at least had some coursework that indoctrinates them into their profession. That indoctrination includes values such as freedom of the press, responsible practices in news gathering, and rigorous fair-minded writing in which accuracy, accuracy, accuracy is the clarion call. News people who do not go to journalism school have to possess writing skills and the ability to work within a media organization. Those organizations have written and unwritten rules about what is acceptable conduct for their employees. People learn these rules quickly and are governed by them. Otherwise they are fired. There are also many professional organizations to which one can belong, ranging from editors' and reporters' groups to others for specialized journalists. Virtually all of them have codes of ethics that are widely distributed to their members. Nearly a dozen new books on journalistic ethics are available, even if they are not the fastest-moving best-sellers on publishers' lists. In other words, information about journalistic ethics is readily available. Journalism and journalistic practice is not exactly a hidden or inaccessible topic. An increasing amount of press criticism is published in newspapers and magazines, and included on radio and television news programs. Mention almost any topic and media coverage of it has been discussed somewhere recently. And what does that coverage and criticism typically address? You guessed it: journalistic ethics. In fact, I would say that the typical citizen probably knows more about journalistic ethics than about medical or legal ethics. Why? Because the topic is front row center much of the time in our major media.

Studies of American journalists and American journalism educators by David Weaver and G. Cleveland Wilhoit, mentioned earlier in this book, suggest that ethics is a serious concern among both groups. Similarly, the several studies of media credibility done in recent years (and stretching back for a half-century) report that the public is very concerned about the ethics of journalists. Although most people support the media and give journalists and others good grades, a vocal minority is dissatisfied. Media people pay attention to these report cards and often act upon them, especially if they believe the criticism is just.

Since the 1920s, every 20 years or so there has been a burgeoning literature on media ethics. There is debate for a few years, and then the topic recedes into the background only to reappear later. That was true until the 1970s, but so visible are media issues and problems these days that the rush of articles and books has not abated. Excellent studies of situational ethics have been rendered by such educators as David Gordon et al. (*Controversies in Media Ethics*, 1998), Ron Smith and Eugene Goodwin (*Groping for Media Ethics*, 1999), and Philip Meyer (*Ethical Journalism*, 1987). Some even suggest that editorial ethics should extend to the business side of the press. Edmund Lambeth's (1992) *Committed Journalism* is a coherent philosophy based, in part, on ethical imperatives as well as practical conditions. These books and others that are notable join several volumes on my shelf by John Merrill, who has been writing on media ethics for at least three decades.

This literature is the tip of a very large iceberg that includes increased instruction in media ethics in journalism schools, a trend that has been traced by Clifford Christians of the University of Illinois. There are centers for media ethics at the Poynter Institute, the University of Minnesota, and Emerson College. There are training programs in ethics for journalism teachers at the University of Missouri and scores of conferences that have been well attended for at least a decade. In recent years, as business schools have begun to train media managers and leaders, they too have urged ethical practices on their charges. Often this is framed in terms of serving the public interest—and, of course, obeying the law, which is often tied up with ethics. Spurred by a spate of business scandals in the financial services and accounting industries, virtually all business schools offer courses in legal and ethical studies, now essential to doing business. In a real sense business ethics and journalistic ethics are merging and blurring and the media are the better for it.

This will ultimately have an effect on the ethics of all media functions, not just news but entertainment and opinion as well. There are codes of ethics for advertising and the topic is much discussed in that industry and in the advertising departments of media organizations. Ethics in the entertainment industry comes front row center when motion pictures, the music business, entertainment television, and other media are under the gun. Only recently, though, has ethics been a topic of much concern in the digital media, notably those centered in and around the Internet. Given the raw nature of the development of much of this industry, ethical imperatives were the least of the concerns of the early dot-com entrepreneurs, but increasingly digital media are professionalizing and susceptible to the same standards as other media platforms.

It seems to me that media ethics is alive and well in the United States. But are journalists ethical? Yes, for the most part they are, I believe, based on studies, personal experience, and the various incentives that encourage ethical conduct. These include the reward and punishment system of American journalism, which rarely rewards reprehensible or unethical journalism; pressure from an increasingly sophisticated public, which is critical of the news it gets; and finally, the legal system, which, in court, takes an exceedingly unkind view of journalists who are regarded by their peers as irresponsible, reckless, or unethical. Mostly, though, journalists, like most people, are ethical because they want to do what is right. And remember, even in the celebrated Jayson Blair case, there was punishment. He was fired, so were his bosses, and the newspaper suffered major embarrassment with a body blow to its reputation.

ARGUMENT SUMMATION: *Journalists and other media people are essentially ethical.*

Although there are notable exceptions as in any profession, ethical behavior is the norm in American journalism. The socialization of journalists, through both school and professional exposure, indoctrinates professional values that emphasize responsible news gathering, freedom of the press, and accuracy in reporting. Journalists who do not follow these unwritten rules of their profession do not have jobs for long. Studies confirm that journalists respond to criticism of media ethics and that there is a healthy debate regarding ethics, thus keeping the profession aware of a necessity for ethical behavior.

SEARCH ONLINE!

Use the following terms and phrases to search for more information on InfoTrac College Edition: *ethics, morals, moral choices, values, value judgments, codes of conduct, social responsibility, ethical codes, situational ethics, accuracy, journalistic context, consistency, rules of conduct, professionalism in journalism and media.*

TOPICS FOR DISCUSSION

1. What do you think being ethical means to most media personnel? Would you distinguish between those involved directly with news gathering and others on the business side? Should news media have a different standard than entertainment media?
2. Where are the main ethical allegiances in news gathering—to the public, to the employer, to the audience? How would you rank such allegiances in terms of importance?
3. Where do you think media professionals derive their ethical standards? If they get them from various sources, how do they know, if they do, which are more valid and reliable?
4. Do you think that codes of ethics are useful in a free-press society? How so? Do you think that a monolithic sense of ethics in the U.S. press would be good or bad for American journalism?
5. Give some evidence to substantiate the claim that "media ethics is alive and well in the United States despite appearances to the contrary." How would we know if American media ethics were in decline?

TOPICS FOR RESEARCH

1. Study the codes of ethics used by media organizations and professional societies. Compare and contrast them. How general are they? How specific? To what extent are they useful?
2. Interview one or more news persons from any medium. Ask them to articulate their theory of media ethics; that is, how do they define ethics in their work? How do they make ethical decisions? Ask for an example of a particularly difficult (or easy) ethical decision they recently had to make. Where does their knowledge of media ethics come from? How do they stay up to date?
3. Examine a major controversy in news or entertainment media in terms of ethics. Pick a case or controversy in which the performance or behavior of

a media professional came under fire. What was the main issue? How was it resolved? Did this serve the public well or not?

4. Write a review essay drawing on at least two recent books on media ethics. Based on these studies, how would you develop your own code of ethics? What advice would you give to a news organization about how they might write a code?

5. Read and analyze a recent biography by a media person. Examine the person's career and decisions on the basis of ethics. Is the person a good, mediocre, or poor model for others? What of his or her ethics?

FURTHER READING

Bromley, Michael, and Hugh Stephenson, eds. *Sex, Lies and Democracy: The Press and the Public.* Boston: Addison-Wesley, 1998.

Christians, Clifford G., Kim B. Rotzoll, Mark Fackler, and Kathy B. McGee. *Media Ethics: Cases and Moral Reasoning,* 6th ed. Boston: Allyn & Bacon, 2000.

Dennis, Everette E., Donald M. Gillmor, and Theodore Glasser, eds. *Media Freedom and Accountability.* Westport, CT: Greenwood Press, 1989.

Didion, Joan. *Slouching Towards Bethlehem.* New York: Modern Library, 2000.

Fritz, Ben, et al. *All the President's Spin: George W. Bush, the Media and the Truth.* New York: Simon & Schuster, 2004.

Gordon, David, et al. *Controversies in Media Ethics.* Boston: Addison-Wesley, 1998.

Kerbel, Matthew R. *If It Leads It Bleeds.* Colorado: Westview Press, 2001.

Lambeth, Edmund B. *Committed Journalism: An Ethic for the Profession,* 2nd ed. Bloomington: Indiana University Press, 1992.

Lowenstein, R. L., and J. C. Merrill. *Macromedia: Mission, Message and Morality.* White Plains, NY: Longman, 1990.

Malcolm, Janet. "The Journalist and the Murder." *New Yorker* (13 March 1989).

Merrill, John C. *Journalism Ethics: Philosophical Foundations for the News Media.* New York: St. Martin's Press, 1997.

Merrill, John C. *Princely Press: Machiavelli on American Journalism.* Lanham, MD: University Press of America, 1998.

Meyer, Philip. *Ethical Journalism.* White Plains, NY: Longman, 1987.

Narone, John C., ed. *Last Rights: Revisiting Four Theories of the Press.* Urbana: University of Illinois Press, 1995.

Patterson, Philip, and Lee C. Wilkins. *Media Ethics: Issues and Cases.* New York: 2004.

Smith, Ron H., and W. Eugene Goodwin. *Groping for Media Ethics.* Ames: Iowa State University Press, 1999.

JOURNALISTIC OBJECTIVITY

If there is a most important tenet of journalistic practice in the United States, it is the concept of objectivity. To its proponents, objectivity does not mean clinical or scientific precision but instead an effort by journalists to produce news stories and newscasts that are emotionally detached and that separate fact from opinion. Objectivity in journalistic practice is often associated with the inverted pyramid news story (news organized in a descending order of importance) and with the 5Ws and H (who, what, where, why, when, and how), or with other systems of sorting out the facts necessary to convey the essence of an event or issue in an orderly fashion.

Objectivity to many means factual reporting, straightforward descriptive presentation. In recent years, though, objectivity as a theory of journalism has also included analytical reporting that goes well beyond simple description. Objectivity is a distinguishing feature of American journalism, especially in comparison with journalistic content in other countries and cultures. At least that is what the proponents of objectivity believe, and it has become the standard wisdom. Some of the world's newspapers engage in polemic and opinionated essays, but the U.S. approach generally has been to keep the views of the journalist out of news stories and to reserve opinion for the editorial pages or bylined columns.

Whatever nuances they put on it, most critics agree that the theory of objectivity or so-called objective reporting is the prevailing journalistic style of the U.S. press and news media. Some may not like it and decry its assumptions, but exist it does, and thus it is often a matter of debate. And what a debate it is. The critics were once mostly outside journalism, but today many are journalists, media executives, and educators who demand a rethinking of objectivity or its abandonment altogether. Still, the notion of objectivity, sometimes relabeled "fairness," is an article of faith in the professionalization of journalism as a systematic attempt to cover the news. As one journalism professor, Michael Bugeja, puts it, "objectivity is seeing the world as it is, not as you wish it were."

CHALLENGE

Merrill: Journalistic objectivity is not possible.

Many readers may think that my position—that journalistic objectivity is not possible—is like building a straw man and then proceeding to demolish it. They will say that nobody contends that journalistic objectivity is possible, and that such a debate simply turns into an exercise in semantic frustration.

First let me say that I sympathize with the position I have just attributed to many readers, but I believe that we cannot ignore such an important journalistic concept. If we did, we would be doing an injustice to a legitimate concern of those who are involved with modern journalism—all of us. Second, many journalists and others talk and write as if they believe in journalistic objectivity. If they do not believe in it, then I propose that they stop using the term.

Perhaps the concept of journalistic objectivity is a straw man to those who seriously think about it, who are sophisticated, and who are realistic about the realities of journalism. But I contend that there aren't many such people and that, generally, laypeople and journalists actually think that a news story can be objective or that there are objective reporters who can be identified as different from other reporters. We often hear the term, as in "I wish he had written an objective story on that speech" or "Bob Woodward—now *there* is an objective reporter." Indeed, Woodward of Watergate fame, who now produces insider accounts on the occupants of the presidency, is often criticized for not taking sides or making political arguments, which he refuses to do. Still, many readers of his work are disappointed that he captures only his reality, that of a quiet observer wide-eyed in the White House.

Let us consider objective reporting. It would be reporting that is detached, unprejudiced, unopinionated, uninvolved, unbiased, omniscient—and infallible, I presume. Where do we find this? The objective report would, in effect, match reality; it would tell the truth, the whole truth, and nothing but the truth. Where do we find this kind of reporting? No reporter knows the truth; no reporter can write a story that can match reality. As general semanticists such as S. I. Hayakawa point out, the "map is not the territory." The story, in other words, is never what it purports to be; it is always much bigger than its verbal image.

All reporters, in addition to being limited in their objectivity by the inadequacy of language, are also *conditioned* by experience, by physical state, by education, and by many other factors. They do not come to their stories as blank slates on which the reality of events is to be written. They may want to be unprejudiced, balanced, thorough, and completely honest in their reporting, but they simply cannot be.

Many people believe that reporters are objective when they are detached from the event being covered. The problem here, of course, is what is meant by detachment. Detached in the sense of being outside the event being reported?

Detached in the sense of being uncommitted to any of the positions involved in the event being reported? Detached in the sense of being uninterested (or disinterested) in the event except as something to be reported? Detached in the sense of holding oneself aloof from the event? Detached in the sense of making sure the reporter's point of view does not impregnate the story?

The obvious answer to all of these questions is that it is really impossible to be detached, that the reporter's subjectivity—values, biases, interpretations, and news judgments—always enters into the production of the story.

Let me briefly mention short remarks on this subject by three legendary journalists; they abjure any pretense of a nonsubjective viewpoint.

> DAVID BRINKLEY: *"If I were objective, or if you were objective, or if anyone was, we would have to be put away somewhere in an institution because we'd be some sort of vegetable. Objectivity is impossible to a human being."*
>
> FRANK REYNOLDS: *"I think your program has to reflect what your basic feelings are. I'll plead guilty to that."*
>
> H. L. MENCKEN: *"We talk of objective reporting. There is no such thing. I have been a reporter for many years, and I can tell you that no reporter worth a hoot ever wrote a purely objective story. You get a point of view in it."*

These brief opinions are representative of some journalists, but I doubt that very many journalists really would say such things, at least for public consumption. If journalists do not really believe in objective reporting, they should stop talking and writing as if they do. They should talk more about being accurate, about being as thorough as possible, about trying to keep overt or obvious opinions or judgments out of their stories. In other words, they should show that they are really aware that objectivity in journalism does not exist.

Sociologist Michael Schudson writes in *Discovering the News* (1978) that journalistic objectivity is a faith in facts and a distrust of values—and a commitment to their segregation. Other scholars believe that most working journalists operationalize objectivity by insisting on verification and attribution, but sometimes admit this is more rhetoric than fact. While some news organizations—*USA Today* comes to mind—virtually ban anonymous sources, arguing that the public deserves to know who is behind a given claim, other news organizations allow unnamed sources, contributing to a growing tendency for this practice to creep into news coverage. Dan Okrent, readers' representative of the *New York Times*, tried to probe this concern by writing to the editors of several leading newspapers, but he received only one response, that being from the editor of *USA Today*.

During the 2004 presidential election, CBS News, in what seemed an effort to verify information about President George W. Bush's National Guard service during the Vietnam War, relied on documents that could not be verified. For days, CBS and its anchor Dan Rather defended the report, based on what were purported to be authentic documents, even quoting documentation efforts. When the documents proved to be false, not only did CBS News lose face, but Rather subsequently announced his retirement. A few months later, in January 2005, an independent report commissioned by CBS but prepared by outside advisers was sharply critical of the network and its practices, which led to the firing of a senior producer and the resignation of three other news executives. The issue was not objectivity per se but whether the network had made a serious effort to gather the facts for a volatile story. CBS News had not.

So even if we apply a rather measurable and realistic definition to journalistic objectivity, we can see that it is really nonexistent. And when we submit the concept to more challenging epistemological standards, it tends to evaporate altogether.

Michael Schudson notes that attribution is valued by the media, but it is sometimes compromised because of other factors. For example, the reporter may plead ethical motivation for withholding names of sources (or even principals in the story). I understand this constraint and will even grant that this is a correct action in some cases. But it doesn't change the fact that objectivity suffers because of it (if in fact objectivity could be said to exist in the first place).

There may be some who think that objectivity is possible in journalism, although how they come to such a belief baffles me. They seem to think that if a reporter checks the facts, verifies all statements, eliminates all first-person pronouns, and makes an attempt to present both sides (as if there were only two sides) of the story, then the story is objective.

The actual state of affairs is this: Every journalist—reporter as well as editorial writer—goes beyond descriptive facts into interpretation. Journalists cannot be objective, even if they would like to be. Every article, every sentence, every newscast, every movement before the camera, every voice inflection on radio is subjective. Even the so-called straight news reporter subjectivizes the story, which is always judgmental, value loaded, incomplete, and distorted as to reality. That is the nature of journalism. In fact, that is the nature of any kind of communication.

News reporters, even those wanting to be as aloof and neutral as possible, are caught in the natural trap of subjectivity. They involve themselves, their ideas, and their values in the story—even though they may ostensibly (verbally) keep themselves out. They are there nevertheless. They decide what aspects of the story to put in and what to leave out. They decide on the emphasis to be given various parts, which quotes to use, which parts of quotes to use, or whether to use quotes at all. When they paraphrase instead of using direct quotes, they in essence become translators and their interpretive powers come into play. Although this reporting is not objective, there is really nothing intrinsically wrong with it.

Michael Novak, writing about the journalist and objectivity, makes the following pertinent observations:

> The myth of objectivity leads to . . . misunderstandings in American journalism. There are no facts "out there" apart from human observers. And human observers become not more, but less astute when they try to be neutral. . . .
>
> Reporters and newscasters know that if they aim at objectivity, at presenting "the facts" without editorializing, they run the risk of giving dignity to nonsense, drivel, and outright lies. What really happened in an event is not, they know, discovered by some neutral observation machine, not even by a camera. Events are not events until they are interpreted by human beings. . . . To list statistics, or outwardly observable happenings, or quotations from witnesses, is to give a very narrow view of the human world. It is to offer interpretation and editorial comment of a very misleading sort. Reality does not come divided into "facts" and "interpretation." (1971, 40)

Others have joined in the charge that objectivity is a myth. Among them is Richard F. Tatflinger of Washington State University who argued that "objectivity is not a possible goal in human interaction and that includes journalism." As long as human beings gather and disseminate the news, then subjectivity will be the rule not the exception (Tatflinger, 1996, 6).

These critiques of objectivity are in the tradition of other thinkers and critics such as Paul Tillich, Martin Buber, and, in the existentialist camp, Jean-Paul Sartre, who have great respect for subjectivity. They have attacked the emptiness of empirical and pragmatic objectivity beloved by Americans especially. They have said that not only is this belief in objectivity contrary to linguistic philosophy (and they could have said also to the principles of general semantics), but it demeans and devalues the individual and the concept of intersubjectivity.

The business of journalism is subjective from beginning to end, and reporting is no exception. There may be an image of objectivity in some stories—a linguistic aura of objectivity—but behind this aura is the reporter's subjectivity. Reporters are not mindless, soulless automatons who roam about, without values, opinions, and preferences, simply soaking up reality and spouting it out completely. They have their prejudices, their biases, their values, their favorite topics, their heroes, and their villains. We may wish that there were some robotized, completely unbiased and bland reporters who could report objectively, but they do not exist.

As Donald McDonald wrote in a seminal article, a reporter's values are necessarily injected into the story.

> The value judgments [the journalist] must make at every critical stage in his investigation and interpretation of the facts must reflect the values he already holds. Again, these values flow from his personal history. They are products of his education, his religious experience, his childhood, family life, social and economic background, friendships and associations, national ties and culture, as well as his emotional life and experiences, and his reason. (1975, 71)

The context in which a story happens cannot be fully reported. But the reporter's inability to explicate the total context keeps a story from being objective. In a story about a political speech, not only the words that a speaker speaks but also how the speaker says those words are part of the story of the speech. What the speaker thinks while speaking is part of the story—a part unavailable to the reporter at the time of the speech. To speculate about it would be subjective. To leave it out is to fail to be objective.

Audience reaction, speaker movements, gestures, smiles, and the like form part of the objective story. The totality of the story is the true story. But the reporter cannot give all this truth, so he or she sifts the objective portions of the story through a mental, emotional, and psychological sifter and thereby presents the audience with a necessarily subjective account of what happened.

Journalists are selective. They are forced by the nature of their craft to select certain facts to report, certain quotations to bring to light, certain individuals to interview, certain perspectives to give, certain aspects of an event to expose. And what happens to the other facts, individuals, perspectives, and aspects of a story? Are they not also part of the objectivity of the story? The answer to this question is that many parts of the story are ignored, or they are slighted, deemphasized, or distorted in some way that keeps them from fulfilling the objectivity of the story.

There may be something that can be called verifiable journalism. If as a reporter I write, "John Doe stole six cows from W. H. Arden of Winchester," and if this is indeed what happened, then that sentence is factual and verifiable. That one aspect of the story is true, in the sense that it has no overt errors in it. But when that sentence is put into a context with other sentences to make a story, then its nonobjective nature is exposed. Then we must begin looking at the story and not just at the sentence.

What are the gaps in the story? What is the totality of the story in the context of reality, and what has it become in its verbal nature in the story? In essence, what happened in reality that is left out in the story? Is there a correlation between the real event and the verbal picture of the event?

Also harming the reportorial objectivity is bias. Many commentators (including scholars such as Rothman and Lichter and commentators such as Ann Coulter or Bernard Goldberg) have criticized the news media for left-wing ideological bias in its news presentation. Others (such as Eric Alterman of *The Nation*) contend that the press has departed from traditional sentiments and principles of the people and is substantially to the right of most Americans.

Many persons will say that journalistic objectivity is not meant to be total, that partial objectivity is what is really meant by those defending objectivity. When we consider such a partial concept, however, we run into trouble immediately: Just how partial can objectivity be? At what point does it cease being objective?

Armand Mattelart, a French Marxist sociologist, calls objectivity the "golden rule of journalistic practice, the cornerstone of its professional deontology, and the equivalent of the Hippocratic oath" (1980, 39). But he does not believe in the concept. He questions it by saying: (1) The concept presupposes on the part of the journalist certain perceptive powers capable of penetrating reality and determining what is important and what is not; (2) the concept postulates that the description of facts (which are *what they are in themselves,* not what the journalist sees them to be) goes no further than the facts themselves; and (3) facts are isolated by objectivity-oriented journalism, "cut off from their roots, deprived of the conditions which would explain their occurrence, and detached from the social system which endows them with meaning and in which they possess an intelligible place." Many writers excoriate those who, like Mattelart, maintain that journalistic objectivity is a myth. But the legendary H. L. Mencken took much the same view as Mattelart, and he was certainly no Communist.

In a 2003 article in the *Columbia Journalism Review,* Brent Cunningham urges us to rethink objectivity and makes two modest proposals:

> First, journalists (and journalism) must acknowledge, humbly and publicly, that what they do is far more subjective and far less detached than the aura of objectivity implies—and the public wants to believe. . . . Secondly, we need to free (and encourage) reporters to develop expertise and use it to sort through competing claims, identify and explain the underlying assumptions of those claims, and make judgments about what readers and viewers need to know to understand what is happening. (Cunningham, 2003, 16)

As the evidence I have cited here and my own views underscore, just because objectivity is a matter of public and professional discussion does not mean that it is anything other than a mythic goal. In a perfect world, a journalism of truth marked by objectivity would certainly be desirable. Of course, I have no objection to discussing this wonderful notion now and forever, but I also recognize that such activity is more of a ritual than anything else. My colleague Professor Dennis, in a colloquy with the Italian semiologist Umberto Eco, put it well when he said, "You must understand that in America, objectivity is ideology." Exactly. Nothing more, nothing less.

ARGUMENT SUMMATION: *Journalistic objectivity is not possible.*

Objectivity may be a worthy goal, but it is unrealizable certainly in regard to the press. In no way can a journalist be detached, unprejudiced, unopinionated, unbiased, and omniscient. The journalist must select, organize, and manipulate facts; that is the nature of journalism. From beginning to end, journalism is a subjective enterprise. No reporter knows the truth; certainly he or she cannot report it. A story of an event is no more than a partial (and poor) image of the real event out there in reality. Journalists are subjectivists, personally conditioned, and are able to provide audiences no more than superficial maps of the real territory.

RESPONSE

Dennis: Journalistic objectivity is possible.

There is considerable irony in this debate, because the prevailing view of objectivity today—shared by journalists and critics alike and persuasively summarized by John Merrill—was heresy only a few years ago. At that time (and for several decades) objectivity was the dominant philosophy that guided most of the nation's newsrooms. Those who criticized objective journalism as a myth that was beyond human capability were hooted down by defensive editors who declared that impartial and balanced reporting could be achieved and that true objectivity was a noble goal.

With great pride, Alan Barth of the *Washington Post* once wrote that "the tradition of objectivity is one of the principal glories of American journalism." Nineteen years later Herbert Brucker of the *Hartford Courant* agreed: "We can do a good job . . . as long as we keep the flag of objectivity flying high. That will give a more honest and more accurate view of this imperfect world than trusting a latter day Trotsky, or any partisan on any side, to tell us what's what." His essay reviewed some of the reasons that objectivity became an object of scorn and derision. Critics declared that "everyone is subjective and journalists have no magic powers to be otherwise." And almost everyone who had ever taken a psychology course agreed.

Sometimes we forget that objectivity is merely a method and style of presenting information. Its defenders, who led the press out of a sorry period of partisan sensationalism in the 1920s, said it had three principal characteristics:

1. Separating fact from opinion
2. Presenting an emotionally detached view of the news
3. Striving for fairness and balance, giving both sides an opportunity to reply in a way that provides full information to the audience

What is wrong with this straightforward set of goals is that they are too simplistic and assume that complex situations can always be reduced to a balanced presentation with two alternative views. Such an approach leaves little room for ambiguity.

Beyond the underlying philosophical problems associated with objectivity was the operational difficulty in the *inverted pyramid* story, which was the mode by which objective accounts were presented to the public. In its pristine form, objective news reports contain the 5Ws and the H, and they organize information in a descending order of importance. This journalistic style was often criticized as cold and lifeless. It was also said to obscure the truth. It was what the sociologist Gaye Tuchman (1972) called a strategic ritual, wherein journalists used four procedures to lay claim to objectivity:

1. Presentation of conflicting possibilities
2. Presentation of supporting evidence
3. The judicious use of quotation marks
4. Structuring information in an appropriate sequence

Objectivity came under attack most significantly during the 1960s and 1970s when there was a flurry of new journalistic styles and standards. Although some of them were not altogether unknown before, they constituted a journalistic movement that expressed dissatisfaction with the status quo and brought change. At the center of this movement was a vigorous assault on the concept of objectivity. Some of the developments in journalism were these:

1. *The New Journalism*—with writers using such literary devices as extensive description, dialogue, interior monologue, and others previously discouraged by spare-prose 5W editors.
2. *Advocacy journalism*—with its unabashed support for particular issues and causes by journalists opposing the impartial, objective tradition.
3. *Investigative reporting*—which took an adversarial stance and sometimes proposed solutions to problems as it uncovered corruption and moved well beyond the scope of disinterested, stenographic reporting.
4. *Service journalism*, or the marketing approach to news—which employed a different definition of news, emphasizing what is commonplace and of interest to the greatest number of people rather than what is unique and new. With this approach both the selection of material covered and the unity of style aim at identifying closely with the audience. Stories aim at all homeowners, not just unusual ones. This form of journalism (discussed in Chapter 10) relies heavily on market research.
5. *Precision journalism*—which is the use of social science methods, including survey research, as reportorial tools to determine what is happening in the community.
6. *Civic journalism*—a journalistic movement of the 1990s (see Chapter 13) that posits that the press should engage citizens and take a more active role in helping a community set its agenda and seek policy solutions, as opposed to doing impartial reporting.

All of these approaches claimed to be more objective than traditional objectivity. New journalists said they provided greater tone, texture, and feeling than in cold, lifeless objective reports. "What we have here," said Tom Wolfe, "is a subjective reality. It is really more objective than traditional reporting." Advocacy journalists also claimed that they came closer to the truth than their more conventional colleagues. "We all have a point of view," they said, "so why not admit it—up front." Journalists all too often presented facts but missed the truth, wrote a 1960s critic, Raymond Mungo. Marketing approach journalists said, "We're giving people what they want. Our news is more pertinent and relevant." And precision journalists added: "We move beyond the limits of intuition. We use computers and statistics to give the most representative picture of the community that is humanly possible within the constraints of a news organization."

In the face of such criticism, support for objectivity crumbled. Although much of the criticism of objectivity as it was articulated and understood in the 1950s and 1960s was warranted, I think that it went too far. As is often the case when a prevailing mode of thought is abandoned, those who push the new view feel a need to drive a stake through the heart of the old one. In this case it does us no service. The wave of new styles and reportorial approaches has definitely enriched American journalism, but it is time once again to look carefully at objectivity before abandoning it altogether. Objectivity fell out of favor because it was seen as an impossible goal. Maybe that judgment was too hasty. Objectivity deserves another chance.

What is objectivity, anyway? According to Webster's *Third New International Dictionary*, objective means:

> publicly or intersubjectively observable or verifiable, especially by scientific means . . . independent of what is personal or private in our apprehension or feelings . . . of such a nature that rational minds agree in holding it real or true or valid . . . expressing or involving the use of facts without distortion by personal feelings or prejudices.

Is this so wild a dream? No one would argue that journalists can achieve perfection, but is it impossible within the context of human frailty to try to be disinterested—not uninterested or indifferent, but impartial? Is it impossible to observe and report those perceptions so that others can verify them if they choose to do so? Can we not reach some consensus about what is happening in our neighborhoods or communities and still leave room for differing interpretations and speculative views? To all of these questions, I would answer with a resounding yes.

It is interesting that my colleague Merrill mentions the Dan Rather affair at CBS in 2004 and 2005. Objectivity—or verified, factual information—was very much at issue in this case. George W. Bush's National Guard record had become an issue in the presidential campaign, and CBS News sought out documents that seemed to be quite damaging, verifying what some critics had claimed about the president's less than admirable record as a young officer during the Vietnam War. CBS News offered the documents as proof positive, the smoking gun—the precise evidence needed to make the case. Because the documents were apparently faked by someone and CBS was at the least careless in its procedures, the news reports that appeared on the *60 Minutes* midweek program were dismissed, and the network's reputation was damaged. When the matter was later investigated, the Thornburgh/Boccardi committee identified the lack of a system within CBS News for rigorous fact checking and verification. It seems to me that CBS was at least suggesting that its evidence was "objective" or that the evidence had been fairly obtained to make the story solid—but the documents clearly were neither. Although some later argued that the charges against Bush were true, but the evidence was faked, the public could not know from the CBS News report precisely what had happened, and thus CBS News fell far short of its duty as a news organization.

I believe that journalistic objectivity is possible if we adopt methods that lead to systematic decisions. We can borrow from some of the admirable new styles that have emerged in recent years and use the tools of rational decision making. This can be not a complex scholarly endeavor that is beyond the daily resources of the media but a practical strategy that will make journalism better and more reliable. I would do this in three ways: first, through strategic planning in the reporting process; second, through the use of systematic tools to analyze communities and gather information; and third, through the clear delineation of the presentation form used.

Strategic Planning   For a number of years American corporations have engaged in strategic planning. Corporate strategies involve an agreed-upon approach, an understanding of the major decision-making points, and a well-calibrated effort to make the best possible choices. The relation of benefit to cost is always a central concern. Practical decisions are made with the expectation that they will yield the best possible results. What we can learn from this approach in journalism is that news gathering and news making involve choices that can be made on a rational basis. They need not be purely subjective. Editor Ronald Buel says that news is essentially data that must be made into a product. This process involves a series of interrelated decisions:

1. *Data assignment: What is worth covering and why?* This will depend on the type of publication and its purpose. If the purpose of a newspaper is to cover the whole community as adequately as possible, it is not difficult to inventory various components of community life. This categorization may mean moving away from the old beat system that emphasizes what happens in public buildings (such as the courthouse) and to consider such issues as lifestyle, the workplace, business, fads and trends, and the environment. Within the paper's particular definition of news, it is not difficult to make rational decisions that can be defined and justified. For example, in the coverage of a political campaign, the paper should be able to explain how it covered various candidates and why some were deemed more important than others. These explanations ought to result in a view of the race with which other observers would concur if given the paper's original assumptions about news. They would also take into account such economic factors as staff size.

2. *Data collection: When has enough information been gathered?* This too is a matter of definition. But there are reasonable standards by which trained reporters know when they have assembled enough information to answer the key questions that make a complete story. Again, outsiders looking in ought to be able to understand the basis for decisions. The test here is whether, within the goals of a particular story, all of the critical questions have been answered with evidence from appropriate sources. This standard of reasonable completeness is frequently used in defense against libel suits, and news organizations are increasingly being asked to explain their thresholds for finished work.

3. *Data evaluation: What is important enough to be put into a story?* Once information is gathered, typically only part of it can be included in the story. What part? And why? Sometimes new reporters make a priority list, especially if they are asked to cut a long story to meet the space demands of an editor who cannot accommodate their first submission. This decision ought to be rational. If, for example, a reporter is covering a trial, it is not difficult to list basic facts, key sources, and interpretations. If this list must be reduced markedly, the real test is what is essential to full and accurate presentation.

4. *Data writing: What words and images will be used?* Good writing means imaginative writing, which involves interpretations that are not always verifiable. Writing adds tone and complexity of perception. Still it is not difficult to write in such a way that the writer's impressions, legitimately expressed, are distinguished from purely factual information. This technique will provide a somewhat subjective portrait, of course, but still it ought to come close to what an average reader might have ascertained had he or she been on the scene. After all, journalists writing for mass media (as opposed to literary or specialized publications) should use words and images that are generally understood.

5. *Data editing: Which story should get a big headline and go on the front page or begin a broadcast, which stories should be buried, which ones should be changed, and which ones should be cut?* Again, we return to the corporate strategy of the news organization. What is most vital to the audience? Once that is understood, decisions can be made about cutting material or providing emphasis. The underlying policies of media organizations are based on values. For example, news of government may be deemed more important than business news because it affects more people. Nonetheless, it is important that orderly, consistent decisions be made so that readers have a clear understanding of the rules of the game. Naturally, values always play an important role. It is not possible to have universal answers to the questions raised in the Buel framework for all societies. The appropriate response in Lagos, Nigeria, will not be the same as that in Austin, Texas.

Mode of Presentation   There are at least three general types of journalistic presentation that ought to be considered.

Descriptive stories can be easily verified. Certain facts are presented and can be corroborated, even if there is disagreement about details.

With *analytic* stories we can usually inventory possible sources on a given topic. They can be listed and individual views set forth. The reporter brings an interpretive or sense-making perspective to the story, but this can be discerned by anyone who reads the story carefully. Also, if the reporter omits a possible source, the reader should be able to see this omission and evaluate accordingly.

Consequential stories are trickier, but they too can be presented impartially as statements of conjecture and speculation.

Armand Mattelart would no doubt see this process as astoundingly presumptuous, with journalists assuming superhuman powers to penetrate reality. But then the very act of being a journalist, of presuming to report what is happening, is by definition presumptuous. However, this process is the social function of journalism and it can be done systematically in a manner that withstands examination. The true test is whether reasonable people in the same cultural setting would have similar, if not always the same, perceptions of the event or issue if they had done their own reporting. Certainly a highly trained lawyer will see a trial differently from the average person, but this difference does not negate the fact that mass communication aims at the mass audience and tries to make connections with a norm. The press is the surrogate of the people in our society—it represents them as their eyes and ears—and it has an obligation to present intelligent and understandable reports that give a reasonably representative picture of society. Objectivity in journalism or science does not mean that all decisions do not have underlying values, only that within the rules of the game a systematic attempt is made to achieve an impartial report.

My concern is that the wave of critics in the early years of the 21st century who decry almost all journalistic activity as politically motivated—especially the popularly received notion that the media are liberal, meaning leaning toward liberal/progressive ideas and candidates (usually Democrats)—has done real damage to the serious professionalism that abounds in the news media. Reporters, editors, and news executives I know want to get it right. They want to pursue truth and offer evidence as part of their reportorial journey. To do less would make them nothing more than unethical information scavengers whose sole purpose is to court power through political-journalistic means. There are such people, of course, and they do seek fame and fortune for themselves through the media. There are dishonest reporters like those publicly rebuked in 2003 and 2004 at the *New York Times* and *USA Today*. The critically acclaimed film *Shattered Glass* documents just such a case. But these are exceptions, rare exceptions from the legions of ethical, information-seeking news people who do believe in a sense of impartiality, even if they can't guarantee fairness or objectivity, which is an elusive goal, a vision of what journalism ought to be, not what it necessarily is at the moment. It particularly rankled critics in the months after 9/11 when Walter Isaacson, then president of CNN, told his correspondents to balance their reports of casualties in covering the Afghanistan War with the realization that the war itself was a direct result of an attack on U.S. soil.

I began writing about the assault on objectivity in the 1960s and 1970s when I documented the New Journalism in scores of visits with alternative journalists, literary journalists, and others. They, as do their counterparts today, found the status quo wanting and often corrupting. Their response was to abandon the values of neutrality for more passionate pursuits. That was a healthy instinct, as are civic journalism and other proposals for change today, but the fundamental construction of objectivity is still a worthy goal, one worth fighting for if the news media are to be truly credible and not simply part of a partisan press as in much of the rest of the world. The U.S. contribution to rigorous news-gathering methods and presentation is worth preserving and can itself benefit from critiques that find some of its present delivery wanting.

My colleague Merrill mentions a conversation I once had with the Italian author and critic Umberto Eco. In a seminar with a group of U.S. journalism deans I led on a study tour, Eco decried the lack of passion in American journalism, which he found to be bland, gutless, and unwilling to take a stand. As he poured on the criticism, it dawned on me that he didn't understand the underlying basis for his complaint and I said, "Professor Eco, you need to know that objectivity is our ideology." I meant that in the sense of a fundamental philosophy, a vision, a goal, one that might displease a European critic but that is perfectly appropriate for our journalistic tradition and, yes, our journalistic faith. Giving up on a rigorous effort to connect scientific precision with literary style in American journalism in favor of sloppy, self-indulgent opinionizing and blatant subjectivity is not an honorable course.

ARGUMENT SUMMATION: *Journalistic objectivity is possible.*

Objectivity is merely a method or style of presenting information. During the 1960s and 1970s new styles of journalism led to an assault on objectivity, which fell out of favor as an impossible goal. However, impartiality is not beyond the capabilities of the modern journalist if procedures are followed providing for systematic decisions. This process should include strategic planning in the reporting process, the use of systematic tools to analyze communities and gather information, and clear delineation of the presentation form used. Following such guidelines would allow journalists to report impartially on their communities or, at worst, properly distinguish subjective conclusion from fact. The goal should be to present the story so that individuals reading the report would have had the same perspective if they had been present themselves. That objective is not impossible in modern journalism, but it does require a systematic attempt to provide an impartial report.

Search Online!

Use the following terms and phrases to search for more information on InfoTrac College Edition: *fact, opinion, impartiality, detachment, bias, opinion, objectivity, objective, advocacy journalism, verification, attribution, news sources, subjectivity, value judgments, balance, fairness, inverted pyramid.*

Topics for Discussion

1. How can a person—a subjective entity—write or present an objective story?

2. What do you think most journalists mean by journalistic objectivity? According to this meaning, do you think journalists are (or can be) objective?

3. Is it possible to give the truth, the whole truth, and nothing but the truth in a news story? How does truth relate to objectivity?

4. If a reporter refrains from naming the source of a quote in the story, or decides not to give the name of a juvenile offender, can the story be objective?

5. The new journalism of the 1960s was said by its adherents to be more objective than Associated Press–type journalism. Similar claims are made for public or civic journalism today. What do you think they mean? Do you think they are right?

Topics for Research

1. Compare and contrast objectivity in science or social science with objectivity in journalism. How do they differ in concept and practice? Indicate how a clinically objective scientific investigation might differ from a report a journalist would call objective. Use specific examples by comparing a research article in *Science* magazine or some scientific journal with a news report in a publication such as the *Wall Street Journal.*

How do the investigators' methods differ? How much evidence is offered? What of interpretation?

2. Write an essay about the concept of fairness. What is it? How is it defined and operationalized in the media? How would you advise laypersons about how they might judge the fairness of the media in covering a particular story or event? Assess, if you like, two or three different accounts of the same event from a standpoint of fairness.
3. Discuss advocacy journalism. What is it? How does it differ from objective journalism?
4. Write a personal essay about how you would try to be objective (if indeed you would) in gathering information about any controversial subject you choose. Be specific and indicate how you would decide which sources to contact, which to quote, how to sum up.
5. Write an essay that takes the middle ground somewhere between Merrill and Dennis on objectivity. Assume that both are giving you their best-case advocacy position. On what points do you agree? Disagree?

FURTHER READING

Alterman, Eric. *What Liberal Media? The Truth about Bias and the News.* New York: Basic Books, 2003.

Cohen, Stanley, and Jock Young, eds. *The Manufacture of News.* Beverly Hills, CA: Sage, 1973.

Coulter, Ann. *Slander: Liberal Lies about the American Right.* New York: Crown, 2002.

Cunningham, Brent. "Re-thinking Objectivity." *Columbia Journalism Review*, July/August 2003, at www.cjr.org/issues/2003/4/objective-cunningham.asp.

DeFleur, Melvin L., and Everette E. Dennis. *Understanding Mass Communication,* 7th ed. Boston: Houghton Mifflin, 2002.

Fallows, James. *Breaking the News.* New York: Vintage, 1997.

Gans, Herbert. *Deciding What's News.* New York: Pantheon, 1979.

Gans, Herbert. *Democracy and the Media.* New York: Oxford University Press, 2003.

Glasser, Theodore, and James Ettema. *Custodians of Conscience: Investigative Journalism and Public Virtue.* New York: Columbia University Press, 1998.

Goldberg, Bernard. *Bias: A CBS Insider Exposes How the Liberal Media Distort the News.* New York: Regnery, 2001.

Hayakawa, S. I. *Language in Thought and Action,* 5th ed. New York: Harcourt Brace Jovanovich, 1990.

Hunt, Todd. "Beyond the Journalistic Event: The Changing Concept of News." *Mass Communication Review* 1 (April 1974): 23–30.

Korzybski, Alfred. *Science and Sanity.* Lancaster, PA: Science Press, 1933.

Lambeth, Edmund B., ed. *Assessing Public Journalism.* Columbia: University of Missouri Press, 1998.

Lichter, Robert, Stanley Rothman, and Linda Lichter. *The Media Elite.* Bethesda, MD: Adler & Adler, 1986.

Manoff, Robert Karl, and Michael Schudson, eds. *Reading the News.* New York: Pantheon, 1986.

Mattelart, Armand. *Mass Media, Ideologies, and the Revolutionary Movement.* Atlantic Highlands, NJ: Humanities Press, 1980. See especially discussion of objectivity, pp. 37ff.

McDonald, Donald. "Is Objectivity Possible?" In *Ethics and the Press,* J. C. Merrill and Ralph Barney, eds., 69–72. New York: Hastings House, 1975.

Merrill, John C. *The Imperative of Freedom.* New York: Freedom House, 1994.

Merritt, Davis. *Public Journalism and Public Life: Why Telling the News Is Not Enough.* Hillsdale, NJ: Erlbaum, 1995.

Mindich, David. *Just the Facts: How Objectivity Came to Define American Journalism.* New York: New York University Press, 1999.

Novak, Michael. *The Experience of Nothingness.* New York: Harper Colophon, 1971. See especially discussion of objectivity, pp. 37–40.

Roshco, Bernard. *Newsmaking.* Chicago: University of Chicago Press, 1975.

Rubin, Bernard. *Media, Politics, and Democracy.* New York: Oxford University Press, 1977. See especially Chapter 1.

Schudson, Michael. *Discovering the News.* Cambridge, MA: Harvard University Press, 1978.

Solomon, Norman. *The Habits of Highly Deceptive Media: Decoding Spin and Lies in the Mainstream Press.* Monroe, ME: Common Courage Press, 1999.

Taflinger, Richard F. "The Myth of Objectivity in Journalism: A Commentary," 1996, at www.wsu.edu:8080/taflinge/mythobj.html.

Tuchman, Gaye. "Objectivity as Strategic Ritual: An Examination of Newsmen's Notions of Objectivity." *American Journal of Sociology* 77, no. 4 (January 1972): 660–67.

Civic/Public Journalism

In the midst of problems with the credibility of the media and their increasingly distant corporate character came a social movement in the 1990s called civic or public journalism. The brainchild of academic journalists and news people, this effort to stop declining confidence in journalism and journalistic content was one of the most talked about new developments in the media during the 1990s—and one of the most controversial. Closely related to a social and philosophical approach called communitarianism, civic or public journalism emphasizes cooperation and community building over conflict and controversy. The founder of communitarianism, sociologist Amitai Etzioni, the author of a book called *The Spirit of Community* (1993), has waged a rhetorical war against Enlightenment liberalism—against individualism and libertarianism. It is also generally related to calls for a civil society wherein cooperation and community also supersede individualism. For journalists this may mean that they play a personal role as change agents, reflecting what they regard as the will of the community as seen in public discourse. In this way, the argument is made, the public (with the public journalist as conduit) sets the agenda for the news, rather than having journalists and editors (as elites) doing so.

In the academic world of journalism and media education, two professors, Jay Rosen of New York University and Clifford Christians of the University of Illinois, were among early leaders in advancing public journalism. Concurrently, a newspaper editor, Davis Merritt, Jr., of Wichita, Kansas, and others championed public journalism in the newsrooms of newspapers and broadcast stations. Among others deeply involved with public journalism were Edmund Lambeth and Esther Thorson of the University of Missouri, Philip Meyer of the University of North Carolina, and Theodore Glasser of Stanford. For newsrooms that adopted civic or public journalism approaches, this usually meant projects of civic betterment or social change. What happened was a gentle version of media crusades of a bygone era. Jay Rosen called it a *constructive act* for a better democracy and most of the proponents emphasized a more democratic journalism, rather than one that was institutionally hidebound and reflecting the views of news professionals who are sometimes out of touch with their audience. By one count about 200 media organizations organized civic journalism projects, some funded by foundations, others urged on by corporate leaders including Knight Ridder's late chairman, James Batten.

Public journalism was never clearly defined and many people thought that it was an assault on the notion of objectivity or an impartial press. And the fact is that although public journalism is enormously popular in journalism schools and at a few news organizations, most of the U.S. press has not adopted this approach and is openly hostile to it. Top editors at the *New York Times* and *Washington Post* have said that public journalism blurs opinion and editorializing with news gathering. The civic/public journalism promoters scoff at the idea of the neutral journalist and argue that a journalism of involvement is the preferred path. Because only a minority of press critics and media leaders support public/civic journalism, it is safe to say that this agenda for change has many hurdles to clear before it is a settled issue. Public journalism may be on the decline and some of its advocates have moved on to other projects, devoting less time to defending its virtues. Foundations that have funded public journalism such as Pew, Knight, and Kettering, for example, have been sharply criticized for trying to influence and control the media's agenda. Although few in the general public have heard of civic journalism, because it is something of an insider's notion, it still has influential proponents.

CHALLENGE

Merrill: Civic or public journalism is a healthy trend for the media.

Public (aka civic) journalism burst upon the media scene in the last decade of the 20th century and is still alive and well in late 2004 as this is written. I think it is fair to say that public journalism is here to stay. Certainly its advocates have a worthy goal. It is to connect the public to the media, to democratize journalism, to get more citizens to be active in public life and politics. In order to achieve this goal, public journalism wants to shatter old myths about press libertarianism begun with the Enlightenment liberalism of the 18th and early 19th centuries. It wants to make the case that press freedom per se is not good. For the public journalist, public service and social responsibility are much more important. Individualism needs to be subjugated to a spirit of communitarianism—to social cooperation and ethical behavior.

The harmony of the community is what is important, along with the public realization that it has access to the media and that, in fact, it can have a big say in what is communicated by the media. Public journalism sees the traditional capitalistic press theory as arrogant, elitist, exclusive, irresponsible, superficial, and egocentric. In short, it has failed to vitalize the public and to help in the betterment of society.

It is refreshing that citizens and media people are beginning to question the old atomistic, individualistic, rights-centered philosophy of the press. And it is good that the emphasis is shifting away from institutional media excesses. All of us should be able to find congenial ideas in the emerging community-oriented philosophy and applaud the more democratic nature of the new people's journalism that is on the horizon. This new public journalism offers social stability and freedom from the chaos and nihilism that rear their ugly heads everywhere. It should seem obvious that the community and its needs come before the individual and his or her rights.

As communications scholars such as Clifford Christians, Jay Rosen, and Edmund Lambeth have pointed out, there is a need for uniform normative ethical standards and for journalists to recognize they need to act in similar and predictable ways. Discipline and commonality of values would ensure a far more smooth-running journalistic enterprise. A people-based journalism is more sensible than a journalist-based journalism—and this is exactly what public journalists are advocating. Public faith in the media is slipping rapidly, and we can see media filled with cheap, superficial, and even pornographic material. Tabloidism is taking over journalism. The Internet is having a profound effect on the total communications system—not only in a technological sense but in a quality-debasing sense. The public journalist would stop this drift. Public journalists and communitarians say that media libertarianism has had its chance—it has failed, and it is failing.

What are some of the characteristics of this new public journalism? Let me mention just a few, largely drawing on an excellent summary in *Good News* (Christians, Ferre, and Fackler, 1993). It is difficult to see how anyone could take issue with them, but I'm sure that Professor Dennis will in his response. Here is what the public journalists propose:

1. Journalists should publish those things that would bring people together, not fractionalize them.
2. Journalists should give the people of the community what they desire, not what the journalists want them to have.
3. Journalists themselves ought to agree on a common ethics and should not fall into the trap of embracing situational or relativistic ethics.
4. Journalists should discard the liberal politics of rights, which "rests on unsupportable foundations"; such rights should be "given up for a politics of the common good."
5. Journalists should deal with positive news, with items that would not tear down community spirit but would solidify and promote the community.

6. Journalists should throw out the old concepts of journalistic autonomy and editorial self-determinism, along with individualism and what they call *negative freedom.*

7. Journalists should make news reports accurate, balanced, and complete, and should localize and featurize the news, making it more relevant to the community.

8. Journalists should hold fast to the underlying normative principles of truth-telling and the public's right to know, which public journalists believe are nonnegotiable principles.

9. Journalists should realize that "universal solidarity is the normative core of the social and moral order."

10. Journalists ought to realize that the Enlightenment philosophy of the press generates confusion about the news media's rationale and mission, and excludes the substantive issues from the media-ethics agenda.

11. Journalists should reject the Enlightenment's individualistic rationalism.

These are only a few of the suggestions made by the communitarians and public journalists, but they are probably the main ones. Runaway individualism and irrational use of freedom simply cannot be sustained by thoughtful, moral people, say the public journalists.

Public journalists want to democratize journalism—making it an enterprise widely available to all citizens and more responsible to journalists themselves. The newsrooms should be more participatory and democratic, with the entire staff having a greater say in policy. The public should recognize its responsibility to take part in the editorial matters of the medium. This could be accomplished, say the public journalists, by sponsoring focus groups of representative citizens, surveying the public about its desires, and bringing citizens into the daily decision making of the news medium.

In addition, public journalism would reconnect the public to the media, increase the media's credibility, and stimulate greater participation of the citizens in the social and political activities of society. Public journalism would help form a community through positive and helpful reporting. It would give more emphasis to the local scene, to features that would help the community solve problems, and would be a positive force for community action.

It is hard to see how anyone could be against public journalism. It is time to be concerned about the limits of individualism and freedom. It is time to place social responsibility and morality ahead of media autonomy. It is time to negate the arrogance and self-centeredness of the media and their elitist leaders. The day has come for a new concept of journalism such as the public journalists are proposing. Anything that makes our press more responsible, more civic minded, more democratic, and more concerned with the public interest is indeed welcome. Public journalism offers such hope.

ARGUMENT SUMMATION: *Civic or public journalism is a healthy trend for the media.*

The new concept of civic journalism has made inroads into journalism during the last couple of decades. It is a good and healthy trend because it takes the emphasis off the atomistic, individualistic, and outdated libertarian philosophy of 18th-century Enlightenment and places it on the good of society, on harmony, stability, and progress of the community.

Public journalism places the group or the community ahead of the individual. It places obligations ahead of rights for the press. It comprises a theory that enthrones a common normative ethics of journalism that promotes positive and helpful news, that scorns negative and divisive journalism, that makes the public and not the media the agenda setter, that calls for accuracy and thoroughness in reporting, that seeks universal solidarity, and that denies the concept of the press as a fourth estate or government watchdog. It is indeed a healthy trend.

RESPONSE

Dennis: Civic or public journalism is an unhealthy trend for the media.

My colleague John Merrill challenges me to rain on a parade that is much discussed in American journalism today, one that arguably tries diligently to improve the quality of public affairs news. I've attended sessions of the communitarianism movement led by the eminent sociologist Amitai Etzioni, and I know that this is a genuine effort to create more civic awareness and to improve the lives of all people. That's a worthy endeavor for everyone in the community. But whether this is a function of journalism is another question altogether. Professor Merrill endorses communitarianism rather uncritically and then goes on to mask his arguments for a new journalistic ethic behind the term *communitarianism*, which is used mostly by pretentious folks in academia and a few community activists; then he shifts gears and moves on to the so-called journalistic movement more often represented in public or civic journalism. This somewhat evangelical effort to change the way newspapers and television stations report on local communities got early support in the work of the Project on Public Life and the Press at New York University, which was originally identified with journalism professor Jay Rosen (*What Are Journalists For?* 2000) and editor Davis Merritt (*Public Journalism and Public Life*, 1995). Public journalism was played out over several years (1992–2004) in election coverage when newspapers in Charlotte, North Carolina, and Wichita, Kansas, agreed to take part in a project that resulted in more issue-oriented election coverage. Studies of the experiment by researcher Philip Meyer found that people read stories that push candidates toward positions on issues that the newspaper thinks are important. And quite consistently, the Pew Center for Civic Journalism has provided support and publicity for public journalism efforts in scores of newspapers and broadcast stations. Some Websites also proclaim an interest in civic/public journalism.

Three major foundations—Kettering, Knight, and the Pew Charitable Trusts—have provided funding for civic/public journalism, both in the academy and at news organizations. These and some other civic journalism advocates often seemed to march lockstep toward a new journalistic ethic that urged the media to get more involved in their local communities, to *join the parade,* as one critic put it, and help frame and solve community problems. Many in the newspaper industry, terrified that their medium is dying, have gotten on the bandwagon too and have mostly uncritically embraced public journalism as just the right medicine for their troubled industry. This is rather like a patient with incurable cancer grabbing onto any potential cure because there is little to lose anyway. I think that the death of the newspaper industry is grossly exaggerated and that its future depends on a mix of ink on paper and electronic delivery modes with greater interactivity between media people and the public. I doubt that content per se is the real problem behind declining newspaper circulation. People aren't rejecting what they get in newspapers; they are simply finding it more efficiently and often in better form on television (McGill and Szanto, 1995). This is, I believe, the fundamental flaw of the public journalism movement: assuming that better content will save newspapers as we now know them. Of course, I'm supportive of anything that purports to improve the press, no matter how remote its ultimate success might be.

But wait. There is yet another problem with the public journalism/civic journalism/communitarian movement: It changes the basic function of the journalist. For decades, social workers have advocated community organization to mobilize the resources of a community in solving a particular social problem, whether health care delivery, drug prevention, or something else. Here, public and private agencies join together to solve problems and develop public policy. That's fine for social workers and for government agencies and private sector interests. It is not fine for journalists, whose job is to cover the news and to report it as impartially as possible. As former *Newsday* editor Howard Schneider put it, "Our job is to cover the parade, not to be in the parade" (*The Cronkite Report,* Discovery Channel, March 22, 1995). The public journalism movement, which really is not a movement for reasons I will detail later, is a traveling road show that urges journalists to become activists and to cast their lot with solutions to problems of public life, to become part of the formulation of public policy by identifying worthy topics and by covering them in four-part harmony. The result is news decisions based on what a newspaper's editorial page thinks should happen or, worse yet, on decisions from its promotion department. This critique is supported by *Washington Post* executive editor Leonard Downie, who says, "Too much of what's called public journalism appears to be what our promotion department does, only with a different kind of name and a fancy evangelistic fervor" (Rosen, 1994, 14).

A decade after it burst on the journalistic scene, civic journalism now has less currency. First, relatively few news organizations have embraced it with any gusto. The major news media still keep a respectful distance with some important regional papers and large chains sounding praise for various and often conflicting reasons. The Wichita, Akron, Charlotte, and Seattle papers are among the largest early adopters, but editors at the *Philadelphia Inquirer* and *Washington Post* have denounced it. An explosive public journalism "case study" played out at the *St. Louis Post-Dispatch* where a leading and controversial advocate of civic journalism, Cole Campbell, was appointed editor in 1996. Campbell tried to implement a regime of civic journalism but hit many roadblocks, including staff upheaval. He resigned in April 2000 after what many described as a "bumpy ride," but had truly tested out some of civic journalism's main notions and made an effort to fully reorganize the newsroom to that end.

Indeed civic journalism's luster is gone and where it exists, the work proceeds rather seamlessly and without much fanfare. Some of its advocates would argue that it has thus achieved a measure of success and certainty, and it is much lionized in the universities as a new ideology for journalism. Perhaps smarting from the legitimate criticism that civic journalism had no real definition, at least not a rigorous one, a spate of books tried to remedy that without much agreement. In 2003, however, a group of academics and journalists formed a Public Journalism Network (PJNET) at a meeting at Kennesaw State University. There they produced a "Declaration for Public Journalism," which articulated a set of principles aimed at "strengthening the relationship between journalism and democracy." The principles were bland compared with the provocative critique that public journalism offered in the mid-1990s and, indeed, pretty much reiterated longstanding journalistic standards and those of so-called community journalism. The Kennesaw Declaration, in my opinion, pretty much threw in the towel as it tried to change public journalism's more contentious image, the one that inspired rejection in so many quarters.

Some of the principles enunciated, however old and shopworn, bear repeating and civic journalism's emphasis on listening to the audience—good advice in the age of digital interactivity—makes good sense. So too does the commitment to truly understanding communities, though this is simply a replay of what every community journalism book since the 1930s has been preaching—a clever way, I think, to embrace traditional values and let any rancor over civic journalism slip away. Certainly the media should cover, analyze, interpret, and editorialize on the important issues and problems of the day, but to *do* something about it makes the journalist a player, an activist, an advocate, and possibly even a propagandist.

No, let's leave that for the elected leaders of the community and for those who represent large institutions and interests. Once the press buys into a given community solution, it takes on a conflict of interest and no longer has a legitimate franchise to criticize. And, worse yet, public confidence in the press as its representative rather than partner in a public policy venture is lost. At stake here is credibility. There are many ways to improve journalism, an effort that is worthy and important, but this is a bad idea, and people ought to step up to the plate and say so.

ARGUMENT SUMMATION: *Civic or public journalism is an unhealthy trend for the media.*

Communitarianism is an academic description of a proposed public philosophy that exists in journalism more often under the banners public or civic journalism and urges the press through its coverage and community to become engaged in solving community problems. This confuses journalism with community organization, a social work concept. Flaws in the public journalism argument are (1) assumptions that better and more engaged content will stave off circulation declines for newspapers, for which there is no good evidence, and (2) that journalists should be activists taking positions on community issues, which would lose them any claim to impartiality. At the same time, credibility is sacrificed. The journalist should cover the parade, not march in it. Civic journalism seemed to peak in the late 1990s and today's version is a rather bland commitment to traditional journalistic values along with a call to action to cover local communities more thoroughly.

SEARCH ONLINE!

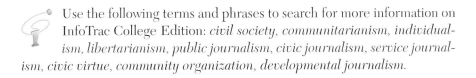 Use the following terms and phrases to search for more information on InfoTrac College Edition: *civil society, communitarianism, individualism, libertarianism, public journalism, civic journalism, service journalism, civic virtue, community organization, developmental journalism.*

TOPICS FOR DISCUSSION

1. How would the concept of communitarianism change the role of the media, and what would be different in newspapers, in magazines, and on television if this were the case?

2. Is there really a difference between a people-based journalism and a journalist-based journalism?
3. Why has the public journalism debate stirred such controversy in American media circles?
4. How do the principles articulated in the 1947 Hutchins Commission Report relate to the communitarian movement and its applications to the press?
5. What are the motives behind those who promote civic and public journalism? And what are the motives of their detractors?

TOPICS FOR RESEARCH

1. Trace the development of the communitarian movement from the Enlightenment philosophers to the present. What are the main ideas expounded and how have they changed or matured?
2. Compare examples of public journalism with more traditional public affairs reporting.
3. Do a survey of local media in your community or state to determine how they feel about public/civic journalism and whether they practice it.
4. Consider the proposition that civic/public journalism failed to meet its promise and is now a marginal effort, hardly a social/journalistic movement, or that civic/public journalism achieved many of its aims and is now so integrated into standard journalistic practices and goals that it no longer sparks controversy.
5. Compare the major assumptions of civic journalism with the traditions of objectivity. How does civic journalism differ from advocacy journalism, if it does?

FURTHER READING

Christians, Clifford, John Ferre, and P. Mark Fackler. *Good News: Social Ethics and the Press.* New York: Oxford University Press, 1993.
Clark, Roy Peter, and Cole C. Campbell, eds. *The Value and Craft of American Journalism.* Gainesville: University of Florida Press, 2000.
Corrigan, Don. *The Public Journalism Movement in America: Evangelists in the Newsroom.* Westport, CT: Greenwood, 1999.
Dennis, Everette E., and Robert Snyder. *Media and Public Life.* New Brunswick, NJ: Transaction Press, 1998.
Etzioni, Amitai. *The Spirit of Community: Rights, Responsibilities and the Communitarian Agenda.* New York: Crown, 1993.
Fallows, James. *Breaking the News: How the Media Undermine American Democracy.* New York: Pantheon, 1996.
Gans, Herbert. *Democracy and the News.* New York: Oxford University Press, 2003.

Glasser, Theodore L., ed. *The Idea of Public Journalism.* New York: Guilford Press, 1999.

Janeway, Michael. *Republic of Denial: Press, Politics and Public Life.* New Haven, CT: Yale University Press, 2000.

Lambeth, Edmund, Philip Meyer, and Esther Thorson. *Assessing Public Journalism.* Columbia: University of Missouri Press, 1998.

McGill, Lawrence, and Andras Szanto. *Headlines and Sound Bites: Is That the Way It Is?* New York: Freedom Forum Media Studies Center, 1995.

Merrill, John, Pester Gade, and Fred Blevens. *Twilight of Freedom: The Rise of People's Journalism.* Mahwah, NJ: Erlbaum, 2000.

Merritt, Davis. *Public Journalism and Public Life: Why Telling Stories Is Not Enough.* Hillsdale, NJ: Erlbaum, 1995.

Perry, David K. *Roots of Civic Journalism: Darwin, Dewey and Mead.* Lanham, MD: Rowman and Littlefield, 2003.

Public Journalism Network, January 2004 update of Kennesaw Summit, at www.kennesawsummit.kennesay.edu.

Rosen, Jay. "Public Journalism," *Editor and Publisher* (12 November 1994): 14.

Rosen, Jay. *What Are Journalists For?* New Haven, CT: Yale University Press, 2000.

Schudson, Michael. *The Good Citizen: A History of American Civic Life.* Cambridge, MA: Harvard University Press, 1999.

Shepard, Alicia C. "The End of the Line." *American Journalism Review,* July/August 2000.

DIGITAL STRATEGIES: THE INTERNET AND NEW MEDIA

Just how the media, their various outlets, and their employees fashion a digital strategy to take advantage of the Internet and other related and associated New Media outlets is in play. Every media company is coping with the digital world, whether adapting to it or leading with new media products, and they've all come through a major period of adjustment since 2000. That was the year of the dot-com crash in the stock market, which sent shock waves through media companies. Many saw their stocks plummet and their investments shaken. Some major executives were fired and many companies tightened their belts and viewed the digital world with wary eyes. By 2004, they had mostly recovered and were exploring ways to harness the Internet and other New Media in an effective way, but many were still risk averse and not experimenting as they had a few years before. Meanwhile many of the early independent entrepreneurs who had launched Web-based companies went out of business altogether or scaled down. In the midst of all this, however, the once singular search engines like Google and Yahoo came into their own as media organizations, not just delivering content but creating it too.

Although it made its debut years earlier as a technology project funded by the U.S. Department of Defense, the Internet was unknown to most Americans until the mid-1990s when high-speed personal computers and efficient software opened this network of networks to ordinary citizens. With the help of browsing software and information portals, the Internet was hailed for its massive capacity for information storage and retrieval, easy accessibility, and interactivity, or instant feedback. Never before had such a marvel existed and its impact was almost immediate as its users rose from under 10 percent of the adult population in 1995 to an estimated 66.5 percent in 2004, or some 218 million Americans. Most people use the Internet for personal communication through e-mail, e-commerce, and access to information.

For traditional and new media organizations the Internet is both a hedge against old technologies (such as printing and broadcasting) and a platform of its own. At first, those who worked in or used old media—the traditional print and electronic mass media—were wary of the Internet, but then they used it as yet another outlet for news, entertainment, and advertising. Most media companies, newspapers, broadcasters, cable organizations, and all manner of media outlets developed Websites and began delivering all or part of their content digitally. New media companies, the so-called dot-com entrepreneurs of Silicon Valley (California) or Silicon Alley (New York), initiated start-up information and news sites that were intact, free-standing businesses, often without the support of conventional media firms. The traditional mass media that have attempted to reach as many readers and viewers as possible joined with more targeted new media players who sought a particular segment of the population, including those with quite specialized interests anywhere in the world. Old media were largely geographic, aimed at people in particular physical places, whereas new media were demographic, seeking clusters of like-minded individuals with similar interests and passions, much like specialized magazines but with broader reach and genuine interactivity.

After initial skepticism, some leaders of media industries proclaimed the Internet to be the universal information highway and were bullish on its development. They imagined the benefits of interactivity as an unparalleled platform for delivering their content (whether information, entertainment, opinion, or advertising) almost effortlessly and without the costs associated with printing and broadcasting. The new media would be interactive, with instant feedback from consumers as well as a constantly updated treasure trove of information.

New media offer massive storage and users can summon up much more detail and content, all customized for them. Professionals within the media have access to information everywhere and can integrate it into their reports without the barriers of extensive and expensive travel or onerous record searching in courthouses and libraries. For journalism, this means a better platform to reach readers and viewers instantly and a chance for those consumers to respond, thus helping shape information based on needs and interests. In effect, instant market research can be combined with news gathering and dissemination. With various Web links, the new media site can connect its viewers with expert information from its own files and news services as well as sources elsewhere. The news consumer can thus be a true participant in the process of shaping his or her own news reports and, at the same time, have an impact on media. At last there is a chance for better and more harmonious communication between the producer and consumer of news media. This is the realization of the *Daily Me*, a visionary customized electronic newspaper proposed at the famed MIT media lab. The result of the Internet and new media for journalism is resourceful new Websites seeking audiences alongside use of the Web by old media to stand their ground against competition. This can be likened to early auto manufacturers operating alongside buggy factories that also made cars.

For journalism the Internet offers the benefits of speed, interactivity, instant digitization of images, multimedia, and infinite storage of background information. Insiders who think about it know that the Internet and new media provide the wherewithal for better and better journalism. For those not professionally engaged in media, common sense tells them the Internet can only enhance what they've been receiving all along. The prevailing view is that journalism will benefit from the Internet. At the same time, many Internet ventures are challenging and competing with old media. For example, bloggers (for Web loggers) emerged in the early 2000s and have played a profound role in delivering information—and gossip—often at odds with the so-called professional news media operations.

CHALLENGE

Merrill: The Internet and new media are debasing journalism.

The Internet may, as the public journalists hope, help democratize journalism. It may facilitate rapid, broad-ranging communication among people with computers. It may make it possible for a wide variety of data to spread over the world. It may, in fact, make every person an editor. No longer can people complain that they don't have access to the media. Economics (and, presumably to a lesser degree, education) will determine who is a journalist, not special training, interest, and dedication. From one viewpoint the emergence of the Internet is a good thing, but as I see it, the Internet largely debases journalism. In fact, it might be said that it eliminates traditional journalism. In effect, that happened to some degree during the 2004 presidential election. The bloggers, whom Professor Dennis seems to admire, added spice, invective, gossip, and misinformation. Some of the bloggers rushed to publish before they had their facts. They were quite happy to palm off their opinions, however half-baked, on an unsuspecting public and, to their shame, the news media often freely quoted this material.

So what, you might ask? Isn't a new age of partisan media a good thing, an outlet for many views that will ultimately enrich our media? Of course you can't stop it and no thinking person would advocate that. But one can try to assess it intelligently and any such exercise comes up pretty empty. What we have are know-nothings in large part using their microphones to promote their views by masquerading as journalists. Bloggers for the most part are not journalists, but instead unschooled amateurs spewing opinions. There have been numerous times in the recent years when unfiltered blogger information has been genuinely damaging to public understanding, not to mention hurtful to people affected by unsubstantiated claims. The blogger Matt Drudge was one of the first to ply his trade on the Web, getting information out early no matter whether it was verified or not. More recently, blogger Andrew Sullivan, once of the *New Republic,* has carried his gay rights crusade to large audiences on his blog—and in the process seems to have created a one man media company. Nothing wrong with this except that information and opinion are joined as one and it is difficult for readers and viewers to sort out facts from interpretations.

Perhaps in a worst-case scenario, professionally produced news media will be a thing of the past. Sure, we'll have more information to choose from. But we probably have too much already. We'll have more writing—much of it almost illiterate and substantially insipid, contributing little to the enlightenment of the public. Chat rooms are already filled with idle and largely ignorant chatter, signifying little or nothing. At a time when we need more expertise and professionalism in our public communication, we are getting increasing amounts of unverified, unresearched, unbridled information. It is little more than a wider sharing of ignorance, distortion, gossip, and propaganda. Matt Drudge may be more interesting than Walter Lippmann, but I doubt if his type of *journalism* is as socially helpful as was Lippmann's. Of course, the traditional and established media (like the *New York Times*) have their own Websites and provide reliable and professionally produced news.

It is true that the Internet will improve—but this will largely be technologically. It will still be an individualistic, personal, amateurish enterprise. Its basic weakness will remain: people spilling their uncritical and often pornographic and vituperative expressions into the cyberatmosphere. It seems to me that we have enough information presently—in fact, perhaps too much. With the new media we will be submerged with undigested, unedited, and unprofessional expressions better suited for the backyard fence or the telephone.

If the Internet is a new kind of journalism, or an extension of journalism, then the question arises: Are Internet users members of the press? Will they be covered by the First Amendment? Are they, indeed, all journalists? If they are, then we should perhaps stop using the term *journalist*. Of course, *journalism* is already a semantically vague term. We even have advertising education flourishing in schools of journalism. Did you ever hear an advertising person called a journalist? Anyway, the concept of everybody being a journalist is a sobering thought for a person who has spent a half-century trying to teach journalism. If our journalism has weaknesses and often performs poorly, then we should try to create better journalists, not expand journalism to include everybody. Societies need a well-trained, dedicated core of people running journalism—the journalists—just as societies need professionally trained doctors, lawyers, and soldiers.

The Internet and new media are here to stay—no doubt about that. But we shouldn't think of users of the new media as part of the press as they put their self-indulgent scribbles forward. No First Amendment for them. Let them take their chances with libel (if you find out who they are), and let the legislatures pass laws abridging their freedom. Freedom is not a society's primary value—morality is. And people who see the filth and frivolous forms of entertainment on the Internet wonder if it, along with television and the vulgarized magazines, will turn the world into a technological haven of insanity and immorality.

ARGUMENT SUMMATION: *The Internet and new media are debasing journalism.*

The Internet and new media are debasing journalism. They are slipping silently and slowly into the domain of journalism—even calling themselves a part of the new journalism. They even want to see First Amendment protection status applied to them. Many users of the Internet are anonymous personal communicators without gatekeepers to provide some kind of credibility to their outpourings. Others are part of a new generation of bloggers who promote opinion over factual reports. They are simply the new letter writers who, in large part, do not mind their writing being seen by others. They like to think of themselves as expanding the public forum, democratizing journalism, and providing a broad base of public communication. Their unedited utterances and biased communication will sap the credibility from the old media, presenting them as stodgy, overly careful, even cowardly journalistic dinosaurs. The new media will further debase journalism and will, if not curbed in some way, completely obliterate it.

RESPONSE

Dennis: The Internet and new media are strengthening journalism.

Conjuring up the image of an endless army of irresponsible Matt Drudges and other bloggers undermining the credibility it has taken news organizations two centuries to establish, John Merrill makes some good points about the darker side of the Internet and new media. He argues that the notion of "every person an editor," fetching up what they want from various information sources, will herald an end to professionally produced news media that are both sense makers and validators of information. He says we'll have more information but less reliable information, more writing but poorer expression, and so on. As for the chat rooms and other news groups made possible by the Internet's interactivity, he says these will be collections of know-nothings—just the kind of people he would like to avoid. Finally, he argues that the proof is in the product and that to date Internet journalism and its news content have been underwhelming, hardly up to the standards of the old media. He does say that the best of the news Websites are, in fact, produced by old media companies such as the *New York Times* and the *Washington Post*, rather than Bloomberg or salon.com or the hundreds of other news sites. That's true, and although some media companies have companion Websites that simply parrot what's in the paper or magazine, others take you to truly new spaces with more diverse and integrated material. One only need compare the Advance Publications sites (Condé Nast and Newhouse) with those of most other local papers, broadcast outlets, or magazines. And who can decry the enormous success of the *Wall Street Journal*'s WSJ.com, which has garnered some 800,000 Web-specific subscribers, thus demonstrating the commercial viability of this new medium?

Professor Merrill's points are largely valid in the short run, but they overstate the case and allow little room for the obvious development that comes with a new medium. Should television be judged by the black-and-white talking heads on the air in its first years, or cable by the dreary public access programs of its early period? I say, no, that the Internet has greatly benefited journalism by allowing for the development of new media, whether Websites, cable outlets, or so-called Web TV alongside traditional media that have cautiously used it as a platform. Old media have mostly embraced new media via the Internet without risking their well-grounded core business and are producing useful products on the Internet that complement what they are doing with traditional printing and broadcasting. Thus any newspaper, magazine, or broadcast, as well as alternative news weeklies, has a Website that mostly reproduces what they do on a daily or weekly basis. The difference is that consumers can retrieve as much or as little as they like. The reader/viewer can also delve into the archives and pull up relevant stories that are days—or months—old to enhance their understanding. These information services, including hundreds of newspapers and electronic media outlets, are offered free of charge to anyone who wants to log on through Yahoo!, Google, Microsoft Network, or other portals or browsers. A few media, as I mentioned, such as the *Wall Street Journal,* do charge subscription fees, and with their great success, this may be commonplace in the future.

Alongside the cautious old media users of the Internet, whole new enterprises such as *MSNBC on the Internet* offer a vast news outlet produced by its own writers, editors, artists, and photographers—but also enhanced by the MSNBC cable network and its offerings, those of CNBC, the most respected media voice in the financial community, and the NBC broadcast network as well as its affiliate stations. Thus, a vast and complex system of information draws on two cable platforms, one broadcast platform, and the Internet and is more than the sum of its parts. Increasingly, sound and full motion video are being added to Internet sites. Specialized news of business, the arts, sports, and other topics can also be delivered with speed through the Internet services. And whereas there was never much of a market for women's news, there are now several high-profile women's Websites. The same is true for ethnic communities and other special interests who want news tailored to their needs and with emphasis on subjects they care about.

And don't forget the democratizing effect of the digital era. True, some bloggers may be outrageous attention seekers, but many more are serious information gatherers and commentators. Ease of entry to the Internet marketplace makes it possible for them to publish and express themselves. Some of these efforts will become viable businesses or nonprofit enterprises; others will simply wither away or be vehicles of personal media. Perhaps one day we'll truly have a right to communicate and that would augur well for the bloggers and their progeny. I say, let them communicate and let their intended audiences as individuals decide whether the material is valuable or worthless. In the 2004 presidential debates when mainstream media were too cowardly to really assess and evaluate who won and who lost, the bloggers stepped up to the plate. Sometimes they were thoughtful and offered hard evidence, sometimes not. But after the first debate when they weighed in, even the conventional news media quoted them extensively after subsequent debates because they were willing to do what the traditional media would not—take a stand.

For years, media critics have argued that most news organizations offer too little content and with too little depth. Instead of the broad and shallow approach of the traditional newspaper, the Internet can offer a compact news menu followed by as much depth and as many alternative sources as people want. What an advantage!

As for the charge that the Internet encourages unethical journalism, unverified reports, and plagiarism (all of which it does), this only suggests that serious purveyors of journalism online need to emulate the best practices of old media. In fact, Internet journalism has a much better chance of delivering accurate and complete information than does the old system. Fact and source checking is much faster electronically and so is seeking out comparative information from other sources, instantly and with assurance. Just because the sophisticated graphics of even the sleaziest Website may be deceptive does not mean that discerning readers and viewers can't apply high standards to the information they want and, in fact, insist upon.

Once the journalistic community had a near monopoly on the news. The idea of alternative or competitive publications or electronic media was all but impossible technically and economically. During this period the news media became more and more autocratic and arrogant. There was no real competition for most daily newspapers. Now that has changed; the traditional news media can and have been scooped by the new media of the Internet and cable. That and the fact that new media can offer truly viable alternative information continuously and instantaneously have made the old media more vigorous and more competitive. The Associated Press was almost unchallenged for its news reports, but when Bloomberg came on the scene, AP suddenly had a challenger with quality news reports going to radio and television stations as well as print media. That has spurred AP to new heights, drawing on its long history in news and making creative improvements as well. CNN.com, ABC.com, and MSNBC all draw on parent media and compete vigorously to be the most visited Website in the world.

In only a few years, a media system of limited alternatives mostly controlled by a few corporations finds itself in the swim with an infinite number of competitors. This, I believe, will result in better and more thorough news for all citizens, whether it comes from old media struggling to keep up or new media linking technology with information to create better and faster news. In the end, what we now call old media and what we now call new media will converge and there will be one media system with infinite voices and variations.

ARGUMENT SUMMATION: *The Internet and new media are strengthening journalism.*

The Internet is not debasing the media any more than the printing press debased the books of its day. The Internet and the World Wide Web are a remarkable invention that allows easy access to an almost infinite storage bin of information. It also accommodates virtually anyone who wishes to create a Website and his or her own media blog. Thus, millions of amateurs exist alongside professional communicators. This is no threat to the mainstream media that are using the Internet to improve their product and make it more relevant to readers, viewers, and other users.

SEARCH ONLINE!

Use the following terms and phrases to search for more information on InfoTrac College Edition: *digital divide, World Wide Web, Internet, The Drudge Report, New Media, Internet journalism, bloggers, digital media, online services, search engines, information overload, portals, vortals, "repurposing" information, media content.*

TOPICS FOR DISCUSSION

1. Dennis believes that in the future the Internet and new media can provide solid, specialized, in-depth news that the old media have been unable to provide. This was said also about television. But the potential does not equal the performance. Will this be the same with the Internet and new media?

2. Do people need an unlimited amount of information? What about the institutionalized gatekeeping and quality control of the old journalism? Don't audiences need an organized and meaningful view of the world?
3. Can Internet users be considered journalists? Why or why not? If they are so considered, then why should we not eliminate journalism education from our universities?
4. Does the Internet lead to increased knowledge and concept clarification among the public or does it lead to more confusion and uncertainty? Is the new media world one that is gravitating toward one big infotrauma.com?
5. Instead of debasing journalism, does the Internet simply supplement journalism? In what ways does it supplement journalism? One could say that conversations supplement journalism. But certainly conversations are quite different from journalism. Is the Internet also quite different from journalism?

TOPICS FOR RESEARCH

1. Write a paper on the impact of the Internet on media content. What has been its impact on traditional media such as magazines and television programming?
2. Examine the Website as a medium of communication by comparing a network television Website with one from a newspaper and magazine. Do a content analysis of each and discuss their graphic presentations.
3. Write a speculative paper about how a Website can differ significantly from a conventional print or broadcast medium. What advantages and disadvantages does the Internet site have over old media outlets?
4. Do an audience analysis of the Internet, a medium that began at zero in your lifetime and now reaches millions, and soon billions, of people. Draw on data sources, scholarly studies, and other materials to study and critique the Internet audience. How does it differ from the audience for any other media platform (newspapers, television, etc.) of your choice?

FURTHER READING

Boczkowski, Pablo J. *Digitizing the News: Innovation in Online Newspapers.* Cambridge, MA: MIT Press, 2004.

Brown, John Seeley, and Paul Duguid. *The Social Life of Information.* Boston: Harvard Business School Press, 2000.

Cairncross, Frances. *The Death of Distance: How the Communications Revolution Will Change Our Lives.* Boston: Harvard Business School Press, 1997.

Callahan, Christopher. *A Journalist's Guide to the Internet.* Needham Heights, MA: Allyn and Bacon, 1999.

Castells, Manuel. *The Rise of the Network Society,* 2nd ed. Malden, MA: Blackwell, 2000.

Dizard, Wilson, Jr. *Old Media, New Media: Mass Communications in the Information Age,* 3rd ed. New York: Longman, 2000.

Irvine, Martin. *Web Works.* New York: W. W. Norton, 1997.

Kawamoto, Kevin, ed. *Digital Journalism: Emerging Media and the Changing Horizons of Journalism.* Lanham, MA: Rowan and Littlefield, 2003.

Levinson, Paul. *Digital McLuhan: A Guide to the Information Millennium.* New York: Routledge, 1999.

Owen, Bruce. *The Internet Challenge to Television.* Cambridge, MA: Harvard University Press, 1999.

Pavlik, John V. *Journalism and the New Media.* New York: Columbia University Press, 2001.

Schafer, Jack. "Blog Overkill—The Danger of Hyping a Good Thing unto the Ground," *Slate,* January 26, 2005. http://www.slate.com/id/2112621.

Selnow, Gary N. *Electronic Whistle-Stops.* New York: Praeger, 2000.

Shapiro, Andrew L. *The Control Revolution.* New York: Public Affairs Press, 1999.

Shenk, David. *Data Smog: Surviving the Information Glut.* San Francisco: HarperEdge, 1997.

RACE, ETHNICITY, AND GENDER

Drop in at any convention of editors, publishers, broadcasters, or journalism/communication educators and almost immediately the word *diversity* is mentioned. Diversity is a euphemism for race, ethnicity, national origin, and sometimes gender or sexual identity. Currently, it usually refers to race and ethnicity and traces its recent history to the government-appointed Kerner Commission Report of 1968, which declared that the United States was not one but two societies: "one black, one white, separate and unequal." The commission found the media of the day especially wanting—lacking diverse, representative staffs and failing to cover news of interest to minorities. For the next thirty-five years leaders of media organizations pledged to hire more minorities—usually defined as African Americans, Latinos, Asian Americans, and Native Americans. Other large ethnic groups such as German, Irish, or Italian Americans are not usually part of this discussion because they are regarded as already assimilated unlike people of color and are assumed to have equal opportunity. However, questions of diversity also increasingly include gender as women's rights, issues, and concerns have been recognized by media organizations and their critics.

Almost immediately there was an effort to increase minority hiring in news organizations and in journalism schools. The American Society of Newspaper Editors took on this goal in the 1980s and pledged to make their newspapers truly representative, with the same ratio of minority staff members as was found in the general adult population by the year 2000—a goal they failed to reach. Other organizations and groups followed suit and the idea of having racial and ethnic minorities well represented on and integrated into news and other media staffs has become accepted. At the same time, there has been a similar effort to make the content of the press more representative. There had been little coverage of minority communities and no concern about this void; again, leaders of the media urged broader, fuller, and more representative coverage. Like some political leaders, they vowed to make the media "look more like America."

Since the mid-1990s, Unity, a consortium of the several ethnic minority organizations of *journalists of color*, has met regularly to promote common concerns and needs. Unity includes the National Association of Black Journalists (NABJ), the National Association of Hispanic Journalists (NAHJ), the Asian American Journalists Association (AAJA), and the Native American Press Association (NAPA). When this group meets in regular conventions, they typically draw several thousand minority journalists who express their concerns and complaints about the staffing and coverage patterns of U.S. media. Acknowledging progress since the Kerner Report, they collectively express disappointment about progress toward full representation and the extent to which so-called mainstream (usually white-owned and -dominated) media seriously portray ethnic and racial minorities and minority communities.

There have long been women's media organizations, including Women in Communication, the International Women's Media Foundation, and others specifically devoted to broadcasting, cable, and new media. In recent years, women have played increasingly important leadership roles in the major media industry and professional societies, which are mostly made up of men.

In an era in which the term *political correctness* has emerged to describe an ideological commitment to particular positions and policy choices, diversity is said to be politically correct. People who question various diversity objectives are dismissed as uncaring, insensitive, or outright racists. Virtually every formal organization in the U.S. media world endorses diversity of staffing and content, but most also admit that goals set long ago have not been met and that true diversity remains a distant dream. The basis for supporting diversity has always been as an extension of democratic theory that posits that all members of the society ought to participate fully and completely in the processes of democracy. In such a scheme, the press is an important instrument in the democratic process. It also follows that full and representative coverage of society requires coverage of ethnic and racial groups and communities.

Some of the arguments made in favor of diversity are moral and philosophical, positing that it should happen because it is right; others suggest that diversity is also good business because it engages more of society as readers, viewers, and workers in media industries. It is almost universally agreed that diversity is a good thing and that all people of goodwill who are not racists should support it. At the same time, there is a backlash against diversity by white males, in particular, who argue that they are being disadvantaged by quotas and preferential hiring practices which, they say, are inherently undemocratic. But clearly the accepted and prevailing sentiment today is that diversity is not only a good thing, but a noble cause as well.

CHALLENGE

Dennis: Diversity needs rethinking and reassessment.

Let's face it, more than three decades after the Kerner Commission Report, there has been considerable progress toward diversity goals, but not perfection. Although accomplishing a great deal that is good in terms of more representative staffs and broader coverage of all people, much of the diversity movement today merely complains, and that neither advances the cause of ethnic and racial groups nor builds bridges to others in American society who were once sympathetic but are now resentful.

Without disputing the rightful claims of African Americans, Latinos, Native Americans, Asian Americans, or women who were effectively barred from newsrooms and covered in the news only as problems for most of the media's history, it is discouraging to see the rise of a new divisiveness that can only hurt everyone.

Diversity's quiet and often frightened critics, whom I have encountered in the newsroom of the *Philadelphia Enquirer* (where a quota policy for minorities caused white males to rebel), argue that quotas and preferential hiring are inherently undemocratic, even un-American. They argue that equality of opportunity is all that is required with regard to participating in the media workplace, not certainty of outcomes. The critics I have met say that they think everyone should have an equal chance at getting into journalism schools, for example, as well as training programs and entry-level jobs. At that point, they part company with minority critics who say that progress must be measured at all levels—when people are hired, at promotion time, in middle management, and in the executive offices as well. The critics argue that this puts the onus on the employer to give preferential treatment to minorities, while no one stands up for the rights of the majority. Richard Bernstein, a *New York Times* reporter and critic who wrote a controversial book about multiculturalism called *Dictatorship of Virtue* (1994), has described *race censors* and *intellectual intimidation* in U.S. newsrooms that lead to thought control. He argues that "truth and fairness are falling victim to the demands of racial and ethnic self-esteem." In an interview Bernstein noted that top editors at one leading U.S. daily praised staff members who joined minority media organizations with a strong political agenda, but denied others the right to join political organizations and even frowned on union membership. To Bernstein and a few other critics, diversity is a political movement aimed at benefiting a few people who rightly want their place in American life and society.

Bernstein and a few other journalist critics of the practices of multiculturalism and diversity are joined by conservative commentators such as Pat Buchanan and Rush Limbaugh, who say that a new favoritism is sweeping the country and that it will lead to greater divisiveness in which principles of fair play and equal opportunity are lost. Several critics have decried these views as a "civil rights backlash" that would undo what 30 years of progress in race relations have accomplished. The troubling question is to what extent the news media should openly become a political battleground for various groups and individuals arguing the rightness of their cause. Should there be color-blind and gender-blind journalism as the Supreme Court once urged, or color-sensitive, ethnically and gender sensitive journalism wherein the personal agenda of the reporter is on display and poised for action? Author and journalist Ellis Cose, whose book *The Rage of a Privileged Class* (1993) captures the dilemma of successful minorities living uncomfortably in a still white world, writes:

> Journalists, of course, are supposed to be different from ordinary citizens, at least when it comes to confronting difficult truths. But race, it seems, can make cowards of us all. It is not merely cowardice, however, that makes honest racial dialogue difficult. The difficulty also derives from the fact that perceptions vary radically as a function of race—or, more accurately, as a function of the very different experiences members of various racial groups have endured.

The racial/ethnic debate gets more complex when one looks carefully at the different groups that are part of the equation, realizing that although they share some common goals about hiring and media coverage, they also have differences with other groups and within their own group. For example, Hispanic journalists, who often prefer the designation Latino, include in their ranks Mexican Americans, Puerto Ricans, Cuban Americans, and others from the Caribbean, Central America, and South America. This is not one lockstep group but people who generally, though not always, share the Spanish language but little else. Still, as has been the case with European immigrants, groups gather together for political reasons to achieve their goals.

Beyond the broad goals of equitable hiring and adequate coverage of minority communities, questions have been raised about problems associated with racial/ethnic identification among reporters. From the beginning, minority reporters, editors, and broadcasters have argued that they have sometimes been typecast and assigned to limited roles covering their own communities, though this is changing. Some newsroom critics say that one cannot be an advocate for a cause, any cause, and also be an impartial reporter. One critic I know says that sometimes this can be overcome in covering a volatile issue or person such as Nation of Islam leader Louis Farrakhan. Most whites and some blacks in one Chicago newsroom were clearly biased against the controversial leader, whereas two reporters, both black and with a more open-minded outlook, developed stories that pointed up beneficial aspects of the Nation of Islam movement—something that a white-only newsroom could not have done.

Prior to the post-Kerner concern over race in the media, it was rare for any ethnic group to openly push its cause in American journalism, although author Gay Talese, an Italian American, once noted how few members of his nationality made it in American journalism. To some extent the danger in ethnic-specific demands and requirements is said to be a lack of openness to the needs of other neglected groups. And occasionally, there has been open hostility. Some Latino journalists, for example, have openly clashed with gay and lesbian journalists on less than friendly terms, and Latinos often argue that minority hiring almost always means black or Asian. Another problem is the presumption that race is all-defining when, in fact, some minority journalists come from truly dispossessed backgrounds and others are people of privilege. One activist minority journalist told me that some media outlets in the United States only take upper-class minorities out of Ivy League schools or fudge their numbers by hiring international journalists of color instead of those born here. "There is a merging and blurring," he said, and "therefore it is difficult to see any real gains."

Another justifiable complaint: The news media, notably newspapers and broadcasters, are light-years ahead of other media and communications organizations in hiring. For example, newspapers at the dawn of the 21st century claimed that 11.5 percent of their staffs nationwide were minorities; broadcasters boasted a heftier 19 percent in the same year. Even though newspapers have been out front pushing diversity, whereas broadcasting has been largely influenced by government mandates and regulations, this is no longer the case. So some newspaper executives believe that these figures will eventually even out—or that print might edge ahead. Magazines don't keep statistics about their racial and ethnic numbers and neither, it seems, do advertising and public relations organizations, all of which are said to lag well behind the news media. As recently as November 2004, media executives in a large multinational company admitted that they were unable to seriously recruit substantial numbers of minorities—or promote women with any sense of urgency—though they said they were trying.

It is important, I believe, not to run too far afield in talking about diversity. Of course, as my colleague John Merrill will assuredly argue, there are all kinds of people who are genuinely left out or discriminated against, including youth, the elderly, people from certain countries and regions of the United States, and so on. Rural people complain that they can't get a break in urban media organizations; former prison inmates say they too confront lifelong prejudice. Enough. While conceding that all these claims may be worthy and warranted, that's not a good way to address the necessarily more focused and prioritized aspects of diversity. To try to embrace everything and everyone at once is a recipe for failure.

Thus, I believe that lockstep assumptions about diversity are misguided, if not wrong. All hail the progress that has been made and the principles underlying those achievements, but we must be careful not to have a litmus test for multiculturalism or diversity wherein all people in the media have to hold the same views. Let's recognize that minorities can also be intolerant and engage in racial censorship in what ought to be a free and open society in which the media are conduits for democracy, not the instruments of groupthink. The media may be guilty, both in their professed (though not often achieved) hiring policies and coverage patterns, of shutting down debate and driving honest differences and perhaps open racism underground. Even racism in the open is preferable to censorship, because honest debate and persuasive arguments can improve the racial and cultural climate for all people everywhere. And, of course, there is something wrong in using the quest for diversity to ignore real differences. Granted, there needs to be greater ethnic, racial, and gender representation in the media work force and in patterns of coverage, but this will only come if differences, rather than similarities, are recognized. Different racial and ethnic groups have different cultures, interests, and values. Native Americans are virtually ignored in the diversity quest, and often Asian Americans are left out of media diversity programs in an out-of-sight-out-of-mind fashion, even though they too are grossly underrepresented in the media.

Some serious rethinking is in order—and it must begin by rejecting the victim-oriented approach of the past and replacing it with dynamic and focused planning for change. Only then will real change come.

ARGUMENT SUMMATION: *Diversity needs rethinking and reassessment.*

Diversity, which translates into equal opportunity and better coverage of minority and female Americans in the news media, may be undermining its own cause through various excesses. Diversity may turn into divisiveness, instead of producing a more civil and humane society. The media should be open and should foster diversity in staffing and in news coverage, but this should not be mandated or prescribed in such rigid fashion that it becomes unfair behavior itself. Diversity efforts in the past have led to many achievements in the staffing of U.S. media organizations and much more is still needed. The same is true for diverse, multicultural news coverage. The main focus now ought to be on careful assessment of major areas of needs and deficiencies, especially in and among media that have not been successful in diversity efforts. All citizens and media people should guard against intolerance.

RESPONSE

Merrill: Diversity does not need rethinking and reassessment.

Let me say that I don't really know just what diversity in the news media means. Dr. Dennis has limited the term mainly to racial categories, namely whites (European Americans) and blacks (African Americans). Of course, there are Hispanics, Asian Americans, and Native (Aboriginal) Americans to be considered, along with a conglomeration of other diverse types. Just how diverse news media staffs should be is, indeed, a big and important question. What about handicapped persons (physically disadvantaged)? What about older people? What about former prison inmates? What about street people? What about Pentecostals, Quakers, Mormons, Baptists, Roman Catholics, Muslims, Hindus, Buddhists? Should all these and many other groups be represented in American newsrooms? And to what degree?

As has been pointed out, there has been considerable progress in diversification of news media staffs since the Kerner Report in 1968. But some groups still maintain that U.S. media are too white owned and dominated. A large segment of the public also believes that minority and ethnic communities are not adequately represented among media agenda setters and reporters. This perhaps explains why the reader of newspapers and magazines finds that they basically present a white world. And a male one at that. Ellis Cose (*Media Studies Journal,* Summer 1994, p. 8) gives a good example of this:

> Today, though we live in a world (as we constantly remind ourselves) that is increasingly multicultural, much of conventional journalism remains fixated on the lives of the white and the wealthy. I was reminded of that earlier this year, when my issue of *New York* magazine arrived. It featured an article that purported to identity the best places to find any number of products and services one might search for in New York City. I was struck by the fact that in a city that is a virtual United Nations—it is said that more than 119 languages and dialects are spoken in New York—practically every face attached to the magazine's recommendations was white. Clearly, New York, as viewed by the magazine's editors, remains a very white place.

A look into most newsrooms of the United States will disclose that European American males dominate, especially in the higher administrative ranks. Let us admit that the rational basis for diversity in the newsrooms is suspect, as Dr. Dennis has said in his *Challenge.* Admittedly there is no real evidence that an African American can, because of his or her color, report—even on racial issues—any better than a white reporter. Nevertheless, greater diversity is a worthy goal in journalism and one to which most American journalists have always paid lip service. The journalist diversity in the media is improving, but is still inadequate.

Diversity is one of the valued principles of American journalism. The greater the diversity of ideas and informational perspectives, the better the news package—this is a widely held belief. Well, why not apply this to the racial, gender, and ethnic makeup of news staffs? A story written by an African American, for instance, may be no better written than one by a European American, but at least it will provide a different angle, viewpoint, perspective, or emphasis. Or at least there is a good chance that it will. Reporters and editors reflect their various cultures—their upbringing, their religion, their values, and their experiences.

Most often, the culture reflected in the media is a white culture—and a middle-class white culture at that. As of 2000 the Bureau of the Census reported that minorities accounted for 30 percent of the U.S. population and estimated that by the year 2050 the population would be 47 percent minority.

No doubt the makeup of media news staffs will reflect this shift; certainly the newsrooms will evidence a much greater pluralism—if not out of philosophical considerations, at least out of economic considerations. And, of course, women are a majority of the population and ought to be treated differently than minorities. Mixing gender into the diversity debate may just diffuse it too much.

I doubt if any reasonable person wants to see what Dr. Dennis in his *Challenge* calls "lockstep assumptions about diversity"—quotas, for instance. But an evolutionary and natural assimilation of many cultural and racial groups into journalism is a worthy goal. And as more and more diverse groups get larger representation in our journalism and communications schools, this natural assimilation into the media is, indeed, taking place.

Forced diversity may, as Dr. Dennis says, be leading to divisiveness in our media. But a white-dominated media system also results in divisiveness. This is really the nature of any institution, especially the press. Divisiveness is natural, to be expected—and a certain amount of it is perhaps good for journalism.

Stuart Silverstein, a writer for the *Los Angeles Times*, once wrote that because minorities have been targets of the "angry white male" backlash, some companies have scrapped diversity training sessions. Other companies run diversity programs "out of economic self-interest, predicting that the initiatives will help attract talented workers, reduce turnover and unleash creativity." This is undoubtedly the case; there are many more black journalists—in print and in broadcasting—than there were 10 to 20 years ago.

Multiculturalism in our society must be reflected (but to what degree, I don't know) in the media that reflect and interpret our society. Therefore, we need more diversity in our news media. Preferably it will come naturally and if it does, it will not be equal; some races, sexes, groups will be larger than others in the makeup of the staff. If it is somehow forced, then we will have a tightly controlled, mathematically determined, highly regimented journalism, and few Americans would want that. For example, if 5 percent of a town's inhabitants were lesbians, few people in their right mind would insist that 5 percent of the town's newspaper staff should be lesbians.

I would say that diversity in the news media is still a great failure. We have too little of it. At any rate I think we need more diversity of all kinds in our news media: conservatives, moderates, liberals, socialists, libertarians, radicals, communitarians, and individualists—as well as well as racial, gender, and cultural *rainbow* representations. In all of this, however, we must remember that freedom is also an important concept for the news media; they should have diversity, but they should bring it about freely with no coercion from outside sources.

Some readers may think that I am weak willed in my dedication to diversity. Not so. I am all in favor of justice (if we can find out what it is), but I don't want anyone to *force* me to be just. As a newspaper editor, I may want diversity on my staff, but I don't want anyone to *force* me to have diversity.

My newspaper may make great efforts to have diversity; your newspaper may not. This, in one sense, is adding to the equation another kind of diversity: some staffs with diversity and some staffs with little diversity.

ARGUMENT SUMMATION: *Diversity does not need rethinking and reassessment.*

Although diversity within the staffs of the news media—at least the kind of diversity that will please everyone—is perhaps impossible to achieve, there is still much that can be done. Media practitioners are still mainly white Anglo-Saxon males, and this is especially true in the higher echelons of media institutions.

One of the basic value tenets of American journalism is pluralism—the idea of a great variety of news and ideas making their way into the media. People pluralism should also be valued, and as large a diversity of people as possible should be found on news staffs. This, however, should be a natural and voluntary process, one that is not forced upon a news medium by any outside force. One does not correct one problem in the media (lack of diversity) by instituting another problem (restriction of press freedom). Voluntary inclusion or self-determined diversity by the media themselves is the correct answer.

SEARCH ONLINE!

 Use the following terms and phrases to search for more information on InfoTrac College Edition: *diversity, minorities, ethnicity, race, race relations, human rights, representation, mainstreaming, political correctness, multiculturalism, minority communities, diversity in hiring, diversity in content, pluralism, market segmentation.*

TOPICS FOR DISCUSSION

1. What do statistics about racial/ethnic representation in various media fields, such as newspapers, broadcasting, and others, tell us? How useful are these kind of data in keeping track of progress? Are there dangers in relying too heavily on statistics rather than looking carefully at different kinds of media organizations (big papers vs. small) and particular jobs (reporter, managing editor, station manager)?
2. What is the philosophical basis for diversity in the media and how does it comport with the theory of democracy?

3. What were the benefits of groups like Unity and what influence does that group have with media executives and leaders?

4. Who are the most visible and important leaders in the media diversity movement? Are they known beyond their media fields among the general public?

5. When you think of visible minorities and women in the U.S. media, who comes to mind? How many of these persons are quite senior? How many younger? Are some media more likely places to find minority journalists and media executives than others?

TOPICS FOR RESEARCH

1. What did the Kerner Commission say about the news media of its day? To what extent are its conclusions still relevant or outdated?

2. Some commentators argue that market segmentation in the media will benefit minority hiring and minority coverage because advertisers wanting to reach particular segments of the audience will have greater influence. What is the relevance of this to diversity, and what do you think of the argument?

3. Consider doing a sketch history in which you compare and contrast two minority media or journalism organizations at the state or national level. If possible, interview active minority journalism organization leaders in the process, either in person, on the phone, or by e-mail.

4. Consider the following proposition: A journalist or other communicator who is an activist for his or her race, ethnicity, or community can/cannot be fair and impartial as a communications professional.

5. To what extent are the digital age and the coming of an Internet culture contributing to diversity? Can Web-based media correct some of the problems associated with the isolation and disconnectedness of minorities and women?

6. Read a week's run of a leading newspaper. Look for news of special interest to women, African Americans, Latinos, Native Americans, and Asian Americans. Pay attention to photographs and then write a comparative essay citing specific evidence from your study.

FURTHER READING

Bernstein, Richard. *Dictatorship of Virtue: Multiculturalism and the Battle for America's Future.* New York: Alfred A. Knopf, 1994.

Biagi, Shirley, and Marilyn Levin Foxworth. *Facing Difference: Race, Gender and Mass Media.* Thousand Oaks, CA: Pine Forge, 1997.

Cose, Ellis. *The Rage of a Privileged Class.* New York: HarperCollins, 1993. Also see "Seething in Silence: The News in Black and White," in Dennis and Pease, *The Media in Black and White.*

Dates, Jannette L., and William Barlow, eds. *Split Image: African Americans in the Mass Media,* 2nd ed. Washington, DC: Howard University Press, 1994.

Dennis, Everette E., and Edward C. Pease, eds. "The Media and Women Without Apology." *Media Studies Journal,* Winter/Spring 1993.

Dennis, Everette E., and Edward C. Pease, eds. *The Media in Black and White.* Thousand Oaks, CA: Sage, 1996.

Fielder, Virginia Dodge. *Minorities and Newspapers: A Survey of Newspaper Research.* Reston, VA: American Society of Newspaper Editors, 1986.

Gutierrez, Felix, Clint Wilson, and Lena Chao. *Racism, Sexism, and the Media: The Rise of Class Communication in Multicultural America.* Thousand Oaks, CA: Sage, 2003.

Jhally, Sut, and Justin Lewis. *Enlightened Racism: The Cosby Show, Audiences, and the Myth of the American Dream.* Boulder, CO: Westview Press, 1992.

Kamalipour, Yahya R., and Teresa Carilli, eds. *Cultural Diversity and the U.S. Media.* Albany: State University of New York Press, 1998.

Lester, Paul Martin, and Susan Dente Ross, eds. *Images That Injure: Pictorial Stereotypes in the Media,* 2nd ed. New York: Praeger, 2004.

Lont, Cynthia M. *Women and Media: Content, Careers and Criticism.* Belmont, CA: Wadsworth, 1994.

Martindale, Carolyn. *The White Press and Black America.* Westport, CT: Greenwood Press, 1986.

Muted Voices: Frustration and Fear in the Newsroom. Reston, VA: National Association of Black Journalists, 1993.

The Report of the National Advisory Commission on Civil Disorders. Washington, DC: U.S. Government Printing Office, 1968.

Smith, Erna. *Transmitting Race: The Los Angeles Riot in Television News.* Cambridge, MA: Joan Shorenstein Barone Center for Press, Politics and Public Policy, 1994.

Torres, Sasha, ed. *Living Color: Race and Television in the United States.* Durham, NC: Duke University Press, 1998.

Wilson, Clint C., II, and Felix Gutierrez. *Minorities and Media: Diversity and the End of Mass Communication,* 2nd ed. Thousand Oaks, CA: Sage, 1996.

Woods, Keith. *Leading the Way: Making Diversity Real.* Chicago: McCormick Tribune Foundation, 2004.

WAR, TERRORISM, AND NATIONAL EMERGENCIES

What should be the role of media in the midst of war, terrorism, or national emergency? At first blush this seems a simple proposition; the answer would assuredly be to cover the news completely and well so the public can be fully informed and thus able to cope with the situation, whether an overseas war or an act of domestic terrorism. But what should the media reveal and what should they withhold to best serve the public interest? Even in a democratic society, this is a matter of much debate. When should full public disclosure give way to secrecy? Should the government ever forbid publication of information in the interest of national security? What do people really need to know, anyway?

These are important questions and they yield different answers depending on the nature of the emergency—an unanticipated domestic attack, as in the case of 9/11 when the World Trade Center and Pentagon were attacked by terrorists using hijacked airplanes; or a war, anticipated or not, such as the Iraq War of 2003, the Persian Gulf War of 1991, or even earlier wars such as Vietnam, Korea, or the granddaddy of them all, World War II. And in such situations do the rules of impartial reporting hold, or do they give way to a policy of "support our side, no matter what"?

In general, the media in the United States and other democratic states assume that there will be no "prior restraint" of publication; that is, free media can gather information and publish whatever they like, subject to post-publication review should they defame people, violate privacy, or appropriate intellectual property. But in the case of war, even in the United States, where government censorship or intrusion on the free flow of information is only rarely invoked, the Supreme Court in the 1931 case of *Near v. Minnesota* invoked an exemption for prior restraint or government censorship in times of war when the movement of troops, naval vessels, and eventually airpower might be compromised by advance publicity. In times of war from the U.S. Civil War forward, the government has tightened controls over the flow of information from outright censorship to strict rules for reporters covering the battlefield—or embedded with troops, which has been the case in the Iraq War.

Most of the guidelines for the media associated with war have involved clear rules of engagement and identifiable parties. There were visible combatants—"our side" versus "the enemy." In most instances, from the Crimean War of the 1850s to the Iraq War, "the first casualty," in the words of historian Phillip Knightley, is "truth." It simply falls victim in high-stakes wars to a desire to support and defend the homeland. And that's true on both sides. One major exception to this was the Falklands War of 1982, which pitted Argentina against the United Kingdom in a conflict involving the Falkland Islands, which the South American nation sought to recover. For both sides the war was potentially lethal and there was much discussion about how much information should be revealed and in what manner. Departing from tradition on these issues, the BBC attempted to provide a relatively neutral, unbiased report for its respected world service. Almost immediately, the British government cried foul, arguing that the BBC had an obligation to support the British cause no matter what. In the early days of the Iraq War of 2003, there was no such problem as U.S. broadcasters and other media people spoke about "our side" and "our troops." The emphasis was on "us" versus "them," or "our side" versus "the enemy," even though the United States began the war with a preemptive strike against Iraq. Later in the conflict, when prisoner abuse at the Abu Ghraib prison in Iraq was revealed, some critics were livid that the media had made the dramatic revelations. During war there is always a concern that the media do not (or perhaps cannot) express empathy for both sides. Thus our troop losses—casualties and fatalities—are charted in precise numbers while the losses of the other side are covered only vaguely, if at all.

Terrorism has long been on the media's agenda but publications, conferences, and various efforts to guide such coverage were intensified after the attacks of 9/11 on the United States. In 2004, the 9/11 Commission, a bipartisan group that looked into the causes and consequences of that national emergency, praised the news media for immediate and continuous coverage that was said to reduce anxiety and provide the American people with valuable intelligence (of the nonmilitary kind) that helped them decide what to do in their daily lives in the midst of a continuing threat. This eventually became part of the war on terrorism. Although there are no general rules for all occasions, the prevailing view is that more, rather than less, publicity amid war, terrorism, and national emergency is preferable to a regime of censorship that breeds suspicion and fuels fear. Not everyone agrees, of course, and many specific circumstances can be cited in which an exception to this view seems warranted.

CHALLENGE

Dennis: News and information media should be mostly unconstrained, even during wars and national emergencies.

The battle between secrecy and publicity is, of course, a venerable one, dating back to the Greeks and Romans. How much information to impart against what to withhold? With some exceptions, I say the more the merrier. That depends, of course, on a responsible, sensible media and I realize that one cannot talk about "the news media" as though they were a monolith. There will always be reckless, self-serving, even truly hateful individuals who will sometimes do the wrong thing. The question, then, is how much should media policy be based on the worst-case scenario. During the 9/11 emergency and its aftermath, people needed as much information as possible to know what to do—whether to flee from their homes to safer locales. They needed to be fully informed about every detail available, whether from official sources or elsewhere. In the case of 9/11, in my opinion, the media took a national leadership role, with the network anchors and others actually doing what a president might have done in the past. It was nearly three days before President Bush had a comforting and expansive statement for the public; meanwhile, the anchors calmly tried to parse information and make sense of the situation. Eventually figures such as New York's Mayor Rudy Giuliani became national figures as interpreters of the events, but many have forgotten that they were largely unable to do this in the first hours after the attacks. It was news reports integrated from many sources and personal observations, plus e-mail messages and even news from abroad, that initially calmed and comforted the American people.

Given the massive number of information sources, it would have been a fool's errand to try to put a lid on information or to censor what was known about the terrorists and the possibility of subsequent attacks. The media reasoned—rightly, I think—that more information was better and that people could make up their own minds. This prevented mass panic and generally calmed a terrorized nation. At the same time, we miss the point if we think that the 9/11 terrorists engaged in such wholesale killing for anything other than massive publicity. That they killed thousands of people and did extraordinary economic damage, not to mention a very real bruise to the national psyche of Americans, was almost beside the point in their quest to make a statement, to create images of terror that would have fallout everywhere. That's what terrorism is about—harnessing the oxygen of publicity to truly frighten and, yes, terrorize people.

In such a situation, should we be leery of what the media publish and broadcast? Judgment calls will probably always be made by sensitive editors who put the national interest above instantaneous revelation, but in most instances we have generally benefited from full, detailed information presented with dispatch. For example, since 9/11 is it not unusual to get news reports about the location of nuclear plants and their readiness for terrorism or problems in and around the nation's ports, railroads, buses, subways, or other public transportation systems. We've also seen stories about how vulnerable our airports and airlines are—even with intensive scrutiny and billions of dollars in security expenses. Does this do a disservice? Does such coverage play into the hands of terrorists? Only minimally, I think. Much of the information published is already accessible on hundreds of Websites and other expert sources. Thus, in putting the public front row center, the media offer these reports with the hope they will goad the government into action. The same is true for coverage of inadequate troop strength and material support in the Afghanistan and Iraq wars. Does this tip off the enemy and lead to more deaths? No one knows, but the probability that such information will inform public policy and help solve problems seems to trump the fear of terrorists' misusing the information.

The same arguments, I might add, can be used with regard to some provisions of the U.S. Patriot Act of 2001, which restricts the free flow of information and some personal liberties and rights. These restraints on freedom and others on the press explicitly are potentially dangerous, I believe, not so much in the short run but for the precedent they set. Whether the media allow terrorism to control their agendas will determine whether we really have any measure of freedom of expression. As said before, careful and thoughtful leadership is needed in the media community. Of course, there will always be some reprehensible conduct in the media among sensation-seeking outlets and those that are simply lazy, irresponsible, or reckless. As long as we reward such conduct by fueling ratings and circulation, we can expect to see more of it.

Having written extensively about the media and war in other venues and having read most of the war coverage literature, I don't think there is much new to say. In my view, the news media should have the fullest possible access to cover a war wherever and whenever they want. This access should be subject to information about how dangerous an assignment is for the individual and some consideration of the consequences of the coverage for the immediate combatants and the public. Good judgment should prevail. Having said that, I believe the "embedding" of journalists in the Iraq and Afghanistan wars truly compromised media independence. Embedded journalists are nothing new— Ernest Hemingway traveled with troops and even wore a U.S. army uniform in World War I—but in the modern era, being on a leash, constrained to do only what military commanders permit, sets a dangerous precedent and compromises freedom of the press. I have no problem with some agreements between the military and the media, but they ought to be fully transparent, with the news media making the judgment call about what gets published except in extreme circumstances. Military leaders and government officials have shown for centuries that in times of emergency they can't always be trusted. The media, on the other hand, have a long and mostly honorable record of doing the right thing. And in national emergencies, from the assassination of President Kennedy to the Iraq War, they did what some said would never happen— suspend advertising and offer 24-hour coverage for days to serve the public interest. This act of good faith ought to buy a lot of public confidence and a franchise for freedom of the press, even in times of emergency. In an earlier essay, Professor Merrill promoted professionalism as the answer to a freer and more democratic media. Here is a chance to make that work.

ARGUMENT SUMMATION: *News and information media should be mostly unconstrained, even during wars and national emergencies.*

The age-old conflict between publicity and censorship during wars and national emergencies has often resulted in constraints on the media that later are shown to be dangerous to freedom of expression and the public interest. Thus in most instances, even national emergencies like 9/11, the media should be left alone to do their work. Free media have mostly proven themselves responsible and have taken a leadership role in national emergencies, even before public officials get to the scene or have much information to offer. Similarly in times of war, with some judgment calls to protect troops and naval and air operations, the media should have maximum access, subject to good judgment and honest communication on both sides, to carry out their function as the eyes and ears of the people. A few bad apples should not the bushel spoil for the rest of the media in those rare instances in which reckless journalists do the wrong thing. Most do the right thing—and deserve the fullest consideration for the good of society.

RESPONSE

Merrill: News and information media should be constrained, under some circumstances, during wars and national emergencies.

Professor Dennis argues that openness is good and secrecy is bad and who could disagree with that? Generally, he's right and history bears this out, but it only takes minor slippage by sloppy, reckless, or truly malevolent media organizations, some of them lurking on the Internet, to cause great damage. I'm a little surprised that someone who witnessed 9/11 from his base in New York City as Dr. Dennis did would so quickly say "anything goes" to people covering highly sensitive and potentially explosive situations. Although of course I don't want to see government censorship bureaus and the monitoring of everything reporters do, I think there has been some highly questionable coverage from 9/11 forward that can only help the enemy, whoever that is. Terrorism has been likened to piracy because it owes little allegiance to governments and passes easily over and around national borders. Controlling such a menace is daunting and the media also have a role to be vigilant. After all, one of the famous Lasswell functions of the media is "surveillance of the environment," and what could be more compelling and a greater public service than trying to help the citizenry avoid the perils of terrorism? So, unlike Dennis, I'm skeptical that it is necessary to list the locations of all the nuclear power plants and to engage in extensive coverage of their vulnerability. If the media discover this, I think that like any citizen they have an obligation to report it first to the authorities—say, Homeland Security—and only secondarily to publish it. In any case, many of these stories make some great leaps of logic and often assume that less is being done than is actually the case. These stories might be more nuanced than they are.

As my colleague has stated, the 9/11 Commission in its report praised the media in their handling of the aftermath of the disaster, if not its pre-9/11 coverage. That's fine; as we've known for a long time, the news media are truly the masters of disaster, as one critic described radio during dangerous storms. I also believe that the media's role is more than that of providing cold, hard information—that there is a human dimension too. The media should comfort the public, calm fears, and try to prevent disasters and panic. For the most part they've succeeded admirably at that. In a situation in which no one has all the answers and there is major uncertainty, it behooves the media to listen to authorities and to accede to their requests to slow the publication of a story if it can be shown to truly benefit the public. That's why thoughtful reporters often accompany the police on raids, for example, in order to both cover the story and take no chances about tipping off the criminals. The same analogy holds for terrorists and others who perpetrate national emergencies. Responsible information, professionally gathered, should be the rule—nothing less, nothing more.

As for the coverage of war, again there is a long history of restraint on the free flow of information for very good reasons—the lives of the troops, the element of surprise in attack, and so on. At times, in dangerous war zones, there need to be rules both to facilitate reporters' getting information for the public and to protect them from undue harm. The military authorities are in a position to have superior information and access to intelligence that will ultimately benefit the public in determining what happened. Done properly and well, compacts between the press and the military as well as the diplomatic corps are essential to assure full and accurate information. Of course the press should be vigilant in not being misled or deceived; that's always part of the reporter's antenna, and ought to be.

Professor Dennis's crabbed view of the embedded reporters is simply silly. They can choose not to go. They go with the troops to be closer to the action and to actually get a more human, and yes, more empathic, sense of the action on the ground as it affects the people in combat—on both sides, I'd add. I think, though, that is it is difficult to have neutral reportage from a war zone. The reporters most interested in being there are generally from the country or countries involved and are covering the action from the point of view of their side of the action. The same is true on the other side; Arab networks such as Al-Jazeera, for example, demonstrate this quite well. I do agree with him on neutral reportage in the sense that sometimes neutral parties during a war can offer a more balanced view for the long haul. However, such parties usually have little interest in being there, so that possibility is often forgone.

My view is that history shows us that some sensible information policies, even constraints, are commonplace during wars and national emergencies and for the most part have not prevented the media from calling things as they are, or were, when necessary. Even the eminent Phillip Knightley knows that although the first casualty of war may be "truth," that's a short-term effect, not a lasting one, because historians can always correct the record later.

ARGUMENT SUMMATION: *News and information media should be constrained, under some circumstances, during war and national emergencies.*

The reality of an advanced information society is that the media must cooperate to some degree with authorities to get information when covering wars or national emergencies. There may be good reason to slow or even withhold certain information from the reach of terrorists, for example, as the events of 9/11 and the war on terrorism have demonstrated. Similarly, there is ample historical precedent for certain restrictions on the media in time of war. These range from battlefield rules on information access and publication to the embedding of troops under military supervision. Historically, this has not seriously compromised either the eventual outcome of war or an honest assessment of it. Nothing is perfect, but the media are necessarily dependent on government and the military for some information during national emergencies and wars, and sensible agreements among all parties are essential to serve the public interest.

SEARCH ONLINE!

 Use the following terms and phrases to search for more information on InfoTrac College Edition: *media and war, media and terrorism, national emergencies, 9/11 effect, Iraq War, war on terrorism, Patriot Act, unanticipated domestic emergencies, media–military relations.*

TOPICS FOR DISCUSSION

1. What kinds of constraints do the media face during times of war, terrorism, or national emergency?
2. What is your recollection of media coverage of 9/11? What about the Afghanistan and Iraq wars?
3. What exactly is the war on terrorism and what is the role of the media in it, if any?
4. What are the dangers of too much "prior restraint" of publication? Too little?
5. Should there be general rules affecting the media in time of war or do they need to be rewritten with each war?

TOPICS FOR RESEARCH

1. Do a study of media coverage of war, selecting two or three wars for comparison and contrast.
2. Consider media criticism of war coverage: What are its main features and what do media critics see as the main problems of access to information?
3. It is said that 9/11 "changed everything." Did it change the news media in their handling of terrorism and related issues?
4. How do the media cover disaster? What is their role and how well or poorly do they fulfill it?
5. Do a report on images of war and national disasters, considering the way that media cover these conflicts visually.

FURTHER READING

Baum, Matthew A. *Soft News Goes to War: Public Opinion and American Foreign Policy in the New Media Age.* Princeton, NJ: Princeton University Press, 2003.

Clarke, Richard A. *Against All Enemies: Inside America's War on Terror.* New York: Free Press, 2004.

Dennis, Everette E., et al. *The Media at War: The Press and the Persian Gulf Conflict.* New York: Gannett Foundation Media Center, 2001.

Hastings, Max, and Simon Jenkins. *The Battle for the Falklands.* New York: W. W. Norton, 1984.

Hess, Stephen, and Marvin Kalb, eds. *The Media and the War on Terrorism.* Washington, DC: Brookings Institution Press, 2003.

Knightley, Phillip. *The First Casualty: The War Correspondent as Hero and Myth-Maker from the Crimea to Iraq,* 3rd ed. Baltimore: Johns Hopkins University Press, 2004.

Neuman, Johanna. *Lights, Camera, War: Is Media Technology Driving International Politics?* New York: St. Martin's Press, 1996.

The 9/11 Commission Report: Final Report of the National Commission on Terrorist Attacks upon the United States. Washington, DC: U.S. Government Printing Office, 2004.

Norris, Pippa, Montague Kern, and Marion Just, eds. *Framing Terrorism: The News Media, the Government and the Public.* New York: Routledge, 2003.

Palmer, Nancy, ed. *Terrorism, War and the Press.* Cambridge, MA: Joan Shorenstein Center, 2003.

Schivelbusch, Wolfgang, and Jefferson Chase. *The Culture of Defeat: On National Trauma, Mourning and Recovery.* New York: Metropolitan Books, 2003.

Shane, Peter M., John Podesta, and Richard Leone. *A Little Knowledge: Privacy, Security and Public Information after September 11.* New York: Century Foundation Press, 2004.

Sieb, Philip. *Beyond the Front Lines: How the News Media Cover a World Shaped by War.* New York: Palgrave Macmillan, 2004.

Steinman, Ron. *Inside Television's First War.* Columbia: University of Missouri Press, 2002.

Thussu, Daya Kishan, and Des Freedman, eds. *War and the Media: Reporting Conflict 24/7.* Thousand Oaks, CA: Sage, 2003.

Zelizer, Barbie, and Stuart Allan. *Journalism after September 11.* New York: Routledge, 2002.

Journalism as a Profession

Although scholars and practitioners debate over what constitutes a profession, most journalists believe that journalism is a profession. There is a Society of Professional Journalists. Journalism is included in various standard listings of professions in the United States. Even the most rigorous critics and scholars studying professional ethics include journalists in their discussions. Efforts to enhance the professionalization of journalists abound in seminars, workshops, codes of ethics, and other activities. Although it is said that freedom of the press, as guaranteed by the First Amendment, prohibits the control or licensing of journalists, newspapers still strive toward professionalism.

Clearly, journalists like to be associated with professionalism and they see no particular advantage in being members of a trade or a simple vocation. Professionalism is associated with competence, with training, with a body of knowledge, with standards of evaluation and improvement. At the same time, with the rise of new media virtually anyone can communicate on a Website or create a blog. Some of these people regard themselves as journalists and, short of a licensing system, which would seem unconstitutional, who is to say they are not? The plethora of new media outlets, from Websites to newsletters and scores of cable channels, has greatly increased the number (and type) of people gathering information, communicating, and possibly doing journalism.

Is journalism a profession? If it is not, should it be? The debate goes on.

Challenge

Merrill: Journalism is not a profession.

Contrary to conventional journalistic wisdom, journalism is not a profession. There really is not much tradition behind the idea of journalism as a profession. It is of recent vintage. For most of American journalistic history, professionalism was not an issue; if anybody thought at all about what journalism might be called, it was usually referred to simply as a trade, craft, or vocation.

Today the term and concept *profession* has proliferated in journalistic rhetoric—in publications, speeches, and conversations. Journalists generally like to think of themselves as professionals and of journalism as a profession. I recently had a journalism student so emotionally tied to the idea that journalism is a profession that the very idea that it might not be distressed her greatly. "That's the reason I wanted to go into journalism—because it was a profession," she stated with apparent consternation.

Journalists seem to be impressed with the general esteem, respectability, and even awe that surround any organized activity carrying the name *profession*. They have observed that law and medicine, for instance, in being accepted as professions, have taken on an elite image and that their practitioners are generally better paid than most nonprofessionals.

It is understandable that journalists, often intellectuals or pseudo-intellectuals, find the lure of professionalism very strong. It would give them the aura of respectability, of public acceptance, of dignity, of exclusivity, and, at least, the collective psychological comfort denied them if they simply functioned as journalists.

The notion that journalism is a profession is undoubtedly growing in the United States, but individual journalists do not really know what journalistic professionalism entails—what being a professional really means. Even two journalists with similar backgrounds may act in ways that each would consider unprofessional. Even members of the Society of Professional Journalists do not agree in many basic and important respects about journalism and its practices.

Professor Jay Black of the University of South Florida, editor of the *Journal of Mass Media Ethics*, writing on "Professionalism in Journalism," maintains that journalism is not a profession. Summarizing six characteristics of a profession (as provided by Abraham Flexner in 1915) that have served through the years as a standard definition, Black shows that journalism does not have these characteristics. The six characteristics are (1) an extensive and complex body of knowledge; (2) knowledge not only of the *what* and the *how*, but also a theoretical grasp of the *why*; (3) a definite and practical goal; (4) agreement with other professionals about the ends to be served and about education necessary for practice; (5) common criteria or standards for practice—agreed upon entrance requirements; and (6) a motivation that is altruistic, not self-enhancing or based on a profit motive.

Dr. Black concludes that "clearly journalism falls short of being a full-fledged profession on several counts" (*World Media Report*, Spring 1987, 13–15). Admittedly, some of Flexner's criteria for a profession are rather vague, but they are helpful. The observer looking at American journalism today can see very easily that journalists really do not have a single identity, nor do they share the same values, nor do they have a common definition of their role.

Originally *profession* meant simply the act of professing; it has developed from that fundamental concept to mean, according to the *Oxford Shorter English*

Dictionary, the "occupation which one professes to be skilled in and to follow . . . a vocation in which professed knowledge of some branch of learning is used in its application to the affairs of others, or in the practice of an art based upon it."

Even now, professionals profess; they profess to know better than others the nature of certain matters, and to know better than their nonprofessional clients what they need to know and in what proportion they need to know it. Professionals claim the exclusive right to practice, as a vocation, the arts that they profess to know.

Sociologist William J. Goode insists that professionals constitute a homogeneous community whose members share values, identity, and definition of role and interests. He has said that members of a profession "are bound by a sense of identity" and "share values in common." The Bureau of Labor Statistics lists these requirements for a profession: (1) prescribed educational standards; (2) licensing; and (3) enforcement of performance standards by the profession itself.

Here are some other characteristics of a profession that are given in the influential *The Professions in America* (Lynn, 1965):

A member of a profession is expected to think objectively and inquiringly about matters that may be, for the outsider, subject to "orthodoxy and sentiment which limit intellectual exploration." (Is this true for the journalist?)

A member of a profession assumes that he can be trusted because he professes to have certain expertise that the layman does not have. (Can a journalist say this with justification?)

A member of a profession believes in close solidarity with other members and thinks that it is a good thing to present a solid front to those outside the profession. (Is this true of a journalist?)

A member of a profession is able to meet various minimum entrance standards for the profession—such as a degree in the professional area or a special license identifying him as a professional member in good standing. (Is this true of a journalist?)

A member of a profession is not only certified or licensed but can expect to be driven out of the profession if he or she does not live up to professional standards. (Is this true of a journalist?)

A member of a profession has a code of ethics governing his or her activities in concert with other professionals and submits to a high degree of group control. (Is this true of a journalist?)

A member of a profession participates in a system of rewards (monetary and honorary) for those who conduct themselves most notably within their code of ethics. (Is this true of the journalist?)

A member of a profession shares in a discrete and substantive body of knowledge available to those in the profession. (Is this true of a journalist?)

Based on this list of characteristics, is journalism a profession? Obviously it is not, although it shares some of a profession's characteristics or approaches a profession in some respects. (A donkey, we might say, shares many of the characteristics of a horse; it *approaches* a horse. But we must say quite definitely that it is not a horse.)

There is no direct relationship between journalists and their clients. A journalist is not a self-employed person; he or she works for an employer. Journalism has no formal minimum entrance requirements; anyone can be a journalist who can get himself hired—experience or no experience, degree or no degree. No journalist is expected (or required) to abide by any code of ethics. No journalist is certified or licensed, at least in the United States. No professional standards are commonly agreed upon and followed by journalists. A person working for the *National Enquirer* is just as much a journalist as a person working for the *New York Times.*

Journalists do not share in common a "high degree of generalized and systematic knowledge." They do not claim the exclusive right to practice the arts (all borrowed from other disciplines) of their vocation. Finally, American journalists do not comprise "a homogeneous community."

Listen to contemporary commentator Irving Kristol: "Even to speak of the 'profession' of journalism today is to indulge in flattering exaggeration. Journalism has not, as yet, acquired the simplest external signs of a profession" (1975, 26).

Even though journalism is not a profession, it can—through increased stress on ethical codes, press councils, peer pressure, licensing of some kind, entrance requirements, and more rigorous standards for journalism education—grow into a true profession. I don't contend that it is impossible for journalism to become a profession, just that it has not yet happened. But I think that it is undesirable that it evolve into a profession.

Philosopher William Barrett, writing about professions, states my feeling very well: The price one pays for having a profession is *déformation professionnelle,* as the French put it—a professional deformation. Doctors and engineers tend to see things from the viewpoint of their own specialty, and usually show a very marked blind spot to whatever falls outside this particular province. The more specialized a vision, the sharper its focus, but also the more nearly total the blind spot toward all things that lie on the periphery of this focus (1958, 4–5).

There appears to be a deep-rooted desire among press people to belong to a select group—a "hierarchical longing within the press," as Lewis Lapham has called it in *Harper's.* It seems clear to me that this tendency, if carried very far, would stamp out unusual or eccentric ideas and, ultimately, also the journalists who embrace them. Lapham wrote that the more the press becomes a profession, the more it will "discourage the membership of rowdy amateurs" and, as it is with other professions, encourage the promotion of people who are "second-rate." No doubt, professionalism would restrict the ranks of journalism, eliminate the nonprofessional from practice, and make the press appear more respectable, at least from the perspective of the elitists making up the profession.

In addition to a loss of diversity, another reason why journalism should not be a profession has been put forward on numerous occasions by James W. Carey of Columbia University: "If journalism were a profession its practitioners would increasingly turn inward on themselves, thinking more and more about their own vested interests and mechanisms for self-protection, and less about their responsibilities to their audiences." Professionals, believes Carey, become ingrown and selfish, with a complacent and arrogant spirit contagious among their members.

I agree with Carey. It would be a pity if journalism, one of the most open, diversified institutions in the country—one that is largely dedicated to public service—were to change into a narrow, monolithic, self-centered professionalized fellowship devoid of an outward-looking service orientation.

So, I maintain that journalism is not a profession and that it should not be.

ARGUMENT SUMMATION: *Journalism is not a profession.*

Journalism is a vocation, an occupation, a craft—but not a profession. It is a calling that is open to all, regardless of education. There are no entrance requirements, no discrete body of knowledge, no elite inner group to depress wayward members, no code of ethics, and no licensing system for journalists. Naturally, journalism resembles a profession in some ways, but it is not yet there. Harper's editor Lewis Lapham was right to view the trend toward professionalization with alarm. He said that the more the press becomes a profession, the more it will discourage eccentricity and innovation, and the more it would encourage the promotion of second-rate people. Journalism as a profession would shrink pluralism and cause journalists to think less of the public interest and more of their own interest.

RESPONSE

Dennis: Journalism is a profession.

Whether journalism is a profession is one of the oldest continuing controversies in journalism. It used to be easier to take sides when the debate was simply whether journalism was a profession or a business. Liberals lined up on the side of professionalism, whereas conservatives liked to see journalism as a profit-making enterprise. But those were simpler times. Today we can look back on a half-century of striving by journalists and journalistic organizations to achieve professional status.

Journalism is commonly regarded as a profession made up of professional communicators, dedicated to professional standards. Journalists themselves believe this, and even some of the most elite of American institutions engaged in the study of the professions consider journalists—warts and all—to be professionals. The Harvard-Hastings Program on Ethics in the Professions, for example, had no problem calling journalism a profession. Neither do such distinguished sociologists as Melvin DeFleur and Herbert Gans, who have contributed mightily to the literature of professionalism generally, as well as journalism specifically.

Admittedly some scholars quibble with this designation, preferring instead to call journalism a subprofession. They would, no doubt, say that the terms *profession* and *professional* are too widely and indiscriminately used in the United States. The commonly understood definitions of *profession, professional,* and *professionalism* vary widely from those who say that a profession is simply a "principal calling, vocation, or employment" to a more rigid view that insists a profession is "a calling requiring specialized knowledge and long, intensive preparation." (Both definitions are found in *Webster's Third New International Dictionary.*)

Most students of the sociology of work, concerned with professionalism, acknowledge that professions evolve. They are not created with all the finishing touches on day one, with their standards and practices intact. Medicine, for example, had little in the way of universal standards or educational requirements in this country until after 1915. Some commentators say that the law did not truly become a profession until the establishment of law schools.

Journalism has most, if not all, of the distinctive marks of a profession and deserves to be so classified. This assertion reflects not a caving in to popular parlance (as with professional actors or professional athletes), but the fact that most of the major criteria that distinguish a profession from a trade or calling are integral to journalistic practice in the United States. What's more, dedication to professionalism is growing in journalism.

Like other professions, journalism shows most of the characteristics of professionalism, with different degrees of intensity. One of the primary marks of any profession (not mentioned in the *Challenge*) is "the kind of work that has for its prime purpose the rendering of a public service." Journalism is, in fact, engaged in a public service—the free flow of information and ideas is at the core of First Amendment freedom in the United States. The press has special protection under the Constitution, not simply to allow newspaper and broadcast owners to make a profit but because, as a matter of law and social policy, we believe that a free press is essential to a functioning democracy. Of course, the press must make a profit if it is to survive, and reporters and editors have salaries and get various ego rewards for their work. But most of them would contend (and with justification) that they render a public service. Certainly law, medicine, architecture, education, and the other professions engage in public service activity and still provide a living for their practitioners. That does not exclude them from the august company of professionals. Under the most rigid definition probably only the clergy, and then only the highly trained clergy, could qualify as professionals.

I accept the standards set out in *The Professions in America* even though they present a rather dated and stodgy view of professionalism. Does journalism qualify under this definition? I believe it does. Can a journalist "think objectively and inquiringly about matters" which by "sentiment and orthodoxy" limit outsiders? Certainly one of the purposes of journalism is to provide an impartial, disinterested synthesis of information. It identifies and explains conflicting viewpoints. This process helps the uninitiated understand what is happening in society without being subject to deliberate bias or distortion. Journalism tells us that a supply side economist says one thing while a Keynesian says another.

Does a journalist have expertise that a layperson does not? Yes, of course. Journalists are experts at news gathering—searching out, assessing, and presenting information; standard definitions of mass communication specify that professional communicators, not amateurs, are required.

Does a journalist have "close solidarity" and "a solid front"? Not in the sense that medicine might, but that is because journalism is so diverse, involving many different kinds of media enterprises and professionals. Certainly journalists are organized through professional societies, unions, and other more specialized subgroups. I can think of few professionals with more solidarity than journalism when a fellow journalist is jailed or when a lively First Amendment issue emerges. Powerful publishers join with lowly reporters to fight a common battle. One of the clichés of the media when a story is attacked or seriously questioned is "We stand behind our reporter."

What of minimum entrance requirements? Although there is no formal licensing, most media organizations do have minimum standards of education or experience before hiring anyone. They can deviate from these requirements if they wish, but rarely do. Increasingly journalists are graduates of professional schools of journalism accredited by a national body that is sanctioned by the government through the U.S. Office of Education. This procedure is not the same as licensing, but there are many other types of conformity and sanctioning within journalism. There is considerable agreement among journalists on a whole range of values and craft attitudes, as studies by communications researchers have shown. It is by no means an *every person is an island* profession.

Can someone be put out of the profession? Not by the government, but certainly by the informal hiring practices of media organizations. Someone who consistently violates professional norms and standards or who is regarded as sleazy by his colleagues may have difficulty getting a job at a reputable publication. A classic case of how the media treats transgressions such as these came at the *New York Times* in 2003 when Jayson Blair, a young reporter, was discovered to have misled his editors—and the public—with stories that were laced with fake quotes or plagiarized in part. This ignited a scandal at the nation's best-known and most respected newspaper. A blue-ribbon committee of respected outsiders and *Times* staff members investigated the reasons why the system for accuracy and fact checking at the paper had broken down. Just as they were preparing their report, the paper's two top editors resigned under fire. The controversy shook U.S. media and a few months later, another scandal was uncovered at *USA Today* where longtime foreign correspondent Jack Kelley was discovered to have faked stories and misled his editors. Again, a blue-ribbon panel was assembled and the paper subsequently sacked its top editor. The point of these two dramatic examples is that there are standards for journalism and clear assumptions about, yes, you guessed it—professionalism.

In another, similar episode in 2004, the CBS News program *60 Minutes* came under fire for using an apparently faked document in a report on George W. Bush's National Guard service during the Vietnam War. In this instance revelations by bloggers had a powerful effect. Dan Rather announced his departure from the network in the aftermath of the controversy, and yet another blue-ribbon committee investigated CBS News and offered a scathing report that led to the firing of one senior producer and requests for the resignations of three other executives. Clearly implied standards are at work, and when they are violated there can be clear consequences. No doubt there will always be an outlet for a disreputable person's work (indeed, Jayson Blair subsequently published a book titled *Burning Down My Master's House*) in the supermarket tabloids or on tabloid television, but not likely at a professionally produced news outlet. Years earlier another media scandal—the celebrated Janet Cooke episode at the *Washington Post* in 1981—caused many media executives to tighten up their hiring policies and develop clear standards for review and assessment. Similarly, the 2003 episodes have led to great soul searching and internal reviews at many news organizations. "If this can happen at the *Times*, one editor told me, "it can happen anywhere." These controversies also had some fallout as a spate of books attacking the press appeared on best-seller lists. Inside the news media, there was much debate pitting the *bad apple* theory against the *system breakdown* notion. When the Jayson Blair story broke, at first *Times* editors claimed that he was simply a troubled, unreliable individual and that his editors bore no responsibility. "How could they have known?" went the cry. Subsequently, however, it became clear that a lack of internal control and vigilance had allowed this to happen and thus it was decided by top management that the executive editor and managing editor of the paper would take the fall with Blair as the newspaper apologized for what had happened. The cost to the *New York Times* was considerable—some four pages of a Sunday paper devoted to re-reporting the flawed stories and, more important, the loss of prestige and the embarrassment of this transgression and violation of the public trust.

Notably the theory of a bad apple versus a system breakdown was also at work in the CBS controversy. No one argued that Dan Rather and Mary Mapes, the producer, were bad people or had deliberately falsified information—in this case, faked documents. Instead, the argument was that the system itself and sloppy practices had been at fault.

Over the years, standards of accountability for media transgressions such as those at the *New York Times, USA Today*, and CBS News have become more stringent—and the consequences have also been more dramatic. In the 1980s, no one suggested that the editor of the *Washington Post* be fired for Ms. Cooke's transgressions. But by 2003–2005, heads rolled—at all three news organizations and at high levels. As for methods of media accountability that help add discipline to the idea of professionalism, there are a few press councils that make public pronouncements and have the power of embarrassment. They provide a voluntary policing function in journalism. Their work is advisory, but it does help guide performance. Journalism has codes of ethics that help define professionalism and assist journalists with ethical dilemmas. On some papers a reporter who violates the code can be fired. In that instance, adherence to the code is a condition of employment. Other methods of accountability that promote professionalism are regular surveys of public attitudes toward the news media, watchdog groups, media critics, and Websites that critique media performance. There is also increasing scrutiny in media reporting on media, led by such journalists as David Shaw at the *Los Angeles Times*, Howard Kurtz at the *Washington Post*, and Mark Jurkowitz at the *Boston Globe*. Programs such as *On the Media* on National Public Radio, *Reliable Sources* on CNN, and a weekly media review on Fox News also weigh in and keep the fires of professionalism burning.

The Editor & Publisher International Yearbook lists several pages of awards, financial and honorary, available to journalists. Some of the most prestigious, such as the Pulitzer Prizes, Nieman Fellowships, and National Magazine Awards, can have a marked impact on their recipients' careers. These awards are given for exemplary performance. Various fellowship programs promote better business and science reporting, coverage of justice, and others aspects of journalism.

The criterion of a "discrete and substantive body of knowledge" is more difficult. Because journalism is part of a system of freedom of expression, it is not possible or desirable to prescribe just what every journalist must know. However, a standard curriculum in the journalism schools includes courses in communication theory, media history, law, and ethics, as well as other substantive topics. It is also generally agreed that journalists should be broadly educated in the liberal arts and sciences. In addition, professional schools have professional practice and skills courses in reporting, editing, photojournalism, and other topics. A substantial literature of journalism includes both scholarly studies and such anecdotal materials as memoirs and media criticism. There are even subfields—journalism history, law, economics, theory and methodology, international communications, media sociology, and others. Each of these subfields has enough of a corpus of scholarship to be worthy of considerable attention by scholars. Journalism studies are also part of a larger literature of mass communication that has strong links to psychology, sociology, anthropology, and political science. Students of journalism have a rich lode to consider if they wish to master the field. Of course, there is no formal requirement that anyone do this. And that to me is always disappointing because many leading journalists are virtually ignorant of the literature of their field and thus doomed (as the historians say) to repeat many mistakes that might have been avoided.

More than half of all journalists in the United States are graduates of journalism schools, and virtually all have at least a liberal arts education. Increasingly, some journalists have specialized education or training in such areas as science, law, politics, or the arts. The diversity of journalism in the United States makes the implementation of one single model of education or training impossible. Some professional communicators in broadcasting must hold federally issued broadcast licenses attesting to certain technical competencies.

Fundamentally, journalists must know enough—gained either in formal education or on the job—to function in their work. If they do not, they are fired or otherwise excluded from the profession.

Just because all journalists do not march to the beat of a single drummer does not mean they are not professional. As the sociologist Morris Janowitz has written:

> Practitioners in any particular profession hold differing conceptions of their tasks and priorities. The differences between the "public health" doctor and the clinician is a long-standing distinction that has had a strong impact on the practice of medicine. Since World War I, journalists have come more and more to consider themselves as professionals and to search for an appropriate professional model. The initial efforts were to fashion journalism into a field, similar to medicine, where the journalist would develop his technical expertise and also a sense of professional responsibility. (1975, 618)

That was the *gatekeeper* tradition, which emphasized the search for objectivity. Other journalists disagree with this view and instead say journalists should be advocates for causes and participate in public affairs. This conflict, according to sociologists John Johnstone, Edward Slawski, and William Bowman (1976, 523), "would reappear to pit proponents of a professionalized objective, restrained, and technically efficient journalism against those advocating a socially responsible journalism inspired by some of the same journalistic norms which were the objects of earlier reforms."

Is journalism a profession? The evidence is resounding. Sociological quibblers can find flaws in all of the professions that might put them outside of purist definitions, but this is not reality. Journalism is a profession not because its practitioners say they are professionals, but because it more than meets most of the criteria that, taken together, define a profession.

ARGUMENT SUMMATION: *Journalism is a profession.*

A profession is defined most narrowly as requiring "specialized knowledge and long, intensive preparation" and involving "rendering a public service." Whether or not journalism was a profession when it began, it has evolved (as medicine or law did) into one and deserves recognition as such. Journalism renders a public service by preserving the free flow of information. Even by the dated criteria suggested by Merrill, journalism possesses the objectivity, expertise, and organizational characteristics of a profession. A discrete substantive body of knowledge is required, in that there is an expectation that journalists be broadly educated and there is a standard curriculum in the journalism schools. A uniform perspective of practitioners is not necessary for a field to be considered a profession; many doctors and lawyers possess differing conceptions of their tasks. Sociological quibblers might find distinctions that could put any profession outside a purist definition, but for all practical purposes journalism is a profession.

SEARCH ONLINE!

Use the following terms and phrases to search for more information on InfoTrac College Edition: *professionalism, trades, crafts, vocations, professional education, journalism education, licensing, educational standards, journalist, journalism, newsperson, professional school accreditation, competency, journalistic norms.*

TOPICS FOR DISCUSSION

1. Why do you think many journalism students and journalists want journalism to be a profession?
2. Do you see any real dangers to journalism being a profession? If you do, what are they?
3. Can journalism be as diversified (pluralistic) as a profession as it can be as a nonprofession?
4. More than half the journalists in the United States are journalism school graduates. What would the proportion be if journalism were a profession like medicine or law? Is common education really important for members of a profession?

5. Is a single code of ethics necessary for a profession? Why not have many codes, all similar but differing somewhat? Should a professional code of ethics have *teeth* in it? Who should decide?

TOPICS FOR RESEARCH

1. Discuss the proposition that the public deserves professionalism in journalism. Indicate why, and document your case carefully.
2. Study codes of ethics in terms of their promotion of professionalism. Do they promote professionalism or not? Be specific, and give examples.
3. How do schools of journalism and communication promote professionalism? Does professionalism apply to all areas of communication? Does professionalism apply to all media functions—information, opinion, and entertainment? Discuss and analyze.
4. Compare and contrast journalism as a profession with any other profession you choose. How do they differ? How are they similar? Be sure you consider the role of education, codes of ethics, licensing, and other issues.
5. Some critics say that professionalism is simply a control mechanism whereby owners of the media control their employees. Is this true or not? Is it a good or a bad thing? How do we know?

FURTHER READING

American Society of Newspaper Editors. *What Is News? Who Decides? And How? Preliminary Report on the World of the Working Journalist.* Washington, DC: Author, 1982.

Barrett, William. *Irrational Man: A Study in Existential Philosophy.* Garden City, NY: Doubleday Anchor Books, 1958.

Blanchard, Robert O., and William G. Christ. *Media Education and the Liberal Arts: A Blueprint for the New Professionalism.* Mahwah, NJ: Erlbaum, 1992.

Fuller, Jack. *News Values: Ideas for an Information Age.* Chicago: University of Chicago Press, 1997.

Gerald, J. Edward. *The Social Responsibility of the Press.* Minneapolis: University of Minnesota Press, 1963.

Janowitz, Morris. "Professional Models in Journalism: The Gatekeeper and the Advocate." *Journal Quarterly* 52, no. 4 (Winter 1975): 618–26, 662.

Johnstone, John W. C., Edward J. Slawski, and William Bowman. *The Newspeople: A Sociological Portrait of American Journalists and Their Work.* Urbana: University of Illinois Press, 1976.

Kovach, Bill, and Tom Rosenstiel. *The Elements of Journalism.* New York: Crown, 2001.

Kristol, Irving. "Is the Press Misusing Its Growing Power?" *More* (January 1975): 26–28.

Lynn, Kenneth S. *The Professions in America.* Boston: Houghton Mifflin, 1965.

Mnookin, Seth. *Hard News: The Scandals at the New York Times and Their Meaning for American Media.* New York: Random House, 2004.

Public Agenda Foundation. *The Speaker and the Listener.* New York: Public Agenda Foundation, 1980.

Reeves, Richard. *What the People Know: Freedom and the Press.* Cambridge, MA: Harvard University Press, 1999.

Rosen, Jay. *What Are Journalists For?* New Haven, CT: Yale University Press, 2000.

Starr, Paul. *The Creation of the Media: Political Origins of Modern Communication.* New York: Basic Books, 2004.

Stephens, Mitchell. *A History of News.* New York: Viking Press, 1988.

Strychacz, Thomas. *Modernism, Mass Culture and Professionalism.* Cambridge, UK: Cambridge University Press, 1993.

ADVERTISING

Advertising is both a communication process and an industry that is inextrica-bly linked to mass media in the United States and in some other societies. It is defined in dictionaries as the action that attracts public attention to a product or business, as well as the business of preparing and distributing advertise-ments. According to the American Marketing Association, advertising is "any paid form of nonpersonal presentation and promotion of ideas, goods, and ser-vices by an identified sponsor." Advertising has also been called "controlled, identifiable information and persuasion." Advertising becomes a matter of con-troversy for several reasons. Its role in society and in the economy has often been debated.

Advertising has a well-established place in American life. The component parts of the advertising industry—ad agencies, media service organizations, media advertising departments—employ nearly 200,000 people and generate about $100 billion in gross revenue annually. Advertising is generally accepted by most Americans who recognize that it funds most of the media they enjoy, provides consumer advice, and promotes a capitalist economy. It has been said that American society is a commercial culture and advertising is an essential ingredient in that formulation.

Advertising is a historical reality and one that provides fuel for most com-mercial media in the United States, but there are those who would prefer a communication system without advertising. Questions are frequently raised about whether advertising unnecessarily stimulates needs and wants and whether it encourages class consciousness, materialism, and other values that are not universally applauded. Such discussion is related to advertising's impact and influence in society, assessed by historians, philosophers, social scientists, and media researchers. The social criticism of advertising often centers on whether advertising is truthful. Few critics today advocate the abolition of advertising, but there is an active movement to control this form of controlled communication, presumably to serve the public interest. Special attention has been given to the impact of advertising on children, the portrayal of women and minorities in advertising, and other topics that have generated controversy.

CHALLENGE

Merrill: Advertising is a negative social force.

A principal deity of a capitalist society and of a competitive marketplace media system is the Great God Advertising. The Great God is everywhere, raising its gaudy face across the land, beaming its insistent messages into our offices, cars, and homes. It fills billboards along our highways, drops in the form of coupons from our magazines and mailboxes, blares at us in all of its resplendent redundancy from our TV screens, and fills our newspapers.

The power and crassness of the advertiser are a negative social force. Advertising contaminates our country from one end to the other. George F. Kennan has called it "the greatest evil of our national life." How can we, asked Kennan, have a healthy intellectual climate, successful education, a sound press, or "a proper vitality of artistic and recreational life" until advertisements "are removed from every printed page containing material that has claim to intellectual or artistic integrity and from every television or radio program that has these same pretensions?" (1968, 201).

These are strong words from one of 20th-century America's foremost diplomats. But that's not all that Kennan had to say about advertising:

> Is it a revolution I am demanding? Yes—a revolution in the financing and control of the process of communication generally. And if this revolution brings in the government as a replacement for the advertiser in many of these processes, I still wish for it. The government's commitment and conscience as an educator—its commitment to truthfulness and integrity in communication—may not be all that we could want. But it has at least *some* responsibility here to the public weal, and *some* obligation to keep in mind the public needs. This is more than one can say about the advertiser. (1968, 201–202)

Another luminary of the 20th century, Aldous Huxley, with his exceptionally keen eye for blemishes in social institutions, devoted the whole of Chapter 6 of his well-known *Brave New World Revisited* (1965) to the "arts of selling," with special emphasis on advertising. He speaks of propaganda in the West as having two faces—one (Dr. Jekyll) the democratic editorialist, the other (Mr. Hyde) the antidemocratic person in charge of advertising.

This propagandist—the advertising expert—has a Ph.D. in psychology and a master's degree in the social sciences. Here is part of Huxley's (1965) depiction of this advertising "Mr. Hyde": This Mr. Hyde would be very unhappy indeed if everybody lived up to John Dewey's faith in human nature. Truth and reason are Jekyll's affair, not his. Hyde is a motivational analyst, and his business is to study human weaknesses and failings, to investigate those unconscious desires and fears by which so much of man's conscious thinking and overt doing are determined. And he does this not in the spirit of the moralist who would like to make people better, or of the physician who would like to improve their health, but simply in order to find out the best way to take advantage of their ignorance and to exploit their irrationality for the pecuniary benefit of his employers. Irrational, exploitive, seeking pecuniary profit, manipulating the audience's desires and fears—this is the picture painted of advertisers. These two men have neatly encapsulated the major characteristics and concerns of advertising in the United States. Obviously such advertising is not a positive force in our society.

Mention Madison Avenue and what comes to mind? The thoughtful, perceptive citizen does not have to read a book critical of the advertising business (such as Samm S. Baker's classic *The Permissible Lie*) to feel antipathy toward the omnipresent commercialism that surrounds us all. Coke and Pepsi battle it out everywhere, each claiming superiority, with their slogans couched in abstract vagaries.

Brand X is best by taste test. Four out of five doctors recommend this mouthwash. Discerning people choose this brand. All one has to do is squeeze the toilet paper to know it's superior. My aspirin is stronger than yours. My automobile is like a bird; just watch it here on TV—it actually takes off and zooms into the night sky. Here come all the ads that hawk their products as new and improved. And there is that advertising that insults one's intelligence; for instance, a commercial on television tells us that its product (a cereal) "might reduce the risk of certain types of cancer." It *might reduce* the *risk* of *certain* types. I am not reassured.

I sit before my TV set and, lo and behold, the alleged "positive force" of the commercials strikes me constantly. I learn useful and important things. I learn that "a double pleasure" is waiting for me if I buy a certain kind of chewing gum. I am urged to "come into Kirshmann's Furniture Store and feel the excitement." If "coffee tastes your way," it's X-Brand. If I drink this kind of beer, "the best comes shining through." And I'll get "taste free in every bite" if I'll eat a certain breakfast cereal.

Important stuff. A positive social force. Just knowing that there are double pleasures, the chance to feel the excitement, things tasting my way, having the best shine through, and getting a "free" taste with every bite—now, that's a positive (useful, socially significant) social force!

But all is well, because the "Creative Code" of the American Association of Advertising Agencies (representing at least 15 national communications groups) has determined to keep this "positive social force" intact and progressing. The public, we are told, has the right to expect advertising to be reliable in content and honest in presentation. And the code assures us that advertisers will "extend and broaden the application of high ethical standards."

Advertising, says the code, will not deal in misleading statements or exaggerations; present testimonials that do not reflect the real choice of the testimonial giver; make misleading price claims; make insufficiently supported claims; or present statements or pictures offensive to public decency. I would say that advertising consistently does *all of these things*. If you don't believe it, just take a few moments and analyze the ads that flood from the media.

Even more insidious these days is product placement advertising, in which a bottle of beer or a car you see on a sitcom or a dramatic program is actually paid for by the advertiser. Unsuspecting viewers of a TV show or movie are unaware that every product they see—from toothpaste to clothing—was not picked for any reason other than as fodder for deceptive advertising. There are few places in visual media where the physical objects one sees are not indirect advertising.

Advertising—a positive social force? I think not. Advertising causes people to buy what they don't need, causes people to discard perfectly good merchandise, causes poor people to want things they can't afford, causes the spread of vulgar culture, and creates exorbitant and unfillable expectations, thus promoting a materialistic society.

Here is what media scholar Michael Schudson had to say about advertising:

> Whatever advertising's direct effect in stimulating and making people buy more goods, it fully merits its reputation as the emblem of fraudulence. . . . A great many [ads] are positively informational. But there is a persistent, underlying bad faith in nonprice advertising. I take as emblematic the old McDonald's slogan, "We do it all for you." That, of course, is a lie. (1984, 13)

As Samm S. Baker (1968) tells us, Madison Avenue condones and encourages half-truths and exaggeration. He adds:

> The overwhelming aim of advertising is to make a profit; to serve the public becomes a secondary consideration. A lie that helps build profits is considered a permissible lie.

Former magazine editor Richard L. Tobin quotes Baker in *Printer's Ink:*

> In a single half hour of browsing through magazines I found more than a dozen ads claiming that their products were smoother; longer-lasting; cheaper; better; washed whiter; stayed fresh longer. . . . Are we really suckers that we swallow these pointless hooks?

Perhaps we are not so foolish as to swallow them, but even if they are relatively harmless from that perspective, it still seems rather obvious that such advertising does not serve as a positive social force.

My coauthor Dennis will surely maintain that much advertising is not of that type, that much of it is straightforward and factual, and that it provides a much-needed public service. I must admit that this is true. There is *some* honest information advertising, just as there is some *helpful* morphine and cocaine. But what about the generality? Advertising, *generally*, is not a positive social force; it does more harm to the society than good, and certainly it should be deemphasized.

Advertising is to a newspaper as intercollegiate athletics are to a university. Both advertising and athletics deemphasize the real purpose of their *carrier.*

Neither is perhaps bad per se, but, to quote two old clichés, each has "gotten out of hand" and we have a case of "the tail wagging the dog." A newspaper (a misnomer these days when only about 10 percent of the total newspaper space contains news) reader must increasingly search diligently for tiny oases of editorial material, surrounded as they are by vast deserts of advertising. Even worse is the Web with its streaming ads, pop-up ads, and other nuisances that appear even in editorial copy. Web advertising is new enough to have a frontier quality and it is everywhere trying to claim every set of eyeballs.

I must contend that advertising is not a positive social force. It is simply the economic foundation for the moneymaking proclivities of media owners and the machine that stimulates exorbitant profits by manufacturers, wholesalers, and retailers. And what about political advertising? I won't even get into that. It's too sleazy. But I suppose that three out of four of the nation's politicians highly recommend it. Undoubtedly, 100 percent of media owners give it the *go* sign. This, of course, must mean that it is a positive social force. But that's Dr. Dennis's position. I don't buy it.

ARGUMENT SUMMATION: *Advertising is a negative social force.*

Advertising clutters our media, overpowers serious news and discussion, encourages unnecessary buying, worsens class envy, and leads to wasteful consumption. Advertisements may largely finance American media, but that would be the only way it could be called a positive force. Advertising exaggerates, misleads, appeals to sex and frivolity, gives irrational testimonials, creates exorbitant expectations, and generally promotes a materialistic society. At best, advertising in the United States is a necessary evil. It could hardly be called a positive social force.

RESPONSE

Dennis: *Advertising is a positive social force.*

If the reader were seated in front of a PC, I would create a Website with a selection of advertisements that urge safe sex practices to avoid AIDS, promote literacy, encourage racial tolerance, and promote environmental improvement. Then I would ask the reader to find equally powerful advertisements reaching mass audiences that promote the opposite of these causes and values, or any other advertising that truly does damage to our way of life, fosters racism, or promotes pollution. I think that the reader would have difficulty with that assignment. I might then ask what in the world Professor Merrill is talking about, but perhaps that would be too easy. So, I will respond to several of his protestations about the evils of advertising.

First, a touch of reality. Advertising is a reality. It has been with us since ancient times and has played a particular role in American culture since before the Revolution. It is so well integrated into our commercial media—and that is most media excluding public television and radio—that they probably could not survive without it. No one I know of, not even Professor Merrill, is seriously suggesting that advertising be abolished or even curtailed by legislation. In fact, I doubt that this is possible because it is well to remember that advertising is protected speech. It is commercial rather than political speech, but it is a form of free expression and it has some constitutional protection. With some irony, advertising executive John O'Toole writes:

> *The Pennsylvania Evening Post* of July 6, 1776, contained the text of the Declaration of Independence and ten advertisements, thereby exhibiting a certain insensitivity to a distinction between news and commercial speech that has taken on enormous importance over the ensuing centuries.

Although once accorded less freedom than political speech, commercial speech has gained important ground during the past 20 years, a trend that is likely to continue. So it seems that my colleague, who sees no problem with the free distribution of all kinds of political and social messages and generally abhors censorship, somehow is uncomfortable with the impact and influence of what he calls "the great god advertising." I refuse to capitalize this rather hackneyed expression.

I am not so silly as to argue that all advertising is elevating and socially responsible, any more than I would make the case for all printed, electronic, and digital communication. Some advertising is misleading, unsavory, and generally reprehensible, but the vast majority of it is not, and if one really believes in freedom of expression, we take the good, the bad, and the ugly as part of the package, while hoping, of course, that positive social forces will reward responsible communicators and shun those who are not. In the case of advertising, ads that make fraudulent claims are subject to legal penalties, just as writers who libel others can be sued and thus punished. But that really isn't the point.

To argue that advertising has a positive social impact, I believe that its value lies principally in providing consumer information to the public. Advertising is the means by which we learn about new products, services, and causes. Discerning people look at advertising with a somewhat skeptical eye because advertising is advocacy for a product and there are simply too many products for any of us to know, understand, use, or for that matter, afford. We know that there are many brands of cereal, all competing for our attention. Some will make nutritional claims, others emphasize taste. Probably no one—not even young children—accepts literally everything in an advertisement, even though it may be true, because there is something called *consumer choice*, and we make our choices based on our own needs, interests, income, and other factors. Advertising thus provides an educational service.

Advertising stimulates the economy. One need only visit a country that lacks democracy to see how few products are available. Although it sometimes seems that our materialistic society has generated more products than we need or can possibly consume, if the choice is between the empty shelves of North Korea and the crowded displays in Los Angeles, I know where I would prefer to shop. Of course, our economy does have a wasteful aspect—we have more firms and more products in the market than can possibly survive. Some do. Some do not. And advertising plays a role in showcasing both to the American public. On the positive side, advertising expands consumer choice and promotes diversity. If it were otherwise, someone would have to make arbitrary choices about which products would be manufactured and which ones would not be allowed to develop. In socialist economies this is done by the government. In our system, ultimately the consumers choose, and they are aided by advertising.

And well beyond content, we need to keep reminding ourselves over and over again that advertising is central to the business model for American media. Although some media depend heavily on user fees, most media need advertising to survive.

There is considerable controversy over whether advertising has any real impact on consumer behavior. Some economists and social scientists say it has little or none. Others argue that it is all powerful. Sociologist Michael Schudson, whom Professor Merrill quotes, has some real doubts about the influence of advertising, arguing that "Advertising is much less powerful than advertisers and critics of advertising claim, and advertising agencies are stabbing in the dark much more than they are practicing precision microsurgery on the public consciousness." Schudson also concedes that "advertising serves a useful informational function that will not and should not be abandoned" (1984, 239).

Schudson is among those who doubt that advertising affects consumer choice all that much, but he does suggest that it may affect the goods available to consumers. Consumers are not the only factors to consider. The entrepreneurs want to create and sell products. They can do this efficiently and try their wares on the public—sometimes successfully, sometimes not—because of advertising.

Modern advertising is not the carnival barker of old, nor is it indiscriminate shotgun messages sent out over mass media. It is carefully calibrated and controlled communication. It is aimed at a particular segment of the market or audience. A particular ad, for example, may target only African Americans or only persons in a particular income bracket or with a given educational background. This also encourages diversity and even stimulates the number and range of media organizations in the marketplace. The magazine industry, for example, exists mainly because of advertising aimed at specialized audiences. There are women's magazines, for example, mainly because there are products and services that are for women only. They advertise in *Cosmopolitan or Oprah!* to reach a selected, target audience. As some critics have said, this is not delicate brain surgery, but it is an efficient way to see that appropriate people know about certain products and issues that will influence them. Advertising ranges from national to local, from display to classified. It is hard to imagine that anyone, even Professor Merrill, would argue against the utility and efficiency of classified advertising unless, of course, it was the personals, which sometimes transgress good taste. And as for product placement, what's wrong with it? The sports equipment in public schools has a brand name and so does almost every other commercial product we use. At one time television and the movies made up fake names, even generic labels and logos, for various commercial products. That seemed silly and contrived. It's better to recognize that people do use a particular brand of ketchup or a line of trendy clothing. Because product placement is so commonplace, it is simply another tool for advertisers to use to garner an audience.

My colleague saves his final stab for political advertising, which he quite superficially denounces. In light of the many attacks on political advertising in recent presidential campaigns, the subject is worth addressing here. There have been political ads that play the race card pandering to people's fears and prejudices. There are misleading, low-grade political ads in almost every political campaign in the United States and other countries. There are also thousands of positive, elevating political ads used by candidates at the local, state, and national levels. And, if past elections are any indicator, the general trend in political advertising has been quite positive, pointing up the virtues of a given candidate rather than tearing down that person's opponent.

The fact that there is so much discussion about the content of advertising suggests that people are paying attention to it. When ads have been sexist, there has often been an outcry against them. Fairly often, these ads are dropped and new ones come on in their place. Is the net result here negative? No, not at all. The sexist ad, which probably was prepared to appeal to people's predispositions, was challenged and brought to public attention, thus unwittingly doing a service to the feminist cause. It is through this kind of criticism and response that attitudes and public images change over time. Minorities and women used to be portrayed in a denigrating fashion or not at all. Now that is changing, reflecting changing social attitudes. That is for the better.

There will always be some offensive and potentially damaging advertisements, but in our system they can be challenged, criticized, and protested. That is not a bad process and probably reflects the advance of civilization generally. After all, our culture wasn't created in a day and it will continue to mature with the help of advertising, which is, of course, a positive social force.

ARGUMENT SUMMATION: *Advertising is a positive social force.*

There is no realistic justification for the restriction of advertising. It is a form of protected speech and is crucial to the financial survival of media industries. Some advertising is generally reprehensible, but the vast majority is not, and there is virtually no advertising that promotes causes or values that truly do damage to American society. Instead, by providing consumer information to the public, advertising plays a positive social role. The public knows that advertisements are advocating specific views and accepts them with skepticism. Advertising is also a positive force for economic stimulation. Targeted advertising is valuable in increasing the diversity and range of media organizations—such as specialized magazines—in the marketplace. Political advertising, even when misleading, reflects the nature of the candidates and rarely goes unchallenged by the opposition or critical news media.

SEARCH ONLINE!

Use the following terms and phrases to search for more information on InfoTrac College Edition: *advertising, advertisement, advertiser, ad agencies, capitalism, commercial media, selling, media sales, commercialism, testimonials, political advertising, public service advertising, social benefit, social force, advertising appeals, product placement, branding.*

TOPICS FOR DISCUSSION

1. What are some of the ways the American media system could be financially supported if we were to eliminate advertising?
2. Can advertising be considered a positive social force because it is a reality that has been with us from ancient times?
3. Does advertising in the United States keep the press free? If so, how? Could the press be just as free if there were no advertising? What does press financing have to do with First Amendment press provisions?
4. Make a case for political advertising. Do you know of anyone who voted for a certain candidate because of advertising? Have you or any of your family? Do you think political advertising is issue oriented?
5. Does most TV and newspaper display advertising appeal to one's reason or to one's prejudices and emotions? Explain and give examples.

Topics for Research

1. Look at public service advertisements that promote an important social cause or issue. Be specific and examine them in terms of their appeals and likely success (or failure).
2. After researching the topic of political advertising, write an essay on "Political Advertising: The Good, the Bad, and the Ugly." Give examples of positive and negative political advertising. What kind works best? Why?
3. Is advertising a positive social force on the movement of goods and services? Compare and contrast the advertisements of two competitors. Do they distinguish their products? Do they make compelling cases? If this were your only source of information about the products, which would you choose based on the advertisements?
4. In recent years comparative advertising, wherein one product promotes itself by attacking a competitor either overtly or with subtlety, has been in vogue. Compare two advertisers who use this approach. Do you think it works?
5. Set up your own criteria for advertising that is a positive social force. Then grade several ads or ad campaigns using your own criteria. Be a tough grader.

Further Reading

Alperstein, Neil M. *Advertising in Everyday Life.* Cresskill, NJ: Hampton Press, 2003.

Baker, Edwin. *Advertising and a Democratic Press.* Princeton, NJ: Princeton University Press, 1995.

Baker, Samm S. *The Permissible Lie: The Truth about Advertising.* Cleveland: World, 1968.

Berger, Arthur Asa. *Ads, Fads and Commercial Culture: Advertising's Impact on American Character and Society.* Lanham, MD: Rowman and Littlefield, 2000.

Cross, Mary. *A Century of American Icons.* Westport, CT: Greenwood Press, 2002.

Huxley, Aldous. *Brave New World Revisited.* New York: Harper & Row, Perennial Library, 1965.

Jackell, Robert, and Janice M. Hirota. *Imagemakers: Advertising, Pubic Relations and the Ethos of Advocacy.* Chicago: University of Chicago Press, 2000.

Kelly, Larry D., and Donald W. Jugenheimer. *Advertising Media Planning.* Armonk, NY: M. E. Sharp, 2004.

Kennan, George. *Democracy and the Student Left.* New York: Bantam Books, 1968.

Kloss, Ingomar, and Makoto Abe. *Advertising Worldwide: Advertising Conditions in Selected Countries.* New York: Springer, 2001.

Napoli, Philip M. *Audience Economics: Media Institutions and the Audience Marketplace.* New York: Columbia University Press, 2003.

Ogilvy, David. *Ogilvy on Advertising.* New York: Random House, 1987.

O'Guinn, Thomas C., et al. *Advertising.* Cincinnati, OH: Southwestern, 1999.

Ries, Al, and Laura Ries. *The Fall of Advertising and the Rise of Public Relations.* New York: HarperCollins, 2002.

Schudson, Michael. *Advertising: The Uneasy Persuasion.* New York: Basic Books,1984.

Sheehan, Kim Bartel. *Controversies in Contemporary Advertising.* Thousand Oaks, CA: Sage, 2003.

Steel, Jon. *Truth, Lies and Advertising.* New York: Wiley, 1998.

Zeft, Robin Lee, and Brad Aronson. *Advertising on the Internet*, 2nd ed. New York: Wiley, 1999.

PUBLIC RELATIONS

Public relations (PR), like advertising, is variously a communication system, a subset of the media system, a series of practices, a profession, and the object of derision and scorn. The leading text by Scott Cutlip and colleagues says: "The term public relations is used in at least three senses: the *relationships* with those who constitute an organization's public or constituents, the *ways and means used* to achieve favorable relationships, and the *quality or status* to the relationships" (Cutlip, Center, and Broom, 1999). Thus, the one term is used to label both means and ends, to name a condition, and to express the conduct or actions related to that condition.

The field of public relations, like advertising, is part and parcel of the communication system in the United States. There are independent public relations firms, public relations offices in businesses and government, and communications consulting firms that do everything from training executives for television appearances to designing an information campaign and strategy for a political candidate or a foreign government. Hundreds of thousands of people work in the public relations field and it would be hard to estimate the amount of money spent on this activity. Public relations certainly has its detractors, but it also has a national professional association—the Public Relations Society of America—an accreditation procedure for professionals, a code of ethics, and a growing scholarly and professional literature. Some critics—especially some journalists—would abolish public relations altogether. That, however, is an unlikely scenario because public relations is nothing more than controlled and organized communication. And in a communication society, public relations has grown because there is simply more demand for communication services. As information increasingly becomes a renewable resource through the recycling of messages, public relations strategies and services are needed to promote and market the product. Public relations differs in an essential way from advertising because it is not generally identified with a sponsor or product. When one sees a guest on the *Today Show*, chances are that person has been booked with the help of a highly paid public relations practitioner or firm, yet the viewer is never told this. Thus public relations can be more subtle and less visible than advertising.

CHALLENGE

Dennis: Public relations manipulates the news.

Pause for a moment and consider the general image that public relations has in U.S. society. Public relations in the minds of many is equated with deception. A *public relations solution*, for example, implies an emphasis on appearances and stage-managing rather than a blunt recitation of facts. Public relations is an arm of top management, whether in the public or private sector; it is a process meant to benefit those creating PR messages. A company's public relations department is not charged with reporting bad news. Instead, the mandate is to put the best face on the situation, to explain and rationalize it. This can be done positively in a fashion beneficial to the public but often is not, because the client, not the public, is paying the bill. Some argue that this is simply exercising the right to communicate and that all persons are entitled to put forth their views, with or without the help of a public relations firm. That is an important factor in the debate over the utility of public relations, because some critics argue that it not only tends to be deceptive but also gives undue advantage to those who can afford to have their own public relations counsel. After years of high-quality professional attainment, the field of public relations still has a somewhat unsavory reputation in U.S. society and the term itself is much disputed. Whether this is fair and accurate or not is not the issue here. It is the prevailing image.

Even the origins of public relations in the United States are unsavory. Public relations historians are fond of recounting the history of this questionable enterprise, which they say was established by Ivy Lee, an ex-journalist who created a publicity agency. One of his clients was John D. Rockefeller, the oil tycoon who had a deservedly bad reputation for his unfair business practices and his cruelty to the people who worked for him. The great muckraker Ida M. Tarbell documented Rockefeller's practices in her brilliant work "The History of the Standard Oil Company," which appeared in *McClure's Magazine* in 1902. Such articles and other social criticism brought pressure on the Congress to clip Rockefeller's wings and those of other robber barons. The result was antitrust legislation and penalties for unfair and illegal competition. Rockefeller hired Ivy Lee to convince the public that he was a kind and loving family man (which he was) and generous as well (which he was not). Lee, for all his genius and his role in modern business communication, helped change Rockefeller's image and, in effect, manipulated the news media and public attitudes. Today, Rockefeller is remembered more favorably than those who campaigned against his excesses. Ivy Lee and public relations must share much of the blame.

Although there have been noble people associated with the public relations field and some of them, like the pioneering Edward L. Bernays, sometimes called the *father of spin*, campaigned for professionalism and ethical practices, it still must be said that public relations packages news and information on behalf of its clients. A vigilant press ought to be able to see through deceptive and dishonest communication—and it does—but still there is an advantage for those who are well represented by public relations counsel over those who are not. Think of the homeless, for example, coming face to face with a giant developer who would remove them from a particular district of a large city. The developer will have a much greater capacity to argue his case in the press with the help of public relations people. There is nothing inherently wrong with this on a case-by-case basis, but considered as a whole, there is no doubt that public relations strategies do influence press coverage and portrayals in the media. It isn't always a matter of money, but usually that is the case. Some social movements, from civil rights to the women's movement, have successfully marshaled public support with limited resources whereas their opponents have sometimes failed to curry support even with superior budgets. These, however, are exceptions to the rule.

The excesses of public relations are less important than the follies and foibles of a sometimes overworked, sometimes understaffed, often lazy and poorly trained corps of journalists in this country. There is simply too much information for most media organizations to cope effectively with it. Instead of hiring legions of specialists to help—they have hired a few—the media make heavy use of handouts (press releases) and other information provided free by public relations people. Clearly, this is not fair and does not serve the American people very well. It is instructive, I think, to note that PR, once a somewhat independent although derivative field, is now mostly owned by giant advertising agencies. And tellingly, a recent book that praises PR also admits that whereas "advertising uses the big bang, PR uses the slow buildup" (Ries and Ries, 2002, 243). The fact that PR is more subtle, more nuanced, than advertising speaks volumes and makes me wonder just how much PR material is deliberately deceptive. The notion of PR as "free media"—that is, embedded in the text of media stories, often without identification—whereas advertising is paid, up-front, and in your face also raises questions about the role of PR and the veil it hides behind.

I know scores of talented public relations people and even more talented journalists. The PR people I know are, for the most part, responsible professionals. They have every right to do what they do, but they are paid promoters for vested interests, and those interests want publicity and public support. The PR people use many ploys to get their way with the news media and to influence the public through other means. To a large extent they succeed and in the process are major information providers for the American people.

ARGUMENT SUMMATION: *Public relations manipulates the news.*

Public relations, by its very nature, is intended to benefit those creating the message, whether the source is public or private. In the information marketplace, public relations manipulates the news by packaging information for the media with a specific client's interests in mind. There have been laudable uses of public relations, but on the whole the practice serves to flood the media with biased news. When the press is unable to verify the reports because of the sheer quantity of information available or out of laziness, distorted public relations reports appear in the media as objective facts, and the news has been distorted to favor the public relations position.

RESPONSE

Merrill: *Public relations provides an essential news service.*

It has been said that public relations is a manipulative force in news presentation. Perhaps it is, to some extent. So what? Many manipulative forces impinge on the news: editors' fears, reporters' biases, advertising pressures, government secrecy. Public relations, in spite of normal manipulative aspects, is a valuable—even essential—adjunct to the news dissemination activities of journalism.

It has been estimated, even by journalists, that nearly 50 percent of the news stories found in the media show some signs of PR influence. Journalists themselves must think PR sources are important to news gathering, because they certainly make use of PR releases and background material that is offered them by the PR establishment. It would be hard to deny that PR sources are helpful in supplying background material and even some hard news to news media.

Much PR material is ignored or discarded, but it is used more often than many journalists might like to admit. I myself have spent five years in college public relations and, having kept careful clipping books and records, I can say that in this small PR sample my public relations–generated news was used up to 80 percent on a weekly basis. Use of releases by radio and TV was much less dramatic, but there is no doubt that newspapers rely heavily on news releases.

Seymour Topping, former administrator of the Pulitzer Prizes, has said bluntly that PR people contribute to the news in a functional way: "Quite a lot of our business stories originate from press releases. Often the first hint of a newsworthy event is first heard of by us from a press release." Topping has gone so far as to say that PR is becoming a news network behind the legitimate news media, "a second network that feeds the real news media more and more of its news" (Blyskal and Blyskal, 1985, 46–47).

The Blyskals also quote Charles Staebler, assistant managing editor of the *Wall Street Journal*, who acknowledges the help provided by PR people. "We look at press releases positively as a source of tips. They can alert us to things that are going on." Staebler estimates that on average perhaps 50 percent of *Journal* stories are spurred by press releases, adding, "In every case we *try* [emphasis added] to go beyond the press release" (Blyskal and Blyskal, 47).

Scott Cutlip, a longtime professor of PR, said the 150,000 public relations practitioners play an important role in setting the public agenda and have a far more important role in opinion making "than the public perceives, or than journalists (who themselves are only about 130,000 strong) are usually willing to admit." Cutlip estimates that 40 percent of all news content today comes from the desks of PR people (Cutlip et al., 1999).

There is no doubt that PR does provide a news service. And in the common or loose sense of providing essential news, meaning a very important service, I think that public relations fills the bill. No one is saying that PR is journalistically relevant in all of its aspects, but in providing basic news, commentary on certain news events, tips on news stories, and access to news sources, the practitioner in public relations is extremely valuable to the news media.

In a strict sense of essential (meaning absolutely necessary), perhaps PR is not essential. A newspaper, for example, could provide news without any help from PR. But how thorough would it be? How many additional gaps would such news presentation have? One might as well say that the news media could present news without interviewing politicians. Certainly it could be done; there would simply be far less political news. So we might say that politicians are essential for the best possible political news, and that public relations practitioners are essential for the best possible news related to the PR person's area of knowledge.

It may be true, as Dennis contends, that public relations manipulates the news. Factors impinging upon the collection and writing of news are manipulative to some degree. I could say, just as well, that reporters and editors manipulate the news. So? *Manipulates* is a word with a negative connotation, so it is not used to describe a journalistic function. But with public relations it is different: From the point of view of the journalist, any news function connected with PR automatically seems to imply skullduggery and self-serving bias, with an accompanying intent to mislead the reader. This may be true in some cases, but in others it is simply not the case. Truthful and conscientious reporting is not the sole province of the journalist. Such reporting can also be found among historians, sociologists, lawyers, and even farmers talking alongside a country road. Why not among PR people?

Because of its financial support by groups, organizations, and persons with vested interests, public relations is a field that is understandably suspect by news media people who pride themselves on being detached and unbiased in their news presentation. Perhaps PR people are prone to accentuate the positive when it comes to news about their special interests. But don't journalists generally accentuate the negative? Is negative bias any better than positive bias? Undoubtedly PR people do feel considerable loyalty to those who pay their salaries. But does employer loyalty necessarily imply dishonesty?

But let us assume PR people are biased. Are they more biased in their normal news-writing activities than media reporters, who usually have their own strongly held values and biases, political and otherwise? This, of course, is a question that cannot really be answered. But it is worth asking.

In spite of biased news from PR sources, which undoubtedly appears from time to time, there is no reason to believe that most PR people are dishonest, at least no more so than others. Surely they intend to be honest and forthright; for one thing, the Code of Professional Standards of the Public Relations Society of America (PRSA) says they must be. For instance, the Code stresses (in Standard Seven) that a member "shall not intentionally communicate false or misleading information and is obligated to use care to avoid communication of false or misleading information." That is strange wording, to be sure, but it points up PR people's concern for providing the truth. Earlier in the same code, PRSA members are urged to "adhere to truth and accuracy" and to refrain from engaging "in any practice which tends to corrupt the integrity of channels of communication" (quoted in Lovell, 1982, 41–42). Not much different from language in a journalist's code, is it?

William Ramsey, president of the PR firm of Bill Ramsey Associates, Inc., insists that public relations people "must communicate better . . . to the public" and that "we must tell the good news of our firm's accomplishments—and level with the public about our firm's or our institution's shortcomings." In fact, he says, "credibility is the key" (Haberman and Dolphin, 1988, viii).

In spite of PR people's attempt to professionalize, to write ethical codes, to use the status initials APR (Accredited in Public Relations) after their names, and to pay allegiance to truth and credibility, they still have a problem with the press. Journalists are suspicious of their forthrightness in news matters. Robert T. Reilly, APR member and professor at the University of Nebraska (Omaha), notes that "Even reporters who have never experienced a problem with a PR person harbor the concept of the practitioner as a self-serving person who will try to interfere with truthful encounter" (1987, 9). He adds this backhanded slap at news reporters: "As reportorial success is measured more and more by exposé, and as media rely increasingly on the profession they criticize, you're apt to see this nagging hostility expand."

But he's right. Journalists will undoubtedly continue to snipe at public relations people—while using considerable portions of their news releases. In retaliation, PR people will take their verbal slaps at what they often see as unrealistic and arrogant journalists who make no real attempt to understand and appreciate public relations.

All right. There's a kind of continuing cold war going on between the two professions. Is that bad? I see it as a good thing because this kind of mild adversarial relationship may help to keep both groups honest. Perhaps here we have another check mechanism in our society. In spite of the unease that exists between the two groups, I still maintain that PR expands the public discourse, helps provide a wide assortment of news, and is essential in expanding the pluralism of our total communication system.

The image of PR is beside the point. The fact that ethical lapses occur in PR is beside the point. The fact that journalists are naturally suspicious of any other person or group in the news business is beside the point. The fact that PR people do have a loyalty to their clients is beside the point. What is not beside the point is that PR people do indeed provide news to various publics (including the general public through the mass media) and, in doing so, provide an essential public service.

ARGUMENT SUMMATION: *Public relations provides an essential news service.*

Public relations generates information for use by the media; it fills gaps in the news and provides services similar to those offered by advertising agencies. PR helps set the public agenda. It may not be essential in the ultimate sense, but neither is a newspaper or a TV station. Public relations may have an ax to grind, but so do advertising agencies. It is true that not all PR is ethical; is that not true of any institutionalized communications endeavor? Public relations serves as a supplement and aid to news media, a gap filler, and, in general, does a valuable job of expanding message pluralism in society. A PR person may do many things other than news gathering and dissemination; but is this not also true of newspaper staff members?

SEARCH ONLINE!

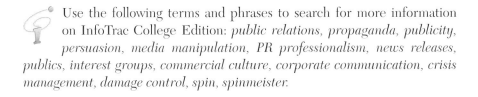 Use the following terms and phrases to search for more information on InfoTrac College Edition: *public relations, propaganda, publicity, persuasion, media manipulation, PR professionalism, news releases, publics, interest groups, commercial culture, corporate communication, crisis management, damage control, spin, spinmeister.*

TOPICS FOR DISCUSSION

1. Is truth related to a PR news release in the same way that truth is related to a news story on TV or in a newspaper?
2. Is it any safer to believe an advertiser than to believe a PR person? In what ways are the two types of practitioners similar? Different?
3. Why would a person who loves independence and truth want to be a part of a PR organization? How can there be so many PR people today who were news media reporters at one time?
4. The assumption is generally made that newspaper reporters are neutral, unbiased, and objective—and that PR people are not. Is the assumption valid? Why, or why not?
5. PR people work for and are paid by their clients. Media news people work for and are paid by their media. What is the difference? How does their employment status affect their loyalties? How do their loyalties affect their work?

TOPICS FOR RESEARCH

1. Study a local firm or nonprofit organization in terms of its public relations program, assuming it has one. What publics do they try to reach? With what methods or tools? How do they measure their effectiveness? How do you assess their efforts and success (or failure)?
2. Assume that you have been asked to document the public relations of your college or university. What is its prevailing public image? Does it differ with different publics—say, students, faculty, and alumni? In your paper indicate how public relations is carried out at the institution, by whom, with what channels or tools, and to what effect. Does the effort work or not? Why?
3. Is there any right to public relations in what is increasingly an information or communication society? Argue the case that all people and organizations involved in public life need and deserve a public relations program. How can the public be protected in such a scheme?
4. Document the ethics movement in public relations. What does professional public relations do to assure ethical practice? Interview a public relations practitioner on this issue. How would you assess that person's approach to ethical public relations? How are decisions made? With what help or sources?
5. Interview a news person about contacts between his or her news organization and public relations personnel. Is public relations a help or a hindrance? Be specific about the impact and influence of public relations, if any, based on this interview.

6. What does the public need to know about public relations? Outline a speech you would give to a civic group about public relations and what citizens should know about it.

FURTHER READING

Bernays, Edward L. *Crystalizing Public Opinion.* New York: Boni and Liveright, 1923.

Blyskal, Jeff, and Mary Blyskal. *How the Public Relations Industry Writes the News.* New York: William Morrow, 1985.

Bogart, Leo. *Commercial Culture.* New York: Oxford University Press, 1995.

Cutlip, Scott, Alan Center, and Glen M. Broom. *Effective Public Relations*, 8th ed. Englewood Cliffs, NJ: Prentice Hall, 1999.

Ewan, Stuart. *PR: A Social History of Spin.* New York: Basic Books, 1998.

Grossman, Lawrence. *The Electronic Republic.* New York: Free Press, 1995.

Grunig, J. E., and Todd Hunt. *Managing Public Relations.* New York: Holt, Rinehart and Winston, 1984.

Haberman, David A., and H. A. Dolphin. *Public Relations: The Necessary Art.* Ames: Iowa State University Press, 1988.

Lovell, Ronald P. *Inside Public Relations.* Boston: Allyn & Bacon, 1982.

Marchand, Roland. *Creating the Corporate Soul: The Rise of Public Relations and Corporate Imagery in American Big Business.* Berkeley: University of California Press, 1998.

Marconi, Joe. *Public Relations: The Complete Guide.* Dallas: South-Western, 2004.

Newsom, Doug, Judy Van Slyke Turk, and Dean Kruckeberg. *This Is PR: The Realities of Public Relations*, 8th ed. Belmont, CA: Wadsworth, 2003.

Pavlik, John V. *Public Relations: What Research Tells Us.* Beverly Hills, CA: Sage, 1987.

Pindsorf, Marion. *Communicating When Your Company Is Under Siege.* New York: Fordham University Press, 1999.

Reilly, Robert T. *Public Relations in Action.* Englewood Cliffs, NJ: Prentice Hall, 1987.

Ries, Al, and Laura Ries. *The Fall of Advertising and the Rise of PR.* New York: Harper Business, 2002.

Stauber, John, and Sheldon Rampton. *Toxic Sludge Is Good for You: Lies, Damned Lies and the Public Relations Industry.* Monroe, ME: Common Courage Press, 1995.

Tye, Larry. *The Father of Spin: Edward L. Bernays and the Birth of Public Relations.* New York: Crown, 1998.

GLOBALIZATION AND THE MEDIA

Any mention of globalization in the early years of the 21st century conjures up images of people rioting in the streets of Seattle or Genoa during global economic summit meetings. Globalization and the new geo-economy have reshaped the global economic map as transnational firms ply their trade in most business endeavors. The media are clearly involved in these developments, which have their origins in the dramatic changes on the world scene at the end of the Cold War through greater economic, cultural, and political cooperation between and among the countries of the globe.

After nearly 50 years of East–West tensions that affected the whole world, the Cold War ended in the early 1990s. This radically affected communication between and among peoples generally and the communication media specifically. The hostility between the United States and the former Soviet Union eased and former communist countries declared themselves democracies. About the same time, most of the authoritarian governments formerly led by military dictators in Central and South America also initiated democratic reforms. There was a new spirit of democracy in much of Asia, and even China embraced a carefully circumscribed market economy and began to loosen up its rigid controls over the media. In most of the world, the preferred form of government is now democracy (defined differently in different places depending on local cultural conditions), and most have adopted market economies, again with different degrees of free market activity in different countries. In all this the press and news media have played a key role, and there has been an increase in independent media— not controlled by the state. One major exception to this trend is in the Islamic world, notably in the Middle East, where theocratic, military, and some near authoritarian regimes continue in states such as Iran, Saudi Arabia, and Syria. In 2003, Iraq's autocratic Baathist regime was overthrown when the United States declared war there. The war and the resistance that followed, however, were related to a declared desire by the occupying coalition and a newly installed local government for democracy and freedom, or some semblance of it.

Along with the sociopolitical changes sweeping the world and the embrace of market economies has come a trend toward globalization wherein cultural products (including media content of all kinds—information and news, entertainment, and advertising) now have an international audience as never before. The old barriers of borders and East–West restrictions have ended for the most part, and there is strong encouragement nearly everywhere for international communication and free trade between and among nations. At one level, globalization of the media seems to be a good thing, with more openness everywhere and the unembarrassed use of the word *freedom* to describe the condition in most countries. This means political and economic freedom and, of course, some measure of freedom of the media. For the news media it means that correspondents can travel freely nearly everywhere on the globe and generally report the news without restrictions and censorship. These trends have also accelerated the growth of large, global media companies such as Rupert Murdoch's News Corporation, Germany's Bertelsmann Co., and the U.S. giant Time Warner. Increasingly there is international ownership of local media in many countries. (Some, including the United States, still have rules that prohibit full foreign ownership of broadcasting.) Political changes along with economic changes have also been encouraged by a climate of deregulation, wherein many rules affecting broadcasting and other media have been greatly relaxed in the United States, Europe, Russia, and elsewhere.

Old arguments about the equitable distribution of all resources to all peoples, including access to communication—once a common feature of the East–West and North–South debate—were muted in the years after the Cold War. At one time, and for nearly 20 years, there was a fierce international debate, largely between developing countries and those fully industrialized, about the New World Information and Communication Order (NWICO), which expressed concern about the inequitable flow of news from the big countries of the West to the developing world with little reciprocity. It was pointed out that cultural products such as movies and news were dominated by the West because of its economic superiority. Connected to this was a UNESCO-sponsored policy that was interpreted by the West as an intrusion on freedom of expression, incompatible with an independent, nongovernmental media system. That debate, though still alive in some university circles, is all but dead in the media worldwide and is no longer a feature of the United Nations Educational, Scientific, and Cultural Organization, which has rescinded the policy and urged a regime of international press freedom attended by market economies, a position quite popular in most countries of the world.

Instead of the New World Order arguments, we now have a great debate over the effects of globalization on media systems, individual media outlets, journalists and other media workers, and, most especially, the general public. The question most often raised is whether globalization in the media will have a liberating and beneficial influence or will constrain communication and deny access to those in poor countries where media markets are less than attractive. The dominant view in the world among governments, business, media companies, and most large institutions is that globalization is a positive influence, with its roots in utopian values promoting true international discourse wherein communication solves problems and the market benefits. On the other side are a few vocal and important critics and some scholars of communication. In recent visits to more than 50 countries and in extensive interviews, we confirm the positive view of globalization as it affects the media, while at the same time recognizing the critical voices of those who worry about the effects of globalization, arguing that bigness is inherently bad and that diversity is nearly always good.

CHALLENGE

Dennis: Globalization greatly benefits people, the media, and freedom of expression.

British commentator Anthony Smith has predicted that in the new communication age, national borders will be irrelevant. If once the nation-state defined the reach of most media, with national newspapers and television systems being the best examples, now human beings have truly conquered time and space and the whole world is within reach. Smith (1991) argues that new technology has tremendous consequences for individuals and institutions and that, although big companies control much of the world's communication content, it has never been easier for new media products to enter the marketplace. Agreeing, banking visionary Walter Wriston (1992) posits that borders are indeed "totally porous," thus rendering "regulatory distinctions meaningless." In other words, governments can no longer control what comes into their countries nor can they stop the "inevitable global conversation" made possible by new media technologies and a global marketplace. This is, of course, what Canadian media guru Marshall McLuhan spoke of when he predicted a *global village* in the mid-1960s. Certainly one sees the global village idea—of messages reaching every corner of the world—in the presence of CNN almost everywhere. Be it a great international hotel or a remote rural village, there is virtually no gathering of human beings in the world today that does not have access to CNN and other global satellite services offering news, information, entertainment, and opinion. Similarly, I have watched the ever popular MTV and other music channels in Moscow, Santiago, Hong Kong, and elsewhere, something that would have seemed magical only a few years ago when a visit to a Nigerian town meant cutting yourself off from the world altogether. The writings of Joshua Meyrowitz show us what this means to individuals as well as whole societies; he points out that it was once possible to *excommunicate* children from the family dinner conversation, sending them to their bedrooms as punishment. Now, says

Meyrowitz, banishment from the family circle means going to a room filled with communication devices and services far more interesting and diverse than the family conversation.

What was possible at first mostly with communication satellites has been greatly accelerated with the coming of the Internet and the World Wide Web. People can now communicate across national borders with instantaneous speed as the Internet spreads along with computer power. Added to this mix is the nearly ubiquitous cell phone and the wireless revolution that has allowed even developing countries to move beyond their limited infrastructures, thus opening the way for people to communicate more freely and over great distances.

The kind of global reach that media have today definitely benefits people, giving them access to a massive range of information and entertainment. This helps the media organization delivering the content by building audiences, mass and targeted, and thus brings revenues into the media's corporate coffers. Global media also benefit noncommercial public media, which beam their messages everywhere, garnering audiences.

The critics worry that a few global companies will not only gobble up all the media of the world but somehow enslave human beings through low-quality programming, cheap information, and entertainment junk food. Such warnings have been with us for a long time. The respected press critic Ben Bagdikian has been worried about big all-powerful newspaper companies for as long as I can remember. But in the mid-1990s, when big media deals were being done on Wall Street, these fearsome newspaper giants could rarely afford to be part of arrangements that involved telephone companies, cable firms, broadcasters, and movie companies. Big media, which now operate with precious few governmental controls, live in the world of competition and to date can be credited with delivering the most diverse, richest storehouse of media content in the history of the world. This has benefited media companies and individuals enormously. Instead of three or four channels coming into the home, there are scores and soon hundreds. True, some of the material is low grade and even denigrating, but much of it is not. When people bother to open their eyes and look at the rich lode of media fare, there can be no doubt that big media companies have been a positive force.

Still, the critics persist in saying that the big players limit the range of information and opinions, thus driving out alternative views. In fact, exactly the opposite is true. A virtual avalanche of Websites has bombarded the world with alternative views so that critics of big media in most countries of the world can make their views known and even invade the space of their big-time competitors. Even alternative journalism—on paper and via the Web—has benefited from the worldwide trend toward vigorous market economies. Magazines of all kinds representing widely varying points of view are thriving today, just to name one media example. This and other media outlets can thank a robust media economy, technological breakthroughs and their many new platforms, and, of course, the loosening of regulatory ties.

I should add that the idea that the nation-state would soon die, and with it the distinctive media of individual countries, couldn't be more wrong. As the economic geographer Peter Dicken has written, "The state is dead, long live the state" (Dicken, 2003, 122). In a globalized economy, the nation-state thrives because it contains distinctive cultures, practices, and institutions, including the media. States are regulators of industry, including the media and telecommunication, and sometimes they are competitors (as with state broadcasting systems) and collaborators when joint ventures are fashioned between outside media companies from Europe or North America and locally owned state enterprises. As media economist Robert Picard has written, some media products are easily exportable, some are not. He notes that "for many media companies, there are numerous benefits in internationalization" (Picard, 2002, 218). In a sense, he argues that many of the fears that critics once had about media globalization just haven't materialized. Newspapers, for example, don't travel far; they tend to produce local content for local audiences. The same is mostly true of radio programming and magazines, though they do have some global reach. Books have a wide berth in international markets, as do television programming and audio recordings, while motion pictures have the most of all.

The crybaby critics have never had it so good; instead of being dispossessed, they are communicating more vigorously than ever—electronically and by the wonders of desktop publishing, which now makes entry into the communication field easier than it has been in history.

All too often those who disparage the global media trends simply argue that bigness is bad, that all media power might be vested in a few hands, and that this is inherently bad. A closer look confirms that there are certainly large conglomerates, not only in the United States and Europe, where the biggest ones reside, but also in Latin America, where virtually every country has only a few well-heeled media companies that own media of all kinds. But at the same time people can now create exquisite desktop newsletters and other new media that are highly professional. They can also log onto an online service and create their own home pages on the Internet. For a lucky few, a small enterprise, such as a Website or even a specialized newsletter or magazine, becomes so successful that a large company will buy it from the individual who started the new publication with little or no capital. Suddenly the owner, if he or she wants to, can sell one enterprise and go start another, thus sharing in the bounty of big media.

Many critics of global media deny the end of the Cold War, the end of public (government) media. Some of them are bitter about the fall of former socialist states that practiced censorship as a matter of course. Only a few years ago, relatively uncontaminated media systems had little contact with the West, but, as the historian Timothy Garton Ash has pointed out, many of these publicly supported media were nothing more than a colossal system of lies. The New

World Information and Communication Order is dead; democracy and market economies are in, and that galls many critics who believe that commercially vigorous media are somehow inherently immoral.

Without defending the dumbing down of U.S. newspapers (a fragile technology desperately seeking a new future), the existence of tabloid television, and other less than elevating content, it is hard to imagine an intelligent person who cannot find a rich range of information on virtually every topic, whether at a public library, a school database, or elsewhere. Much of the yield of new media is available free in an institutional setting, such as a school or library, or on a home PC. Globalization may have its flaws, but to date it has been far better than a world divided between East and West, North and South. And many hope that the deep chasm separating much, though not all, of the Islamic world will eventually be bridged by globalization and true international communication. With interactive digital media, people can talk back to the media and communicate directly with friends and peers anywhere in the world. Of course, there are some modest problems of access for all people to various video services and information, but I would counsel patience because methods for access and the navigation of complex files are being extended and developed every day.

I see new media as a tool for the citizenry and the large firms that produce these products as mostly beneficial in virtually every society they enter, normally by invitation from locals. There will always be room for localism in the media industries, but person-to-person contact over long distances also enhances the global conversation. Both greatly benefit freedom of expression and globalization, which follows the trends set by international business—a process that brings jobs and wealth to many. All this is just beginning, but the idea that big companies, which must court public favor, are malevolent has not yet been proven.

ARGUMENT SUMMATION: *Globalization greatly benefits people, the media, and freedom of expression.*

Globalization is a reality. The world now has a global economy wherein goods and services are marketed across borders by transnational firms that have a presence in several countries. Media, once creatures of the nation-state, are now also increasingly global. Global media companies and media such as CNN, the BBC, and MTV have worldwide reach. The main benefit of global media, both mass media and digital media such as the Internet, is that for the first time interactive communication among all people everywhere is possible for most of the world. At the same time people are better informed and get a wider range of information and entertainment than ever before. People worry that a few companies will dominate world communication, but many small entrepreneurs are also flourishing, and entry into the communication market is easier than it has ever been in human history.

RESPONSE

Merrill: Globalization harms national and local media, thus impairing freedom of expression.

We have just been told in the *Challenge* that globalization is a good thing and that we should be grateful for it. That will come as startling news to people who demonstrated at various global summit meetings complaining that globalization is virtually destroying local economies. Has Professor Dennis heard of the outsourcing of jobs and the real pain that developing nations feel as they fall farther and farther behind trying to compete in a global media market? If the gap between rich and poor, North and South, was wide in the past, it is even wider today. We've also been told that the New World Information and Communication Order, pushed vigorously by UNESCO for more than two decades, is all but dead in the media worldwide. To some degree it may be ailing around the world but, in my view, it is far from dead. In every developing country I visit I have to try to defend Western journalism—and especially U.S. journalism—from the same old criticisms of the last 20 years. It may be that the partial demise of communism has muted much of the criticism of Western journalism—especially the debates surrounding press freedom. But this NWICO is not dead yet. Indeed, every survey I know of has shown that the United States is extremely unpopular in much of the world in the wake of the Iraq war, though this could, and likely will, change eventually. We've seen the rise of Arab language media in several countries, largely to combat U.S. cultural and media imperialism. And though some of those media broadcast outside the Arab world, they are hardly tied into any global economy.

All this fuels the old complaints of Western information imperialism, inequity of worldwide news flow, Western stereotyping of developing countries, and the spreading of values and traditions harmful to indigenous cultures. And the danger of Western multinational media conglomerates is stressed probably more than ever before, with good reason. Western-style advertising—especially in the Muslim world—is perceived as demeaning and harmful to religious values. Nonrational, emotionally charged advertising raises unrealistic expectations in the developing countries. All is not peace, light, and harmony on the world scene. Dennis sees no danger in the growth of big media companies increasingly controlling world communication, and quotes Anthony Smith as saying that it has never been easier for people to get exposure to new media products. It's easier than ever for people to get exposure to AIDS too, but who would call this a good thing?

In his *Challenge* Dennis also quotes visionary Walter Wriston as positing that borders are now "totally porous," thereby rendering governmental regulation of incoming messages meaningless. Even that is doubtful, as he himself acknowledges in touting the localism of newspapers and magazines, for example. We should be clear that the capacity to receive messages from abroad or having locally controlled media at home is not necessarily the same thing as having freedom of the press. What about the freedom from government control of domestic media? What about the availability of national leaders for reportorial interviews? What about a whole variety of governmental controls over the press, both foreign and domestic, in several countries that are assuredly not democracies? In many places in the geo-global economy, governments still have a very strong role and can discourage outside media from distributing there and local media from veering off a very safe course. Of course, our real hope is with the Internet, but it is by no means universally available in some countries where modems, phone lines, and other technological innovations are not yet widely available.

Dr. Dennis mentions that he has watched MTV and other music channels in places such as Hong Kong and Moscow in recent years, something that was not available only a few years ago. All right; let us admit that more Western programming is reaching more of the world's people. But is the bulk of this material good for the world's people? Does it have a positive or negative impact on the various cultures? Does it do little more than perpetuate stereotypes and lower moral standards? The new global reach of the media, according to my colleague, benefits people by giving them a massive range of information and entertainment. This is a statement of opinion, and certainly one that needs evidence. How do we know that a range of information, and especially entertainment, is of benefit to people?

Common sense, you may say. I wonder. I have access to tremendous amounts of entertainment, but I doubt if it benefits me very much. In fact, it is quite probable that the more we are exposed to television and the print media, the less we live authentic, active, and productive lives. It might benefit me (especially if I live in a Third World country) far more to grow vegetables for my family than to sit and watch *Oprah!* reality TV or even PBS's *News Hour.*

Dennis mentions that the fear of entertainment junk food (and I would add screaming heads on cable) is unwarranted and that such a concern has been with us for a long time. True, we can live with junk in our media, and granted there is plenty of substantial material. But junk food, especially in the form of titillating, splashy, and mindless advertising, seems to be proliferating everywhere— and is now flowing in large quantities into other countries and cultures.

If big media companies increase pluralism and alternative views, as my colleague contends, then we might assume that what we really need is one big multinational media company in the world so as to provide the greatest diversity in media messages. It would presumably spawn large numbers of short-lived mini-media, rising and falling as they constantly fertilize the Big Medium. As to desktop publishing and online services and connections being products of the big media conglomerates, this is quite dubious. Besides, computer networks and individuals talking to individuals via the Internet are not journalism; certainly they do not constitute news media, any more than one person talking to his neighbor over the back fence.

It seems to me that having media fall into fewer and fewer hands is bad. The fewer the big companies, the less real diversity will be found in the total media picture. Bryce Rucker's *The First Freedom* (1968), as well as a number of works by recent media critics such as Ben Bagdikian (*The Media Monopoly*, 2000) and Herbert Altschull (*Agents of Power*, 1995), attest to this. Freedom of the press may not be affected directly by the big conglomerates and media companies, but alternative perspectives reaching sizable audiences will tend to be squeezed out. Admittedly, research needs to be done on this hypothesis, but common sense suggests that it is true.

Dennis seems to believe that it is a healthy thing that some small specialized newsletters and magazines will be successful and will then be bought up by big media companies. That is exactly what will probably happen. Big companies cannot stand seeing small individual publications succeed. They want to own them. This further consolidates media in fewer hands and limits the individualistic flavor of the total media system.

People who see bigness and consolidation of media as harmful, contrary to Dennis's contention, are not bitter about the fall of the former socialist states. We do not deny the end of the Cold War. But we do not think that the Cold War's end means that all is now good with capitalist expansionism, cold bottom-line publishing, and dog-eat-dog competition. We still believe that variety is healthy in the media, that media values are not universal, that Western big media companies dominate world news flow and flood alien values into the developing countries. Dennis triumphantly contends that "democracy and market economies are in" and all's well with the world. We critics of big media companies do not necessarily believe, as Dennis says, "that commercially vigorous media are somehow inherently immoral," but we do believe that it is considerably more difficult for a wealthy media company to enter the Kingdom of Media Morality than it is for a small public-service-oriented medium. Frankly, we need to get beyond the Cold War, which is old news now, and look at the contours of the world as it is today. What we have is a complex matrix of countries, cultures, and societies, but we also have the very real gaps between the information societies, mostly in the West, and the developing world. And do I need to add, there is still a deep North–South divide? No, the world is not a happy, democratic, market-oriented place. Far from it.

Globalization, says Dennis, may have its flaws, but it has been far better for the world than the mixed bag of repressive regimes represented by the Cold War, the current Islamic world, and such places as Castro's Cuba. I wonder.

Look at the countries of Africa, and many in Southeast Asia. Where are the healthy influences of the media? Are they helping fight the AIDS pandemic? Bolstering the economy? Preventing the spread of illegal drugs? How is Western-influenced globalization helping these unstable countries? Where is the national harmony and stability?

Where are the reliable news and quality entertainment in the media? Sure, the Soviet Union is gone, but a kind of tribalism has taken its place all over the globe, and world stability and security are no better than they were. In fact, there are indications that nationalism, bloodshed, suffering, and hunger have grown throughout the world since the end of the Cold War. As the great globalized media companies spread their views of political disputes, revolutionaries, terrorists, nationalists, and tribal animosities, ideas are planted here and there in fertile soil. Is it any wonder that they grow rapidly?

As an institution grows, as a company expands, as a conglomerate globalizes, the individual shrinks in personal dignity and impact. This is a sociological truism. As a media company extends its tentacles into ever more projects, programs, and global enterprises, the news function of the company tends to get less attention. Entertainment and bottom-line considerations take over, and the news medium is transformed into a business.

Individual liberty suffers under such a system. Cooperation, stability, and lockstep thinking among the functionaries take over. Local media are minimized or subsumed by the big media, and the number of voices in the marketplace is restricted. The whole trend of international publishing—exemplified well by the giant Bertelsmann company of Germany and several similar media behemoths in Britain and North America—is little more than an indication of capitalism gone wild. The health of the world's media system is anchored in local and national media, reinforcing indigenous values and providing homegrown entertainment and news. Localism, not globalization of the media, is the way to foster individualism and pluralism and to communicate with an increasingly tribalized international audience. There is a reason those people have been demonstrating.

ARGUMENT SUMMATION: *Globalization harms national and local media, thus impairing freedom of expression.*

The new trend toward globalization, toward big media companies expanding worldwide, is an unhealthy trend. There is no evidence of benefits to people, or to freedom of expression, within the countries receiving messages. Small local and national media are squeezed out of existence by the big companies, just as the mom-and-pop stores are killed by a Walmart coming into the community.

National values are endangered by the increase in alien cultural media material—especially advertising and entertainment of a sensational, vulgar nature.

SEARCH ONLINE!

 Use the following terms and phrases to search for more information on InfoTrac College Edition: *international, global, globalization, global media, comparative media, cross-cultural communication, multinational firms, geopolitics, cultural imperialism, conglomerates, media barons.*

TOPICS FOR DISCUSSION

1. What are the dimensions of globalization? How is it defined and to what extent are media the conduits for this process?
2. Discuss some of the most visible media barons and big media firms, such as Time Warner, Bertelsmann, Rupert Murdoch, Sumner Redstone, and others. What impresses you about them? What does not? Do they have too much power?
3. One of the topics raised in discussions about the New World Information and Communication Order a few years ago was the licensing of journalists. Is this justified? Does it impair free expression? Why or why not?
4. Among the world's information societies are the United States, Japan, Canada, Western Europe, and others. How have these countries advanced their cause in a global media economy? What about developing countries?
5. Debate the proposition that for media, bigness is bad and diversity is good.

TOPICS FOR RESEARCH

1. Observe the topics covered on a television network evening news show for a week and assess whether these topics are (a) diverse and (b) drawn from virtually every continent.
2. Examine the basis for the notion that growing hegemony of the media is the main result of globalization versus the idea that globalization drives diversity of communication.
3. Write a paper examining how globalization of the news affects what media products people get in individual countries. What impact have the Internet

and digital communication had on developing nations? Will that change? When?

4. Compare and contrast arguments for and against media subsidies to assure diversity, as with government funding of public TV in the United States or newspapers in Western Europe. Consider any policy issue that pits the public interest against private interests.

5. Document cases of New Media enterprises on the Web that have been successful in reaching global audiences. Are global media available via the Web in your own community—either produced there or received there? What influence, if any, do they have?

FURTHER READING

Altschull, Herbert. *Agents of Power.* White Plains, NY: Longman, 1995.

Artz, Lee, and Yahya R. Kamalipour. *The Globalization of Corporate Media Hegemony.* Albany: State University of New York Press, 2003.

Bagdikian, Ben. *The Media Monopoly.* Boston: Houghton Mifflin, 2000.

Debeer, A., and J. C. Merrill, eds. *Global Journalism.* 4th ed. Boston: Allyn & Bacon, 2004.

Dicken, Peter. *Global Shift: Reshaping the Global Economic Map in the 21st Century,* 4th ed. New York: Guilford, 2003.

Gerbner, George, Hamid Mowlana, and Kaarle Nordenstreng. *The Global Media Debate: Its Rise, Fall and Renewal.* Norwood, NJ: Ablex, 1991.

Grunwald, Henry. "The Post–Cold War Press." *Foreign Affairs,* Vol. 72, no. 3 (Summer 1993): 12–16.

Mattelart, Armand. *Multinational Corporations and the Control of Culture.* Atlantic Highlands, NJ: Humanities Press, 1979.

Meyrowitz, Joshua. *No Sense of Place: The Impact of Electronic Media on Social Behavior.* New York: Oxford University Press, 1986.

Morris, Nancy. *Media and Globalization.* Lanham, MA: Rowman & Littlefield, 2001.

Picard, Robert G. *The Economics and Financing of Global Media Companies.* New York: Fordham University Press, 2002.

Rantanen, Terhi. *The Media and Globalization.* Thousand Oaks, CA: Sage, 2005.

Rucker, Bryce. *The First Freedom.* Carbondale: Southern Illinois University Press, 1968.

Smith, Anthony. *The Age of Behemoths: The Globalization of Mass Media Firms.* New York: Priority Press, 1991.

Sommerville, C. John. *How the News Makes Us Dumb: The Death of Wisdom in an Information Society.* Downers Grove, IL: InterVarsity Press, 1999.

Sparks, Colin. *The Media and Globalization (Media & Culture Series, 194).* London: Sage, 2004.

Tunstall, Jeremy. *The Media Are American.* New York: Columbia University Press, 1977.

Vincent, Richard L., ed. *Towards Equity in Global Communication: McBride Update.* Cresskill, NJ: Hampton Press, 1999.

Wriston, Walter. *The Twilight of Sovereignty.* New York: Scribner's Macmillan, 1992.

Media Debates Web Resources

There are now scores of Websites devoted to the media industries, media accountability and criticism, ethics, law, and related topics. Some are commercial enterprises, hoping to make a profit as they direct their material to media insiders and the interested public. Others are self-serving promoters of their own causes and issues. Some of these are especially ideological and bear careful scrutiny. Here, in our opinion, are some of the best, most interesting, and most provocative sites that will prove helpful as one encounters debates in and on media.

Jim Romensko's Media News (found at Poynter.org)—A lively daily report on media issues and problems keyed to current news. The best source for other media industry links, professional societies and associations, media pundits and analysts, as well as radio/TV and alternative newsweekly sites.

IWantMedia.com—a Website focusing on diversified media news and resources. It provides quick access to timely media news and relevant industry data, updated throughout the day.

FAIR.org—Fairness and Accuracy in Media, a left-leaning watchdog organization, offers a wide range of critical materials and some surprisingly generous links to other, less biased sites.

CJR.org—*Columbia Journalism Review*, a journal of media criticism.

Mediabistro.com—This site covers news of the book, magazine, film, TV, and other media industries.

Mediaaccess.org—A public interest law firm that is especially interested in litigation and regulation affecting the electronic media.

AIM.org—A mother lode of complaints about the media from a conservative perspective. Some critics say this site, organized by media critic Reed Irvine, likes conspiracy theories about the media.

Mediapost.com—an integrated publishing and content company whose mission is to provide an array of news and directories for media planning and buying.

Projectcensored.org—Project Censored is a longstanding annual compilation of stories deemed important by the project (at California State University, Sonoma) and ignored or under-covered by the media. A perspective on the media's sins of omission.

Dailyhowler.com—An online journalism review that takes on the celebrity-chasing press corps with some commonsense ideas.

Poynter.org—Useful, professionally oriented journalism material from the Poynter Institute, a media training center, that gives special attention to media ethics. Features material on writing, editing, and other journalistic skills.

Mediaresearch.org—Another conservative source of media criticism and analysis, Media Research is associated with pundit Brent Bozell, a frequent TV and cable news source.

Pewcenter.org—The Pew Center for Civic Journalism and other Pew Foundation media activities and polls are found on this site, which promotes civic/public journalism for a foundation that has been one of its major funders.

AJR.org—Provides access to the *American Journalism Review* and its various resources.

Indexonline.org—This is a good source for issues of genuine censorship worldwide.

In addition to these sites, nearly every media industry, professional society, magazine, and association has a site that has useful material.

Note that Web sources are always subject to change and need to be scrutinized carefully to see when they were most recently updated. Virtually all of the major gateways and portals (Google, Yahoo, MSN, and others) take you to sites related to the various chapter topics in this book.

Index

237